Coastal Recreation Management

Management

JOIN US ON THE INTERNET VIA WWW, GOPHER, FTP OR EMAIL:

WWW: http://www.thomson.com
GOPHER: gopher.thomson.com
FTP: ftp.thomson.com
EMAIL: findit@kiosk.thomson.com

A service of I(T)P

OTHER TITLES AVAILABLE FROM E & FN SPON

Leisure and Recreation Management
3rd edition
George Torkildsen

Sociology of Leisure: A reader
Chas Critcher, Peter Bramham and Alan Tomlinson

Recreation and the Law
2nd edition
Valerie Collins

Recreational Land Management
2nd edition
Bill Seabrooke and Charles Miles

Coaching Children in Sport: Principles and practice
Martin Lee

Arts Administration
2nd edition
John Pick and Malcolm Anderton

Leisure Studies
Journal published on behalf of the Leisure Studies Association

For more information about these and other titles published by us, please contact:
The Promotion Department, E & FN Spon, 2–6 Boundary Row, London,
SE1 8HN. Telephone 0171 522 9966

Coastal Recreation Management

The sustainable development of maritime leisure

Edited by

Tim Goodhead

Head of Maritime Management
Southampton Institute
UK

and

David Johnson

Head of Maritime Science
Southampton Institute
UK

E & FN SPON
An Imprint of Chapman & Hall

London · Weinheim · New York · Tokyo · Melbourne · Madras

**Published by E & FN Spon, an imprint of Chapman & Hall,
2–6 Boundary Row, London SE1 8HN, UK**

Chapman & Hall, 2–6 Boundary Row, London SE1 8HN, UK

Chapman & Hall GmbH, Pappelallee 3, 69469 Weinheim, Germany

Chapman & Hall USA, 115 Fifth Avenue, New York NY 10003, USA

Chapman & Hall Japan, ITP-Japan, Kyowa Building, 3F, 2-2-1
Hirakawacho, Chiyoda-ku, Tokyo 102, Japan

Chapman & Hall Australia, 102 Dodds Street, South Melbourne, Victoria
3205, Australia

Chapman & Hall India, R. Seshadri, 32 Second Main Road, CIT East,
Madras 600 035, India

First edition 1996

© 1996 E & FN Spon

Typeset in 10/12 pt Palatino by Saxon Graphics Ltd, Derby
Printed in Great Britain by St Edmundsbury Press, Bury St Edmunds,
Suffolk

ISBN 0 419 20360 5

A catalogue record for this book is available from the British Library

Library of Congress Catalog Card Number: 95-72976

♾ Printed on permanent acid-free text paper, manufactured in
accordance with ANSI/NISO Z39.48-1992 and ANSI/NISO Z39.48-1984
(Permanence of Paper)

Contents

Contributors

Brief details of the qualifications and experience of those who have contributed to this book are given below.

Jenny Anderson, BA (Hons), MSc, PGCE, MILAM, MTS Jenny Anderson is Coastal Resources Subject Leader at Southampton Institute. She has published articles on watersports participation and undertaken consultancies on the subjects of jetskiing, youth sport and attitudes towards safety in outdoor recreation. Her most recent research is the National Watersport Audit for the British Marine Industry Federation and other national bodies.

Rob Andrews, PGCTL Rob Andrews is a senior lecturer in Maritime Leisure at Southampton Institute. He has spent 18 years in the Marine Leisure sector, working for the Royal Yachting Association and the Sports Council. His current research is an investigation into the physiological impact of competing at Olympic level in windsurfing. As an Olympic coach he has represented Great Britain at the Olympic Games in 1984, 1988 and 1992.

Christopher Atwell, BSc (Hons), MRIN Christopher Atwell is a lecturer in the Maritime Faculty of Southampton Institute. His teaching and research interests are Marine Safety and Management, Navigation Systems and Port Operations. Christopher is involved in EU research in the field of Vessel Traffic Services and their contribution to maritime safety.

Tim Badman, BSc (Hons), PGDip Tim Badman is Coastal Recreation Officer with Hampshire County Council and the Sports Council (Southern Region) and is responsible for the implementation of the Region's Coastal Recreation Strategy. He was formerly the organizer of the Heritage Coast Forum.

Dr Rhoda Ballinger, BSc (Hons), PhD, PGCE Rhoda Ballinger is a lecturer in Marine Geography in the Department of Maritime Studies and International Transport at the University of Wales College of Cardiff. Her research and teaching interests include coastal management and environmental management of tourism and recreation.

Andy Fairclough, BSc (Hons), PGCTL, FRGS Andy Fairclough is a senior lecturer in Maritime Leisure at Southampton Institute. He began his career as a research oceanographer at the Bermuda Marine Biological Station. He then spent six years as a training manager for a large outdoor centre developing and running vocational courses for watersports professionals. An experienced yachtmaster with over 20 000 miles at sea he now specializes in meteorology, oceanography and watersports instructor training.

Tim Goodhead, BA (Hons), MSc, MPhil, MILAM, MRIN Tim Goodhead is Head of Maritime Management at Southampton Institute. Previously Tim has been employed as an Instructor at the National Sailing Centre, Chief Instructor of a Sailing School and as a manager of a Water Sports Park. As a senior lecturer at Portsmouth Polytechnic he specialized in the economics of property management. Tim is also a RYA Area Coach.

Ian Harris, BEd (Hons) Ian Harris is a lecturer in Leisure Management at Southampton Institute. Previously he was a teacher of physical education at secondary schools in Essex and Hampshire, with responsibilities for the organization of outdoor education and many activity courses. Ian now specializes in watersports training and instruction. He is also a member of the Hayling Island lifeboat crew.

Richard Hill, BSc (Hons), MSc Richard Hill is an environmental scientist with Posford Duvivier Environment. His specialisms include resource management and marine pollution control with specific projects on marinas and the Braer oil spill.

Zelda Hill, BSc Econ (Hons), PGCE, MBA, MILAM Zelda Hill is a senior lecturer in Marketing Communications at Southampton Institute. With over 16 years' experience as a lecturer, her most recent research activity has concentrated on the water-based leisure industry including the industry's expectation of graduates.

Martin Hughes, BEd, MILAM, SNAC Martin Hughes is course leader for the BA Maritime Leisure Management course at Southampton Institute. He is a RYA Council member and Vice Chairman of the Windsurfing Divisional Committee for the RYA. Martin has devoted significant time to the development of the UK's windsurfing schemes and is currently involved in developing water-based NVQs and an extensive international research project.

David Johnson, BSc (Hons), MSc, MILAM, MIEEM David Johnson is Head of Maritime Science at Southampton Institute. His management experience is gained from running his own limited company for eight years and from a former position as Chief Executive to an environmental charity. David is also an Associate Environmental Auditor and his research interests include coastal zone management, sustainable development and assessment and auditing of leisure impacts on the environment.

Nicholas Kasic, BA (Hons), PGDip, SMIT Nicholas Kasic is a researcher with the Maritime Research Centre at Southampton Institute. He is currently working on his PhD investigating small boat crime and recently organized a Maritime Crime Forum. His specialisms include port security, crime prevention and security management.

Dr Sue Lewey, BSc (Hons), MPhil, PhD, MIBiol, CBiol Sue Lewey is course leader in Maritime Environmental Science at Southampton Institute. Her PhD work on the physiology of brown algae included a study of the effects of herbicides on marine algae. Sue has much experience in cruising and racing keel boats and advised the RYA on the impacts of TBT antifouling in the 1980s.

John Pearson, BSc (Special), MRIN John Pearson spent 25 years as an Instructor Officer in the Royal Navy, lecturing in meteorology, navigation and communications systems. He is now a senior lecturer at Southampton Institute. John has significant sailing experience and combines this with his practical experience as an environmental forecaster at sea.

Dr Helen Pickering, BSc (Hons), PhD, ARICS Helen Pickering is a Research Fellow in the Centre for the Economics and Management of Aquatic Resources at the University of Portsmouth. Her specialisms include research and consultancy in coastal zone management, coastal property rights, water-based leisure management, fisheries and the environmental performance of the oil industry.

Prof. Malek Pourzanjani, BSc (Hons), PhD, CEng, MIMarE, MSNAME, MRIN, MASEE Malek Pourzanjani is Head of the Maritime Research Centre at Southampton, having formerly been Head of the Marine Dynamics Group at the University of Exeter. His PhD is in marine simulation and ship manoeuvring and he has been involved with numerous research projects sponsored by SERC and MoD. Main areas of current research are in navigation systems, ship motion prediction and simulation, risk assessment, safety management and human factor studies.

Dr Gareth Rees, BSc (Hons), MASc, PhD Gareth Rees is Head of Environmental Management at Farnborough College of Technology. He worked on the major UK Government funded project considering the health effects of sea bathing. In 1994 he was Special Adviser to the House of Lords Select Committee on European Communities considering amendments to the EC Bathing Water Directive. Gareth has also been Director of Coastwatch UK since 1987 and is adviser to the World Health Organization United Nations Environment Programme Mediterranean Action Plan on recreational water quality issues.

Tim Savill, BSc (Hons) Tim Savill is a senior lecturer in the Coastal Resources Group at Southampton Institute. His commercial experience includes environmental consultancy work for the oil industry and involvement in the development of the Ocean Surface Current Radar (OSCRII) system. Currently lecturing in small craft operations and offshore surveying he is also involved with research investigating the application of neural networks to remote sensing data.

Prof. William Seabrooke, BSc (Hons), PhD, FRICS Bill Seabrooke is the Chairman of the Centre for Coastal Zone Management, Professor of Land Economy and Head of the Department of Land and Construction Management at the University of Portsmouth. He is management adviser to the Beaulieu Settled Estate, Hampshire. His research interests are estate management and valuation, recreation and leisure management, land use appraisal and coastal management.

Jane Taussik, BA (Hons), DipTP, MRTPI Jane Taussik is a town planner with local government experience gained before moving into teaching. She is a member of the Centre for Coastal Zone Management at the University of Portsmouth, where her research concerns the contribution of the planning system to coastal zone management. She has developed, and is Course Leader for, the University's Masters level course in Coastal and Marine Resource Management.

Cliff Wheeler, BSc (Hons), MRTPI Cliff Wheeler is a senior lecturer in the Built Environment faculty of Southampton Institute. He lectures on a wide range of planning and environmental subjects to both Real Estate Valuation and Leisure Management students. Cliff has maintained an interest in coastal matters since the mid-1960s and specializes in coastal property issues.

Preface

I must go down to the sea again, to the lonely sea and the sky,

(John Masefield, *Sea Fever*, 1902)

This romantic concept was both a tradition and a reality until well into the nineteenth century. The sea was for those who made their living from it or across it – fishermen and traders. The coast, where land meets sea, was a focus for those practical activities with human settlement confined in the main to small fishing communities or trading and naval ports, some of great economic and political importance in the ancient and medieval world.

That age-old pattern changed with the impact of the railways in the nineteenth century, and developing social attitudes to the 'seaside' as an amenity for leisure and pleasure. In the last 50 years, however, a growing population with car ownership as the norm, and increasing affluence and leisure time, has brought a new dimension to society's expectations of, demands upon, and use of the coast.

At the turn of the century the demand was for resort activities – the seaside holiday or day out – with sandy beaches, swimming, the pier, pleasure steamers, public entertainment and catered accommodation. Those demands are now met in more exotic or sophisticated ways. The coast is under different pressures. For example, some 3 million people take part in sailing activities and their needs have been met by providing about 75 000 berths in 370 locations around the UK. In total one in five young adults are involved in watersports. The environmental, economic and social equation is new, and the implications for the coast massive.

As maritime leisure continues to grow and pressure on natural resources and personnel increases, the need to make organized, intelligent and safe use of our coastal waters for leisure and recreation has become painfully clear. Conflict between water users and an increase in the number of accidents involving a range of user groups have led to serious questions being asked at government and national governing body level about the way in which we should manage this resource.

Attitudes to leisure are also changing. The public no longer look at recreation as a passive experience. More and more people want to make constructive use of their free time; to learn a new skill, to seek a new challenge or thrill or simply to enjoy unfamiliar surroundings. The maritime environment can satisfy all these desires. It can be both welcoming and threatening, busy and remote. It is perhaps the most unexplored, challenging and poorly understood of all our recreational resources.

The maritime leisure industry has responded to increased demand by finding new ways of enjoying the seas and waterways. New sports and pastimes have appeared. Windsurfers, jetskis and catamarans were almost unheard of ten years ago. Older more established activities like yachting and scuba diving, which were previously reserved for the rich and famous, or brave adventurers, have become accessible to the general public. New materials and equipment, changed attitudes and economies of scale have brought these opportunities within the grasp of the masses. In the small boat category, powercraft, sailboats and windsurfers have become fast and abundant. This, combined with the vast improvement in personal protective clothing and equipment (wetsuits etc.), has meant that enthusiasts can pursue their chosen interest all year round, and the opportunity for people to get into difficulty some way offshore, in winter, is now a real concern.

Coastal recreational management is becoming an increasingly complex challenge. How can we manage a constantly changing common resource and, at the same time, hope to satisfy a diverse range of recreational user groups, all of whom have slightly different requirements of their environment?

Even within a single user group there are different needs resulting from diverse knowledge, experience and ability. If we take windsurfing as an example the newcomer to the sport needs a safe protected calm environment with flat water and light winds; he or she is therefore likely to conflict with bathers and anglers who have similar needs. By contrast the experienced short-board sailor seeks strong winds, severe sea conditions and waves, and is therefore more likely to co-exist with surfers, powerboaters and offshore sailors.

From another standpoint, if we consider the number of different maritime district councils and harbour authorities with responsibilities to control and regulate our waterways, and the number of national governing bodies which represent our leisure interests, the complexity of the management task becomes clear. The task is made much more difficult by the fact that many groups fail to understand the requirements of other groups and that management decisions are often made by people who do not have a wide enough understanding of the issues involved.

To address these issues various forms of coastal zone management have been implemented in places with the greatest degree of pressure on them – and with some success. Inevitably there are problems particularly with the cost of policing these schemes and with keeping users confined to their land fixed zones once they are afloat in a moving tidal environment.

The intention of this book is to provide a practical overview of the issues facing coastal recreational managers and account for how these are currently being addressed.

The book is presented in four parts. The first introduces the concepts of increasing demand for water-based recreation in maritime areas and the need for management to ensure sustainable enjoyment opportunities. Part Two covers the environment for maritime leisure in its widest sense – in terms of physical conditions, limitations, water quality and institutional controls. Part Three details the variety of water-based leisure activities from individual pursuits, to sailing schools, marinas and yachting and their relationship with commercial port operators. Part Four covers management solutions. Each chapter, written by different contributors, presents an analysis of the issue, followed, where appropriate, by case-study examples.

ACKNOWLEDGEMENTS

The editors would like to thank Katie Barber and Amanda Killingback for their support in preparing and producing this text. The publisher and editors would like to thank all individuals for permission to use material from lecture notes and other sources. We have made every effort to contact copyright holders, but if any errors have been made we would be happy to correct them at a later printing.

PART ONE
Concepts

Maritime Leisure   1

1.1 INTRODUCTION

This chapter introduces the concept of maritime leisure, the historical development of water based leisure and current water sport participation patterns.

The maritime environment provides a rich resource for the pursuit of our leisure. No matter how active or passive the activity may be, recreational opportunities provided by coastal, estuary and inshore waters are increasing. Maritime leisure includes an expanding range of contrasting activities and local environments, such as surfing in Newquay, water skiing in a sheltered harbour, bird-watching on mud flats in a river estuary, building sandcastles on the beach at Skegness, racing round the world in a maxi yacht, learning to canoe in the Menai Straits, jet skiing in the London Docklands, diving off the South West Coast of Scotland, and just gazing at the sea from a clifftop static caravan in Devon.

A clear summary of the scope of coastal recreation is given by Laffoley (1991). He states that

> Recreation can be divided into major infrastructural developments and into the individual sports and recreational pursuits. Major infrastructural developments can take the form of marinas, non marine moorings, dinghy and boat parks and leisure centres, complexes and piers. Sports and recreational pursuits can be divided into those that are predominantly aquatic based, those that occur on the inter tidal or terrestrial coastal fringe and those that are air based. Aquatic based recreation can be categorized into angling, bathing, canoeing, jet skiing, non commercial fishing other than angling, leisure barges, power boating, towing, sailboarding, sailing. SCUBA diving, snorkelling, surfing, tourist

Coastal Recreation Management Edited by Tim Goodhead and David Johnson. Published in 1996 by E & FN Spon, London. ISBN 0 419 20360 5

boat trips, water skiing and windsurfing. Terrestrial and inter tidal based recreation consists of all purpose terrain vehicles, bird watching, car sand racing, clay pigeon shooting, four wheel drive vehicles, golf courses, horse riding, hovercrafts, sand yachting, trail biking and walking. Air based recreation occurs in the form of overflying by hang gliders, microlights and light aircraft. Parascending may also occur.

Although it is impossible to estimate how many people visit the maritime environment as part of their leisure time what is obvious is that the numbers visiting and taking part in activities have increased greatly in recent years (O'Neil, 1993). Maritime leisure participation includes the activities of people who choose to spend their free time outdoors beside, in or on water. Throughout this book the focus is on the management of those who spend their time on the water actively pursuing a recreation or sport. We are more concerned by those who use some type of craft or vessel in a maritime environment and consequently less concerned with major leisure activities such as shore-based fishing, swimming and general beach activities. The emphasis is therefore on coastal watersports.

1.2 WATERSPORTS AS A LEISURE ACTIVITY

Between three and four million people are involved in watersports in the UK (Mintel, 1992). Watersports participation is a leisure activity that takes place on a daily basis from home, or as part of short breaks and longer holidays in Great Britain and abroad. Watersports may range from less active to more active, from non-competitive to competitive, from solitary to group activities, from casual to highly organized. The main motivation to undertake them may range from challenge and exhilaration to peace and solitude.

The watersports industry is diverse, widespread and fragmented. There is evidence of approximately 5000 companies catering for this market (Sells, 1993). The British Marine Industries Federation, the trade association for 75% of companies operating in the small-craft and water-sport sector, claims that 35 000 craft were constructed in 1993 with a turnover of more than a billion pounds. Worldwide water-based recreation is big business. The export market is becoming increasingly significant to British boatbuilders with sales in the Middle and Far East in the mid 1990s (Tate, 1994).

There are obviously both positive and negative impacts of the growth of leisure in the maritime environment. The interface of leisure activities with the maritime environment is both 'an enormously complex and powerful phenomenon' and 'ubiquitous and complicated' (Miller and Ditton, 1986). This can be assessed by numbers of people involved, types and nature of activities, capital invested, the potential for conflict and the differential sensitivity of the resource itself. The benefits are usually assessed in economic terms. In addition to environmental problems, social systems can also be disrupted with evidence of increased crime, dislocation, racism and stratification in maritime communities.

Leisure is a prominent feature in people's lives in industrialized countries (Henley, 1991). Rises in car ownership, increases in disposable income, demographic changes such as the decrease in family size, the changing role of women, increases in educational attainment, growth in leisure opportunity, choice and access, technological innovation and the influence of fashion, have all helped to popularize watersports over the latter half of the twentieth century.

Leisure is recognized as a right by most people in Britain. We have moved from a time when only a few had the chance to enjoy leisure, to a time when most of us have leisure opportunities, from a leisure class to a leisure society. Leisure used to be seen as the opposite of work but increasingly leisure and work are seen on a continuum. With higher unemployment, early retirement, longer life and greater leisure potential the work/leisure relationship is changing.

> Leisure is important therefore in the rhythm of our lives. It is to do with activities, usually chosen for their own sake, and in relative freedom, and which bring intrinsic satisfactions. (Torkildsen, 1992)

Instinctively we are drawn to water whether it be ocean, lake or river. In Britain the earliest travel for pleasure was inspired by the desire to visit first inland spas and then the sea for medicinal purposes. Water has great value as a visual amenity. Urry (1990) has argued the need to travel today for pleasure is generated by a necessity to escape the pressures of everyday routine. Water has restorative qualities. Passive observation of the maritime environment in itself has been described as a fundamental tourism activity (Miller and Ditton, 1986).

As a nation we are also becoming more aware of health. This is due to more attention being paid to personal appearance and well-being, but also to the general ageing of the population. As people have more free time they will need to use less of it for rest and recovery and more of it for physical and mental activity. A specific trend has been an awareness of the need for quality use of leisure time – an active use of mind and body. There is increased understanding about different roles of leisure; for example the difference between consumerist, media-influenced and consumption-based leisure, and active, participative leisure. For quality leisure experiences people feel the need to gain expertise in activities. As there is more choice of leisure activities it may only be possible to become expert in a few of these activities – these experts or 'leisure connoisseurs' are becoming increasingly important to many markets. Many active activities lend themselves more to the 'expert' approach (Darton, 1986).

The most recent General Household Survey shows that nearly two-thirds of adults take part in at least one activity although gender, age, class and ethnic contrasts persist. Most popular of all are informal activities, especially outdoor, countryside, and individual as opposed to team-based sports.

According to the Sports Council,

> The widespread popularity of these types of physical recreation supports the contention that there has been a divergence of trends between individual activity and group activity, reflecting broader trends towards a more personal type of leisure experience. (Sports Council, 1988)

Fastest growing are many of the newer, more adventurous and more glamorous countryside sports, and those associated with healthy lifestyles. Individuals will give more priority to outdoor sport and exercise due to their contribution towards personal and family health (Martin and Mason, 1993).

The range and diversity of leisure activities on the water are growing. Traditional favourites such as canoeing and sailing are being both challenged and complemented by a new generation of activities led by the windsurfer, but closely followed by a range of innovations, many of which depend on fuel rather than wind or human energy for propulsion (Chapter 7). Despite this it is important to recognize that coastal recreational management is concerned mainly with a small and specialized sector of the leisure market.

1.3 THE HISTORY OF WATER-BASED RECREATION

1.3.1 EARLY ORIGINS

The earliest types of craft were made from reeds, bark, logs, skins and then the 'planked boat' (McGrail, 1981). All over the world people using a variety of raw materials, methods and ingenuity have wanted to exploit the possibility for transport on water. It must be assumed that people have always pottered on the water, making use of whatever was available; the divide between work or survival, and play or leisure, must have always been blurred.

Until the Industrial Revolution there was no distinction between work and leisure for ordinary men and women. Agricultural production followed the rhythm of the seasons with times of intense hard work and quieter times. Sporting activities now known as folk games were played in the fields during the day. In medieval times travel on land and water was burdensome, unpredictable, dangerous and demanding. Travel for pleasure was inconceivable to most and was confined to day excursions, fairs, festivals and travelling to sport or entertainment.

1.3.2 THE BIRTH OF YACHTING

Before the eighteenth century then, water sport participation for pleasure was restricted to royalty and aristocracy. Monarchs of most coastal nations had some form of regal craft to carry them on occasions. In the sixteenth century a small craft named *Rat of Wight* was built for Queen Elizabeth I of England 'for national entertainment'. Evidence of early yachting in household accounts of Hurstmonceux castle in 1643 made several references to 'my Lords yaught' (Pelly, 1989).

In 1660 King Charles II returned from years of exile in the Netherlands where the idea of sailing purely for pleasure had become attractive. All trade in Netherlands was dependent on water for transport. The yacht was the normal possession of a person of any consequence. Yachting became a social yardstick, a status symbol. It is not surprising that a class of vessel gradually developed for visiting, entertaining or just showing off. Charles was an enthusiast. The Dutch presented him with a 60 ft yacht. He later built and owned 20 yachts. In 1661 the king took part in the first recorded yacht race from Greenwich to Gravesend. Some felt that he spent too much time and money on yachts but he made the sport respectable and encouraged other enthusiasts to build their own pleasure craft. Charles is also noted because he commissioned Captain Grenville Collins to produce a book of charts of the British coastline.

1.3.3 THE FIRST YACHT CLUBS AND EARLY RACES

In 1720 the first known sailing club, Water Club Harbour of Cork (now the Royal Cork Yacht Club) was established. The highlight of the club's season was sailing in formation with quasi naval activities and practice mock naval battles. The 25 members of the club wore splendid uniforms.

They had extensive rules and records of their activities were lovingly kept. It was primarily a social club and consequently much food and drink was consumed (Heaton, 1972).

Owning a yacht was a very expensive business. By necessity the original yachtsmen were royalty, noblemen, or wealthy gentry who did not handle the sails but left it to the 'common seamen'. Yachts often had crews of 25 and upwards. Early London regattas had Royal patronage. The yachts were beamy, bluff bowed, rigged mainly as cutters, with gaff mainsail, stayrig, and jib on a long bowsprit (Heaton, 1972). Organized races mainly involved merchants and businessmen. In other parts of the country annual seaside regattas were held by local fishermen who would compete in sailing or rowing races, tugs of war, mud wrestling and other sports. Eventually clubs also grew from these regattas, run by men who earned their living from the sea.

By the mid 1770s there is evidence of the first yacht race off Cowes on the Isle of Wight. Interest grew in this area culminating in the formation of the Royal Yacht Club at Cowes. It was noted as an aristocratic establishment and was later transformed into the Royal Yacht Squadron, which became the home of yacht racing as we know it today. The Royal Yacht Club became established as a powerful influence in all yachting matters. The first Cowes week took place in August 1826 for a prize of 100 guineas under the flag of the Royal Yacht Club. By 1845 the Cowes event included 80 vessels under sail. The importance of the Cowes week comes from its tradition, continuing Royal patronage, regular good breezes, exacting tidal courses, the waterfront which presents a good grandstand, and the ability of the River Medina to accommodate a large number of yachts.

By 1846 16 yachting clubs had been granted the title Royal by the Crown and from this point the growth of yachting clubs was rapid in Europe. Before the first half of the nineteenth century few left harbours and estuaries for pleasure because of the dangers of being attacked. However the earlier royal patronage and increasing affluence allowed time for sailing for its own sake among those rich enough to afford it (Johnson, 1975). Thus the origins of yachting lie both with the rich who used craft as status symbols and maritime working folk who used their livelihood skills to sail them.

1.3.4 GROWTH OF THE SEASIDE RESORT

The eighteenth century saw a considerable increase in sea bathing in Britain and drinking sea water was seen as a general 'pick-you-up'. The dips were ritualized and structured and were prescribed only to treat serious medical conditions. They were normally carried out naked. The beach was regulated by the dippers, women who were responsible for immersion. For the first time leisure was taking place not at inland spas but at the coast which eventually became accessible to a greater range of people.

Seaside resorts became more popular over the next half century. By 1800 Brighton was considered the most fashionable resort in Europe. Steamboat services were introduced between population centres and seaside towns improving accessibility in 1815. In 1823 the first pier was constructed at Brighton. The attraction of the pier was that one could have the impression of being at sea, look back at the land and appreciate it from a different perspective. It was influenced by the Romantic movement originating in the Italian Renaissance.

The invention of the steam engine and expansion of the railways to the seaside resorts lead to more day visitors reaching the coast. In 1848 100 000 trippers left Manchester by train for the coast. By Whit week 1850 it had risen to 200 000. Seaside hamlets, fuelled by the railways, grew into resorts. The beach became a built-in escape from the rigours of everyday life. It became very noisy and crowded, full of unpredictable social mixing, involving inversion of social hierarchies and moral codes. The beach which had been a place for medicine was now a place for pleasure.

1.3.5 THE INDUSTRIAL REVOLUTION – THE SEPARATION OF WORK AND LEISURE

The Industrial Revolution caused a separation of work and non-work activities. There was mass migration from the country to the towns, leading to overcrowding and poor quality living environments. Several Acts were passed to enable local authorities to provide leisure facilities to improve the quality of life. Public parks, museums and galleries, it was claimed, would reduce crime, trespass and drunkenness and were therefore a contribution to the national economy. This was later called 'municipal socialism'. The 1875 Health Act was followed by four more Acts concerned in part with leisure provision. The initial power of the first Act was to provide and manage public walks or pleasure grounds. Parliament gradually sanctioned wider and wider extensions of use – one of which was the hiring of pleasure boats in 1890.

Leisure opportunities grew as legislation increased free time. A half day on Saturday and the first bank holiday were introduced in 1870. The former gave an incentive to the growth of organized sport and the latter, coupled with the extension of the railways, a boost to the growth of the seaside resort. Until then there was limited official free time due to the strength of Puritanism which meant that Sunday was intended for rest, recovery and prayer rather than leisure. The success of Thomas Cook as the first tour operator meant that the middle classes were travelling further than ever before both home and abroad. The ruling classes were beginning to pursue leisure activities that deliberately excluded the working classes. Team sports, originating in public schools, filtered down through grammar schools and into society.

1.3.6 THE INFLUENCE OF COMPETITION AND RACING

Yacht racing started as early as 1661. Competition is an essential component of all sport. Innovation, national and regional prestige are closely associated with the urge to win or to improve one's own performance against the elements. Throughout British sport gambling has been closely integrated with competition and therefore the need for rules to ensure equality.

> The America's Cup story is an historical exercise in exaggeration. Every important aspect of it is more expensive yet more rewarding, more acrimonious yet more demanding of sportsmanship than any other aspect of yachting, more technological effort is injected into the preparation of the contenders than any other sailing boats, but as a spectacle of sport it is one of the most tedious. It remains the most important of all yacht racing events. It is the oldest international trophy in any sport; the first contest was in 1851. It has the longest unbroken sequence of wins in any sport. (Johnson, 1975)

Regattas took place at all levels. In the River Hamble in Hampshire, for example, these regattas were held in September and largely relied on fishermen for active support. Financial support came from the gentry. Prize money was well worth the effort of dumping heavy fishing gear ashore and fishing boat sailing races were important events of the day and were contested without too much regard to the rules. Rowing races in excise cutters also took place. As yachts became more numerous more classes were provided. A crude handicapping system was developed. Crowds came to watch the rowing races and aquatic sports (Robinson, 1987).

Much later in 1900 yachting became part of the Olympic Games revived by De Coubertin in 1986 and with this came the idea that the owner became more than a passenger. The Olympics had a strong emphasis on amateurism. Yachts raced without time allowances in six different tonnage classes. British helmsman Lorne Currie won two gold medals. In 1920 dinghies were introduced into the Olympics. Yachting has never attracted the public imagination in the way that athletics has. Within the sport perhaps Paul Elsvstrom of Denmark made the greatest contribution by winning four successive gold medals (from 1948), demonstrating the importance of a physical training programme and generally raising standards. Ocean yacht racing came into existence in a regular sense.

1.3.7 FASHION AND STATUS

Towards the end of the nineteenth century yachting achieved a fashionable image. Major yachting venues were Cowes and New York. Kaiser Wilhelm II promoted Kiel to compete as a yachting centre. People of quality and rank visited in high season whether they were interested in sailing or not. The dates of Cowes week are fixed between the conclusion of racing at Goodwood and the opening of Grouse shooting on the Glorious 12th. There was great interest in new steam yachts among the rich, especially Americans. One notable American industrialist was Cornelius Vanderbilt who raised the profile of the sport with his 276 ft steam yacht *North Star*. Some were over 300 ft long, displaced over 'one thousand' tons and had crews of 90 men. Yachting became inseparable from money, power and fashion. Some of these magnificent vessels were fitted out like large country houses. The era of the very large sailing yacht lasted from 1900 to 1930 under the influence of Sir Thomas Lipton and others. This was the Golden Age of yachting.

1.3.8 SMALLER CRAFT

By the start of the twentieth century, however, for the majority of participants the world of yacht racing was changing. Racing in large yachts was considered by many as needlessly expensive. There were no mass-produced boats. They were all individually designed. Wages had risen, crews often numbered 25 on sailing yachts. Sailing schools did not exist. Skills were learnt from parents or by sailing as crew. This is why the tradition of the paid hand continued for so long. The middle classes were used to paying for domestic help at home and extended the idea to boats. On the River Hamble many local men took jobs on yachts over the summer where food and conditions were so much better than on fishing smacks and crabbers (Robinson, 1987).

Under the new Dixon Kemp rules smaller and cheaper boats could be built and still enter the races. Some owners traded down but this also opened the sport to more people of comparatively modest means. Many classes of 'raters', as they were known, sprang up around the coast. They were not only cheaper to build and run but they took up less anchorage.

1.3.9 THE WORLD WARS

During both world wars sporting activities, were severely curtailed. After the First World War watersports resumed quickly, notable changes being fewer hired hands on the water, more women, use of radio with BBC weather forecasts and the replacement of the gaff rig with the Bermuda rig.

The interwar years, despite the Depression, saw the expansion of voluntary organizations with an emphasis on health and fitness. Many new clubs were set up at this time for amateurs who sailed their own boats. New classes such as the National 14 dinghy provided racing at a relatively low cost and called for new levels of fitness besides sailing skill. It was a restricted class, which meant that the shape and design could be altered as long as the boat conformed to certain limited number of measurements. Its design was improved by Uffa Fox. The International 14 was extremely important in the development of dinghy sailing and racing. Many leading clubs had one design racing classes. In 1932 the Star keelboat was introduced to the Olympics (it was included until 1972). The Star taught the Sailing World a great deal about organization. It had a strong owners' association, organizing club, area, regional and world championships, in addition to keeping a tight control on the rules.

At the end of the Second World War the revival of normality in sailing circles took much longer than anticipated. It was a frustrating time. Mines had to be cleared from the coasts and bomb damage in harbours repaired. There was some river sailing but with shortages of paint, white lead, varnish, tar, labour and other materials many owners struggled to make their boats seaworthy again. The war also had a positive impact in that new materials such as aircraft alloys, resin-bonded plywood, and GRP led to a revolution in yacht building.

1.3.10 BOOM IN SMALL BOAT SAILING

Mass production of small dinghies in the 1950s revolutionized watersports participation. The market was led by the USA with factory-produced boats built from glass reinforced plastic (GRP) which reduced costs greatly. The 'do it yourself' boatbuilding boom really came into its own. In several countries yachting magazines published designs for small boats. Development of marine plywood and waterproof glue meant the average handyman or woman could construct a boat (as opposed to traditional skilled labour-intensive boatyard lofting, steaming, bending and shaping). Cruising turned into a family activity. One marked change at this time was the increase in the number of women afloat.

Many new sailing clubs grew including some near towns and cities, and on inland water. These people wanted to learn how to sail and sailing schools came into existence. France led the way with both club-based training programmes but also with seamanship schools where people could spend a fortnight's holiday. Britain lagged sadly behind until the 1970s.

Another consequence of the increased number of small power boats was the phenomenal growth of water skiing. Water skiing originated from the towing of snow skiers behind ponies in the early 1900s (Elson *et al.*, 1985). The British Water Ski Federation was formed in 1949. Other watersports also founded their amateur club origins at this time. In 1953 the British Sub Aqua Club was formed. By 1965 there were 6813 members, and by 1975 there were 23 204 members – a fourfold increase in a decade.

The mass production of boats and growth of associated sports has inevitably led to more crowding. Even before the growth of the last three decades there was evidence of crowding at the most popular destinations. This account comes from as early as 1963.

> My decision to go to the Channel Islands meant the Solent again for the season in spite of many vows never to go near the place again, the whole area having become a nightmare of so-called yachtsmen dashing madly about in high speed runabouts, and others who consider it de rigueur when moving with the motor on, in crowded anchorages or to have the throttle open to the full. The question of the damage and danger they create with their heavy wash is no concern of theirs, fancy hats and other such nonsense taking all their attention. (J. T. Morse in Hayes (1983) *The Cruising Association 75th Anniversary*, The Cruising Association)

1.3.11 GROWTH OF CRUISING

The next three decades saw a major expansion in amateurs cruising and subsequently racing round the world. The Ocean Cruising Club was founded in 1951. Members had to achieve a passage of 1000 miles in open water. In 1966 Francis Chichester set off to sail round the world in *Gipsy Moth*. In 1969 the first single-handed non-stop round-the-world voyage was completed by Robin Knox-Johnson. The voyages were widely publicized. In the late 1970s synthetic materials were coming into use for sails and rigging and immediately became popular for their lightness and ease of handling. There were new and lighter anchors, radars and echo sounders, a new and detailed range of pilot books were produced by Adlard Coles. The development with the greatest impact was that of self-steering. The new gear gave an immediate stimulus to single-handed sailing.

By 1974 the Ocean Cruising Club had 877 members. Opportunities for non-boat owners expanded through chartering and holiday companies. In 1963 the Yacht Charter Association was formed to represent the interests of owners and charters in the UK. It was an important milestone. By 1971 the Fastnet Race exceeded 200 entries. All this activity inevitably raised the profile of watersports. It was in the 1970s that a number of sailing holiday companies were formed and grew rapidly, servicing the growing interest in sailing holidays.

1.4 WATERSPORTS PARTICIPATION

Participation in all watersports increased during the 1980s and '90s. With few sources of empirical data on actual participation magazines readership and club membership are useful sources of information (Tables 1.1 and 1.2). However, circulation trends need to be treated with caution as they reflect magazine readership as much as specialist interest.

Research into leisure participation in general is in its infancy. The earliest leisure surveys date from the 1960s when a Pilot National Recreation Survey was produced by the British Travel Association and the University of Keele. Another survey 'Planning for Leisure' was conducted by Sillitoe as a government social survey during the same period. In 1983 the Sports Council conducted a survey on watersports. It included sailing, power boating, board sailing, canoeing, rowing, sub aqua, water skiing and jet skiing. The General Household Survey included questions on leisure in 1973, 1977, 1980, 1983, 1987 and 1990. Reference is made to watersports in the survey. In 1994 respondents could identify yachting or dingy sailing, canoeing; windsurfing, board sailing and other watersports (e.g. water skiing, sub aqua and rowing) as separate categories.

Table 1.1 Leading watersports specialist magazines, 1980–92

Name	Circulation	
	1980	1992
Sailing		
Yachting Monthly	34 313	45 200
Yachting World	25 133	31 700
Yachts and Yachting		22 000
Practical Boat Owner	47 346	66 000
Windsurfing		
Boards	10 024	22 700
Windsurf		20 300
Water skiing		
Water Ski International		17 000
British Water Skier		14 000
Surfing		
On Board Surf Magazine		15 000
Grounds		4000

Source: Mintel (1992).

Table 1.2 Club membership

	1970	1980	1984	1988
RYA Clubs	1504	1408	1524	1497
Members	31 089	41 361	51 026	63 927
UKBSA Clubs	Nil			250
Members	n/a	n/a	n/a	n/a
BCU Clubs	383	414	601	(600)
Members	5800	10 800	10 234	(12 500)
Rowing Clubs	562	460	478	500
Members	16 200	n/a	n/a	12 000
BSAC Clubs	331	862	918	1000
Members	13 721	27 075	33 988	37 000
BWSF Clubs	75	155	(158)	165
Members	5730	10 375	n/a	10 000

Source: Leisure Consultants, 1989 with additional information.

In addition current knowledge about water sport participation is derived from a limited number of one-off surveys produced in the last ten years. Comparison between surveys is difficult because of variations in definition of leisure, reference periods, sample size, rates of participation and finally what is included in the term water sport. Leisure Consultants, authors of *Boating and Other Watersports* (1989) commented:

The watersports market is very ill documented in statistical terms. It is not just a question of there being very little information available on boating and watersports. The figures that do exist differ greatly in terms of coverage and reliability... evidence on changes in participation in watersports is bitty and inadequate. (Leisure Consultants, 1989)

An estimated three to four million people participate in watersports. Accurate statistics are hard to obtain. Individual watersports have different potentials to exploit demographic and lifestyle trends.

1.4.1 INTRODUCTION TO WATERSPORTS

The issue of how people first take up watersports is complex. Studies of motivation and choice are immature. However the long-term success of the watersport industry depends on new entrants coming into the sport. Initial research (Table 1.3) suggests more than half of new sailing participants are introduced by friends or relatives. The figure drops to a quarter when considering new power boating entrants. New sailing entrants are significantly younger than power boaters reflecting the strong family profile of sail as opposed to power.

Table 1.3 Introduction to watersports

	Frequency	%
Family own boat	111	31
Friends' own boat	103	29
Club	24	7
Family holidays	19	5
School	13	4
School activity at centre	13	4
Ordinary holiday in UK	9	3
Scouts/cubs	8	2
Try it out day	7	2
Activity holiday as child	3	—
Activity holiday as adult	3	—
Local authority centre	3	—
Sea cadets/rangers	3	—
Work/forces	2	—
Non-participants	29	8

Source: Anderson (1994), Boat Show Survey, unpublished.

A more formal method of introduction is through the British-based sailing and windsurfing schools which were first established in the late 1970s. There are approximately 77 RYA-listed sailing schools, with one in Ireland and one in Europe. In the Southern area (Chichester to

Southampton) there are currently 10. However if non-RYA-listed schools are added, the number expands to 25 (BMIF, 1992). They offer sailing cruising, motor cruising, shore-based, dinghy sailing, power boating, keelboat and other specialist courses. These are complemented by over 170 RYA listed windsurfing centres, based all over the country, with just over 50 offering residential accommodation. Four National Sports Centres have a remit for watersports

1.4.2 HOLIDAY PARTICIPATION

For many adults and children the first opportunity to sample watersports is on holiday either abroad or in this country. About 60% of the UK population took holidays of four nights and over in 1994. This proportion has been fairly static since the late 1970s. A holiday is now seen as a necessity rather than a luxury by those who can afford it. Many people have their first encounters with watersports on holiday. Some may just dabble in watersports, others spend a day on a hired boat, or charter a yacht for a couple of days, while others choose a holiday within which the principal point is acquiring watersport skills. It is a diverse industry meeting a wide range of needs. Leisure Consultants (1989) estimated that approximately 3000 organizations in the UK offer some form of activity holiday to British residents. About one-third of these are offered abroad.

As in the case of watersports participation it is not possible to quantify trends in the activity holiday market due to lack of data. Problems of comparable definitions and measurements arise but formal activity holidays involving an element of tuition or supervision are estimated to account for at least two million holidays a year and a spend of over £250 m (Wooder, 1992). A 1988 Sports Council report estimated that 10% of all holidays taken in Europe were built around a specific activity or sport. A more recent estimate is that nearly one in four holidaymakers take part in some kind of activity holiday and more will have gone on activity-based trips (Martin and Mason, 1993). The established children's activity holiday business must be added to this.

As well as an important role in introducing people to watersports, holidays also serve to offer equipment and appropriate environments in which to participate. This is particularly true for those trying watersports such as yacht chartering and flotilla sailing, as equipment is so expensive and location is crucial. It is over 80 years since the first evidence of a yacht being chartered for pleasure when the Workman family of Belfast chartered a boat in the West of Scotland (Pelly, 1989). The move towards more active, 'real' or authentic, and greener holidays suggests that this sector should expand, and despite the recession, the outlook for activity holidays looks encouraging.

1.4.3 FREQUENCY OF PARTICIPATION AND MOTIVATION

Watersports are also mostly seasonal in nature. Two-thirds of participants do not take part in any watersports in winter (Levens, 1991). As would be expected those with their own equipment show a higher frequency of participation than those without. The temperature of water and air are important but wind patterns also make a significant impact especially with serious participants (Chapter 8). This seasonal nature is emphasized further by traditional holiday-taking patterns in Britain and the fact that many participate in watersports only on holiday.

Almost half of all participants are attracted by the challenge, exhilaration and excitement of watersports, which is one of the reasons for the growing interest in power boating and the new generation of small craft. The attraction of power boating to certain sectors of the population is that immediate gratification can be gained without the slow process of gaining competence in sailing skills.

In a recent survey at the London Boat Show (Anderson, 1994) 250 participants were questioned as to whether they would increase their commitment towards watersports. The major constraints to increasing participation were, as predicted, time (40%) and money (30%).

As a leisure activity, watersports in general are perceived as an expensive activity. Costs of participation have been estimated as £3965 for total annual overheads of sail cruiser owners, £265 for dinghy owners, and £2919 for power cruiser owners (Levens, 1991). Two-thirds of participants are non-boat-owners and costs are obviously less. Sailing accounted for 67% of total expenditure on watersports in 1991 (wetsuits 15%, windsurfing 12% and water skiing 6%). The current recession has dramatically depressed the watersport leisure and tourism market in Britain.

Watersports such as water skiing, dinghy sailing and windsurfing, require strength, agility and speed. Others such as power boating require less strenuous activity. There is evidence that some recreation activities are also experiencing high drop-out rates. The rates of discontinuance vary by activity type but this is obviously an important matter to those in the industry and worthy of further research.

1.4.4 THE FUTURE OF WATERSPORTS PARTICIPATION

A few research studies at the end of the 1980s and start of the '90s attempted to forecast future demand for watersports. It is a difficult area to make predictions about due to the number of variables involved, in particular the perilous uncertainties involved in predicting innovation and fashion. Table 1.4 lists those factors seen to be important by those attempting to predict the future of watersports.

Table 1.4 Analysis of factors seen to be important in predicting the future of watersports

Population structure	Less 16–24 yrs
	More 45–54 yrs
Lifestyles and values	Health awareness
	More active use of leisure
	Influence of fashion
	Green consumer
	More flexible use of time
Economic trends/UK economy	High cost of equipment
	Affected by downturn in economy but overall rising affluence
	Interest rates
	Increases in personal disposable income
	Exchange rates
Official policies	Less subsidies from government
	More planning controls
Weather	Participation related to temperature
	Good weather encourages use and trading up (in boats)
	Change of attitude towards sun tans
Water pollution	Increased awareness of effects to health
Facilities	Access issues
	Lack of new investment

Source: Compilation of various consultants' reports (pre-1992).

In brief, experts consider that rates of participation and expenditure will increase but at a slower rate than in the previous two decades. The steady growth forecast in active outdoor sport participation and expenditure on boating is illustrated in Table 1.5.

Table 1.5 Participation and expenditure

Forecast of participation in active outdoor sport[a]		Expenditure on boating[b]	
1990	19.1 m	1990	£652 m
1991	19.1 m	1991	£638 m
1992	19.3 m	1992	£697 m
1993	19.4 m	1993	£772 m
1994	19.5 m	1994	£863 m
1995	19.7 m	1995	£952 m
1996	19.7 m	1996	£1039 m

Sources: [a] Leisure Forecasts Report, Leisure Consultants (1993); [b] Keynote UK Leisure and Recreation (1992).

Of all the watersports power boating and jet skiing are projected to show higher rates of annual growth. Power boaters are almost twice as likely to want to increase their commitment as other water users (Anderson, 1993). Basic equipment can be relatively cheap or easy to hire and few participants are members of clubs. However, it should be noted that typically the initially high growth rates of a new sport taper off; the problem is predicting when the novelty of one sport will wear off to be overtaken by a newer craze. Power boating has a particular appeal to older affluent entrants to watersports. In many areas the proportion of powerboats in marinas has increased dramatically (Sidaway, 1991).

Companies producing a middle-range class of power boating saw significant increases in business in 1994. One company, the only quoted boatbuilder (Fairline), revealed a surge of profits from £161 000 to £350 000 at the start of 1994 (following a 16% advance in sales to £17.6 million). Smaller power boat production has suffered at the expense of the rapid rise of the jet ski where sales in 1994 are thought to be up by as much as 20% (Tate, 1994).

1.5 CONCLUSION

The future of maritime leisure is a bright one. The industry is set to grow in the years to come, with people spending an increased amount of time on leisure pursuits. In particular growth is expected in the watersports sector of the leisure industry, as illustrated by a number of reports. *Boating and Other Watersports* (Leisure Consultants, 1989) was commissioned to give an overview of watersports in Britain and what the future prospects are up to the year 2000. In summary it claimed that one million more British adults would take part in watersports, as the general trend is towards a greener lifestyle. However, as it points out, the result of this will be a growth in the conflicts over accessible water space and the environmental impacts of the increased pressures of land and waterside development

REFERENCES

Anderson, J. (1993) *Changing Patterns of Watersports Participation*, unpublished report, Southampton Institute, Southampton.
Anderson, J. (1994) *Participation in Watersports*, Insights, English Tourist Board.
BMIF (1992) *British Marine Industry Guide*, BMIF.
Darton, D. (1986) *The Leisured Society*, Leisure Manager.
Department of National Heritage (1993) *The Report of the Watersports Working Group*, HMSO.
Elson, M., Lloyd, J. and Thorpe, I. (1985) *Providing for Motorised Watersports*, Sports Council.

Glyptis, S. and Jackson, G. (1993) Sport and tourism: mutual benefits and future prospects. Paper given at The Leisure Studies Association Conference: 'Leisure in Different Worlds', Loughborough University.

Heaton, P. (1972) *The History of Sailing in Pictures*, Peter Heaton.

Henley (1991) *Leisure Futures*, Henley Centre for Forecasting.

Henley Centre (1992) Time Use Survey, in *Social Trends*, HMSO.

HMSO (1993) *General Household Survey*, HMSO.

Johnson, P. (1975) *The Guiness Book of Sailing Facts and Figures*, Guinness Superlatives Ltd.

Keynote UK (1993) *Leisure and Recreation*, Keynote Market Information.

Laffoley, D. (1991) Use of coastal land and water space: recreation. In N. C. Eno (ed.), *Marine Conservation Handbook*, 2nd edn, English Nature, Ch. 6.4.

Leisure Consultants (1989) *Boating and other Watersports*, Leisure Consultants.

Leisure Consultants (1992) *Leisure Forecasts 1992 – 1996*, Leisure Consultants.

Leisure Consultants (1992) *Activity Holidays The Growth Market on Tourism*, Leisure Consultants.

Levens, G. (1991) *Survey of Boat Owners*, British Marine Industry Federation.

McGrail, S. (1981) *The Ship; Rafts, Boats and Ships. From prehistoric times to medieval era*, HMSO.

Martin, B. and Mason, S. (1993) Current trends in leisure: new views of countryside recreation, *Leisure Studies*, **12**(1), 1–7.

Miller, M. and Ditton, R.D. (1986) Travel, tourism and marine affairs, *Coastal Zone Management Journal*, **11**(1/2).

Mintel (1992) *Watersports*, Leisure Intelligence, Vol. 4.

Morse, J. T. in Hayes (1983) *The Cruising Association 75th Anniversary*, The Cruising Association.

O'Neil, S. (1993) The future of the coast, *Sport and Leisure*, Jan./Feb.

Pelly, D. (1989) *The Illustrated Encyclopedia of World Sailing*, Marshall Cavendish Ltd.

Robinson, R. (1987) *Hamble: A Village History*, Kingfisher Railway Productions.

Sells Marine Market International (1993) Ben Business Information Services Ltd.

Sidaway, R. (1991) Marina development and coastal recreation: managing growth, *Ecos*, **12**(2).

Sports Council Report (1988) *Sport in the Community*, Sports Council.

Tate, M. (1994) Boat Show on a crest of a wave, *Observer*, 21.8.94.

Torkildsen, G. (1992) *Leisure and Recreation Management*, E & F N Spon.

Urry, J. (1990) *The Tourist Gaze: Leisure and Tourism in Contemporary Societies*, Sage.

Wooder (1992) Multi activity centres, *Insights*, English Tourist Board, May, B71–B82.

Sustainable Enjoyment: The Need for Leisure Management at the Coast

2

2.1 INTRODUCTION

Management is both an active human occupation and a continuous process by which people and organizations achieve results. In this chapter a distinction is drawn between the management of the coastal recreational experience and the management of the coast as a resource or arena within which such experiences take place. In future the two are likely to be seen as synonymous.

In 1965 Michael Dower warned that the wider countryside was not prepared for the influx of a mobile population looking for recreational · opportunities. Thirty years later the same might now be said of the coast. The pressure for participation in recreational activities in coastal areas (described in Chapter 1), and potential conflict with other users, has been one of the key factors which has prompted the attention now being given to the planning and management of the coast as a resource. Recent publications and government initiatives have highlighted confusion and concerns, emphasized by the need to implement European Union Directives and Regulations, about the administration and future development of maritime areas. Coastal resource planning and management is generally perceived as a public-sector role. A key aim is to balance the needs of recreation against those of commerce, economic development, wildlife and natural history, visual and aesthetic requirements and those of communities vulnerable to flooding. Traditional command and control management techniques are inappropriate and management by objectives and consensus, undertaken by multi-disciplinary teams, is widely accepted as the way forward.

There is also a clear need for management of maritime leisure activities at an individual or group level, on a voluntary or professional basis, publicly, privately and commercially; locally, regionally and nationally. The demand for coastal recreation, particularly in the most

Coastal Recreation Management Edited by Tim Goodhead and David Johnson. Published in 1996 by E & FN Spon, London. ISBN 0 419 20360 5

popular places and at the most popular times, can often outstrip the capacity of an area to accommodate that demand. Maximizing opportunity for maritime leisure requires responsible management of each recreational activity taking place in, on or around the coastal zone. Coastal recreational managers are responding to these specific challenges. A range of public, private and voluntary management organizations has evolved within which managers operate but coordination of the different organizations then brings its own problems.

There is obviously no panacea for integrating and resolving these two sets of management issues. However, the concept of 'Coastal Zone Management', based on principles of sustainable development, is gathering momentum worldwide and providing a framework for management which has hitherto been lacking. In the UK much of the attention has concentrated on the development of national policy for coastal matters, but a growing number of regional and local initiatives are also being developed or are already in place. Problems differ from area to area but are only likely to be resolved if all users and vested interests, including those concerned directly with coastal recreation, collaborate and agree strategic guidelines and then effect practical solutions.

2.2 MANAGEMENT PRINCIPLES AND PROCESSES

2.2.1 PRINCIPLES

Early studies of management were dedicated towards the understanding and improvement of the economic efficiency of both individuals and commercial organizations. Drucker, (1955) in his core text *The Practice of Management*, identified the following key management responsibilities which remain applicable to any management situation:

- management is concerned with responsibility for the future as well as the present;
- management should make what is desirable first possible and then actual;
- management is not just passive, adaptive, behaviour – it means taking action to make the desired results come to pass;

- the manager's job is to make a visible and measurable contribution to the success of the enterprise.

More recently a body of work on recreational management has developed recognizing that the management of 'people service' programmes differs in some fundamental respects from the management of commercial, profit-orientated operations. Any form of recreational management should be considered as a social as well as an economic process which accommodates and initiates recreational opportunity. It must also safeguard the natural environment within which it is accommodated.

A wealth of management theory is available which can be applied to any management topic. Classical management theory (as expounded by Fayol and Taylor) identifies five management processes (planning, organizing, commanding, coordinating, controlling) and 14 management functions (discipline, chain of command etc.). Efficiency of management is perceived as measurable. This structured approach underwrites many of the management frameworks within which coastal recreational activity operates (e.g. local government) but is often inappropriate to dynamic multiple-use resource management. Behaviourist or human relations theories (such as those of Maslow, McGregor and Herzberg) emphasize the requirements of individuals within the organization and the importance of people's needs. They suggest that these must be balanced with the objectives of the organization itself. Motivation and leadership theories, group dynamics and behaviour between different groups are all important elements of these theories.

Latterly systems approaches have emerged within which elements of any organization – people, tasks and technology – are drawn together. A management system allows each individual manager to determine his or her own way of addressing problems or opportunities by drawing on a series of known and tested techniques and management tools and by creating new techniques. This must also include a means of measuring and checking how well objectives are being met.

Ultimately, any form of management is carried out in the context of an organization formed by a group of people (see Torrington and Weightman, 1994). The contingency approach to organizational structure suggests that each organization responds to a variety of circumstances or contingencies. Formal structuring is closely related to size. The larger the organization, the greater the need to adopt a high level of formal structuring.

Coastal recreational management needs to incorporate a mix of each of these theories. Torkildsen (1986) maintains that classical management theory, adapted and modified to meet the needs of different organizations, can be used as a basic framework for the management of recreational services, facilities and programmes. From this he identifies the following five management functions:

Recreational management functions

1. Conceptualizing
2. Establishing objectives
3. Carrying out the plan and obtaining results through people
4. Seeking improvements and appraising results
5. Assisting subordinates – inspiring and motivating them

Source: adapted from Torkildsen (1986).

But recreational management is also very much concerned with anticipating and servicing the needs of people and, in doing so, encouraging teamwork.

The role of managers is to help the team identify goals and objectives, identify roles and objectives for individuals, monitoring the team and individual goals. Motivation is clearly important. Water-based recreation offers opportunities for managers to achieve recognition and status, in terms of both personal proficiency at an activity and building supportive work teams. Job satisfaction, social contacts and being part of a select group are often as important as salary and working conditions which often tend to be poor. The principal factors which influence effective teamwork are listed below:

Principal factors which influence effective teamwork

1. Leadership
2. Nature of tasks required to be performed
3. The knowledge, skills and motivation of the team members
4. The size of the group
5. The group's stage of development
6. Group cohesiveness (extent to which the group sticks together)
7. Group norms and organizational norms
8. The roles played by individuals
9. The environment in which the group has to work

Source: adapted from Cole (1993).

Of these leadership is a key influence within recreational management. Adair's model of leadership, which relates the needs of the task, the group and the individual, is very relevant as illustrated in Figure 2.1.

In this case the leader can be individual/group orientated in his or her approach in order to realize individual competence within small teams sailing dinghies.

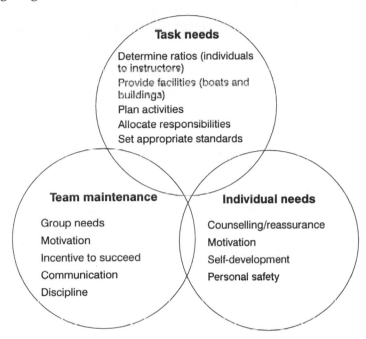

Task needs

Determine ratios (individuals to instructors)

Provide facilities (boats and buildings)

Plan activities

Allocate responsibilities

Set appropriate standards

Team maintenance

Group needs

Motivation

Incentive to succeed

Communication

Discipline

Individual needs

Counselling/reassurance

Motivation

Self-development

Personal safety

Figure 2.1 Functional model of leadership needs as applied to a hypothetical sail training situation. (Source: After Adair, 1982.)

However, priorities would change if the weather turned or the safety of the groups was compromised. Task needs would then take precedence. In the execution of tasks it is important to distinguish between 'compliance' and with the task and 'identification' with it. In recreation management, particularly activities where safety is of great importance, a high degree of identification with the task is essential. Again, this reinforces the importance of group identity and motivation.

Recreational management organizations can be viewed as open social systems whereby inputs, such as expertise, finance and equipment are converted (by the management process) into a recreational experience. For open systems, each of these stages – inputs, conversion, outputs – influence and are influenced by the environment.

Coastal recreational management is in many ways similar to countryside management given its reliance on the coast as a resource. Systems of 'Management by Objectives' are perhaps the most appropriate. Bromley (1990) suggests that such a system will enable the manager to:

- provide a suitable framework to work towards objectives;
- develop a suitable management culture of open discussion and mutual trust;
- manage change and help teams work through problems;
- generate commitment.

2.2.2 PROCESSES

In practice management processes can be seen to focus upon the relationship between four key management activities, summarized by Cole (1993): planning, organizing, motivating and controlling. However, this should not be seen as a 'linear' process but a 'cyclical' process of continual reappraisal and review. Indeed, slavish adherence to 'management by objectives' can lead to a narrow, 'blinkered' approach and a failure to 'see the wood for the trees'.

2.2.3 MANAGEMENT PLANNING

The planning function of management is the decision-making process which managers use to set out aims and objectives for their operation. Such decisions, about business direction and resourcing, can be classified as strategic, operational or administrative. The large number of stakeholders, with an interest in the coast, influences this process particularly at the strategic level, as explained later in this chapter. In operational terms specific targets, performance standards and manpower planning are important elements.

2.2.4 ORGANIZING

The process of organizing is concerned with creating the means to deliver aims and objectives. Cole (1993) defines this as a process for:

- determining, grouping and structuring activities;
- devising and allocating roles arising from the group of activities;
- assigning accountability for results to both groups and individuals; and
- determining detailed rules and systems of working, including those for communication, decision-making and conflict resolution.

The detailed organization of coastal recreational management becomes critical in terms of operation and safety (Chapter 8, Sea School Management).

2.2.5 MOTIVATING

Gaining commitment from staff and volunteers is essentially a human management process or skill. Its effectiveness is largely determined by the style of management, or the level of influence the manager has, in terms of directing the group to achieve results, once planning and organizing processes have taken place. It is essential, however, that managers demonstrate and encourage a high degree of 'identification' with the objectives and operating standards of this enterprise; mere 'compliance' with management tasks is not commensurate with good quality.

2.2.6 CONTROLLING

Control management processes aim to measure performance against set standards and effect any necessary corrective action. Timely feedback, information generated by control systems, is essential for accurate control management. For coastal recreational management both budgetary control measures and physical control measures such as safety checks, are important.

More recently Total Quality Management (TQM) concepts have been applied to recreational operations. These ideas are based on customer care principles in which quality is defined by the customer. Customer satisfaction is obviously crucial for any recreational service operation. Total quality policies rely on commitment from management and are then applied through organizations.

2.3 RESOURCE MANAGEMENT: RECONCILING COMPETING DEMANDS

The coastline is a vital finite national resource. Resource management is only one aspect of coastal management and planning, a body of information recently summarized by the government (DoE, 1993). And within the coastal resource, maritime leisure is only one of a list of major legitimate uses which take advantage of the benefits a varied coastline offers (Gubbay, 1990).

The boom in leisure activity requires resource managers to take recreational impacts more seriously than previously. The situation on the coast is made more complicated by the essential differences between terrestrial and marine resources, illustrated below:

Key differences between terrestrial and marine resources

Key features*	Terrestrial environment	Marine environment
Private property rights	Highly developed system covering all facets of resource use	Limited Generally in sea bed only
Degree of naturalness	Highly modified environment	Largely unmodified with 'high level of naturalness'
Spatial nature of resources	Fixed in short to medium term	Many mobile
Spatial nature of resource/use/users	Largely single user and location specific	Multi-use environment
Spatial nature of use impacts	generally fixed in short to medium term	Often geographically and temporally widespread

Source: Kerr (1994).

The impacts of recreational uses range from interference with the right of other users to the diversion of incompatible uses to other locations. In this context aspects of coastal recreation are seen as pressures or threats which need to be managed. The flow diagram in Figure 2.2 summarizes the overall situation.

Of all these potential conflicts, that prevailing between coastal recreation and nature conservation has attracted the most attention. Impact of recreation on nature conservation can create short- or long-term damage and disturbance which can be either reversible or irreversible. English Nature (1991) recognize disturbance as perhaps the major area of conflict, particularly in estuaries, affecting resident and migratory bird populations. The following specific conflicts are also detailed:

- loss of habitats caused by land-claim for recreational developments such as car parks, marinas and slips, jetties and piers;

- loss of intertidal habitat caused by amenity barrages impounding water upstream of the barrier which can then be used for recreational activities;
- damage to intertidal and terrestrial coastal fringe habitats mainly by terrestrial-based sports such as sand-yachting and horse riding;
- dredging of marina berths and access channels and disposal of dredgings.

Selman (1992) defines this resource management problem as one of environmental planning in its broadest sense for which an imaginative combination of legal remedies, negotiation, mediation and persuasion are required. He explains:

> If societal or individual use of the environment is deliberately or unwittingly selfish we need to modify ownership, or the user rights associated with ownership.

This is a rather extreme reaction to the imperfections of the market for allocating resources to their best use. However, the market mechanism gives insufficient weighting to the intrinsic or existence value of the natural environment. It operates largely on the basis that 'things' have value in use and/or value in scarcity. Furthermore, value in scarcity is only recognized in conjunction with 'ownership' and transferability from one owner to another. Flora and fauna which are incapable of being owned or transferred are considered to be 'wild' and have no economic value.

For this reason most coastal resource management is undertaken by the public sector, often as part of the local authority planning department's role. A rare exception to this is the Beaulieu estuary in Hampshire which is part of a private estate. Government guidance set out in the Planning Policy Guidance note on Coastal Planning PPG20(DOE/WO 1992) confirms this as follows:

> The coast is a popular destination for recreational activities and there have been growing pressures on its capacity. The natural beauty and landscape variety of the coast, its nature conservation interest and its various natural resources for recreation, such as water, beaches and cliffs, make it a major attraction. In most coastal areas the aim should be to balance and reconcile these interests and contain the impact of these activities through appropriate management measures.

This need to reconcile conflicting uses is supported in the UK by an increasing environmental consciousness. Key indicators identified by the Department of the Environment (1992) are:

The pressures:

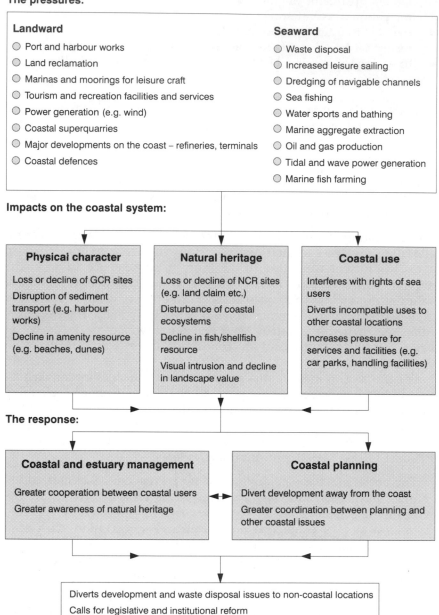

Landward	Seaward
○ Port and harbour works	○ Waste disposal
○ Land reclamation	○ Increased leisure sailing
○ Marinas and moorings for leisure craft	○ Dredging of navigable channels
○ Tourism and recreation facilities and services	○ Sea fishing
○ Power generation (e.g. wind)	○ Water sports and bathing
○ Coastal superquarries	○ Marine aggregate extraction
○ Major developments on the coast – refineries, terminals	○ Oil and gas production
○ Coastal defences	○ Tidal and wave power generation
	○ Marine fish farming

Impacts on the coastal system:

Physical character	Natural heritage	Coastal use
Loss or decline of GCR sites	Loss or decline of NCR sites (e.g. land claim etc.)	Interferes with rights of sea users
Disruption of sediment transport (e.g. harbour works)	Disturbance of coastal ecosystems	Diverts incompatible uses to other coastal locations
Decline in amenity resource (e.g. beaches, dunes)	Decline in fish/shellfish resource	Increases pressure for services and facilities (e.g. car parks, handling facilities)
	Visual intrusion and decline in landscape value	

The response:

Coastal and estuary management	Coastal planning
Greater cooperation between coastal users	Divert development away from the coast
Greater awareness of natural heritage	Greater coordination between planning and other coastal issues

Diverts development and waste disposal issues to non-coastal locations

Calls for legislative and institutional reform

Figure 2.2 Coastal resource management. (Source: DOE, 1993. Crown Copyright is reproduced with the permission of the Controller of HMSO.)

- during the 1980s people have expressed an increased willingness to accept the economic costs of measures to protect the environment;
- the membership of environmental groups in the UK has increased significantly since 1981;
- around 9 out of 10 people say they are interested in the environment.

The coastal resource manager therefore aims to manage the coast, not only because it is all too easily destroyed by a range of human activities but also for its own sake.

Perhaps the most pressing issue for coastal resource management is the problem of coordinating activity and decision-making across the coastal zone. Particular difficulties are experienced in the area immediately above and below low water mark, especially in conservation terms for the protection of intertidal habitats.

2.4 RECREATIONAL MANAGEMENT: MANAGING THE RECREATIONAL EXPERIENCE

Growth in the number of people participating in watersports and changes in lifestyles, technology and disposable incomes (Ratcliffe, 1992) all add to the complexity of the equation making this the most dynamic of activities to be managed. Torkildsen (1986) introduces his chapter on leisure and recreation management by stating that

> good management of recreation is concerned with meeting objectives and targets, achieving optimal use of resources, achieving financial objectives, meeting priority needs and offering the most attractive services to meet recreational demands.

The coastal recreational manager should have a clear understanding of the products or services being supplied. His or her function, whether in the public private or community sector, is to provide settings and opportunities for people's water-based recreational experience.

Recreational managers are 'selling' the benefits of their attraction or sport and marketing becomes an important mainstream activity. Marketing is defined as a social and managerial process leading to an exchange of products(s). Companies may be orientated in various ways – to production, to their product, to selling or to marketing. Many coastal recreational enterprises naturally assume a marketing orientation. Customer satisfaction must also be included in this definition. Many functions of recreation provision are led by consumers' requirements and therefore market segmentation becomes very important to the manager. Customers' needs and wants must be identified by market research, thus enabling targeting of different segments. Leisure interests themselves are often used as a market segmentation indicator but other typical parameters are social class, family life cycle stages, age demography and occupation.

Seabrooke and Miles (1992) define 'the recreational experience' as a service which comprises both active participation which occurs at the source of the supply (in this case the coast), together with elements – particularly anticipation and reflection – which occur back home. The 'experience' can range from informal recreation to formalized leisure pursuits. The recreation experience and the nature of most recreation sites are complex and the marketing associated with them is correspondingly complex. Although the need for leisure and recreation is important in the context of individual self-fulfilment the way in which that need is expressed is manifestly variable: it varies from person to person, from time to time and place to place. The way in which sites are perceived also varies according to the nature and context of the use which it supports and the degree of imagination and sensitivity of the users. Visitors who are new to a site or visit infrequently may need to be informed about the site and how best to use it. Managers should not assume that all visitors will use a site in the 'planned manner' when this is in any way unclear.

Watersports are particularly good at stimulating a variety of sensations, such as excitement, exhilaration and the feeling of social well-being gained from enjoying the experience with other like-minded people. Novelty of the experience is also often a key source of enjoyment. An activity tackled for the first time, in a new location, or challenged by an ever-changing and unique set of physical conditions provides a different experience. As with any leisure activity, participants make a conscious decision to undertake the activity. Choice is freedom, and freedom is pleasure and also responsibility.

The location and spatial distribution of activities is fundamentally important. The recreation manager should be able to identify, systematically and objectively, the potential uses of any site, the likely duration of those uses, and the capacity of the site to accommodate recreational pressures. Market research will help define any such assessment but value is the yardstick by which management effectiveness is measured. 'Value' is formulated and expressed in many forms; it is a social expression of worth. All managers are charged with responsibility for maintaining or enhancing the worth of the resources to which they have access. Management decisions which result in a diminution in the worth of resources can expect harsh judgement.

However, 'worth' can be expressed in a variety of ways and relate to a variety of time horizons. Each form and time horizon may be valid yet may not lead to an effective, sustainable allocation of resources.

As a general rule most resource allocation decisions are strongly influenced, if not solely determined by, financial expressions of worth and, although long-term views are often espoused, short-term criteria often hold sway over long-term sustainability. In the natural environment, however, the 'worth' of resources is often expressed in terms which are inherently non-financial: they may relate to natural science, culture or aesthetic values. Unlike financial values which are usually tied to the 'use' to which a site or the resources associated with it can be put, these other values are tied to the qualities associated with the simple existence of the site, its qualities and characteristics. Such values can easily be swept aside as managers strive to maximize use values and the collective failure of managers and planners to take proper account of 'existence' values leads, inevitably, to long-term deterioration of the natural environment and to resource management which is manifestly unsustainable in the long run.

Seabrooke and Miles consider valuation of the site, or what it can provide in terms of recreational opportunity, in terms of location factors, site attraction and carrying capacity.

2.4.1 LOCATION FACTORS

The relationship between location of a site and its accessibility to the people for whom it is intended to be attractive is fundamental to any resource evaluation. The 30-mile radius, rule of thumb distance, that daytrippers will casually venture from home by car is probably conservative for many coastal locations. It is estimated that no place in the UK is more than 83 miles from the coast and parts of the coast often draw people from great distances.

2.4.2 SITE ATTRACTION

The most positive influence on the value of a site in recreational use is its capability to attract visitors. For water-based recreation the site may:

- offer special physical water conditions (sheltered, safe/exposed, exhilarating);
- be where facilities exist such as marinas or clubhouses;
- be near to competition areas (e.g. The Solent);
- be naturally beautiful, such as some harbours or beaches.

Seabrooke and Miles define five broad headings under which the attractiveness of a site may be categorized – distinctiveness, quality, availability, quality of management and price. Matching the physical characteristics of the site with specific activities is a routine stage in evaluation.

Skilful marketing can assist site attractiveness. In coastal areas quality schemes, such as the EC Blue Flag Award, have exerted considerable influence on whether or not people choose to visit any particular site.

2.4.3 CARRYING CAPACITY

Management needs to balance attracting visitors without causing an unacceptable deterioration. This is normally a physical factor – pressure leading to erosion or crowding can result in physical damage with a resultant knock-on effect for the recreational experience and return visit potential.

The quality of management determines to a large extent the type of use and viability of recreation facilities.

Managing the coastal recreational experience requires the ability to:

● research and appreciate leisure demands;
● communicate with and manage people;
● make decisions particularly in the interests of safety;
● understand the variety and mix of watersports;
● ensure financial viability;
● plan ahead to create opportunities and anticipate the need for future provision.

Practical common sense and an empathy with those using the facility are also important.

2.5 COASTAL ZONE MANAGEMENT

The concept of Coastal Zone Management (CZM) has developed from the struggle to find a mechanism to balance the demands on the coastal resource, promote its sustainable use and manage individual activities including those associated with coastal recreation. It is now recognized that coastal areas need to be managed in an integrated way. Recreation should be considered as one part of the whole and not managed independently of other activities in the same area. Indeed, the nature of property rights in the coastal zone, particularly relating to the surface or body of water, notably the established concepts of common property and open access resources, largely determines that recreation must co-exist with other maritime activities. The need to work in harmony with the numerous agencies involved with the coast is therefore an important element of the job of coastal recreation managers. This approach was articulated at the World Coast Conference (1993):

A national CZM programme should facilitate integrated decision making through a continuous and evolutionary process for cooperation and coordination among sectors, integrating national and local interests in the management of activities concerning the environment and development [through] education, public awareness and an equitable process for the participation of all stakeholders.

The Marine Conservation Society also see CZM as being about increasing awareness of the wide range of issues facing the environment of the coastal zone and the cumulative effects of coastal development. Coastal zone managers need to interpret what they do and attempt to educate users about the qualities of the resources they are trying to manage. First introduced in legislation in the USA in 1972 and subsequently by Sweden and Australia, the ideas of CZM have been adopted internationally (OCED, 1993). They are rooted in environmental concerns about the vulnerability of the coast and have grown in parallel and in response to calls for sustainable development.

The most often quoted definition of sustainable development was made in *Our Common Future*, the report of the World Commission on Environment and Development, also known as the Bruntland Report (1987):

Development that meets the needs of the present without compromising the ability of future generations to meet their needs.

Sustainability has emerged during the 1980s as a unifying approach to concerns over the environment, economic development and the quality of life (see Mannion and Bowlby, 1992 for a fuller discussion), and is seen as a dynamic process – not an absolute state.

Coastal management is the central issue for the 'Oceans' chapter of Agenda 21 (1992), the Agenda for Action which arose from the United Nations Conference on Environment and Development of the Rio Earth Summit. In Agenda 21 the coastal states of the world 'commit themselves to integrated management and sustainable development of coastal areas and the marine environment under their national jurisdiction'.

The European Union (EU) is currently moving towards a Strategy for Integrated CZM and coastal zones feature as a theme of the Fifth Environmental Action Programme 'Towards Sustainability' (EC, 1992). The Institute for European Environmental Policy, in a briefing paper, have illustrated a possible outline for an EU Strategy (Mullard, 1994).

In the UK the coastal zone has been the focus of attention both at national, policy-making level and in terms of regional and local CZM initiatives. In 1994, following a consultation exercise, the government announced their intention to formulate a statement of policy guidance for the coast; to set up a standing forum on CZM; to highlight good practice on coastal management plans and to review bye-law powers relating to coastal management.

The objectives of CZM have been summarized as:

- promoting sustainable use;
- balancing demand for coastal resources;
- resolving conflicts of use;
- promoting environmentally sensitive use of the coastal zone;
- promoting strategic planning for coasts.

The national standing forum (the Coastal Forum) held its first meeting in December 1994. Coastal groups at all levels (Gubbay, 1992) continue to deliver the objectives of CZM but progress is slow.

Depending on the spatial and temporal scales considered, some land and water uses can occur contemporaneously or sequentially: others cannot. Multiple and sequential use strategies for the coastal zone have a major role to play in the sustainable use and conservation of coastal resources (Selman, 1992).

2.6 CONCLUSION

There are certain basic principles, which, with modification, may help in devising a management regime for any specific purpose. However, while established management theories are applicable to coastal recreation management, the coast is such a diverse recreational resource that no particular management or administrative model is appropriate for all situations. It is therefore impossible to prescribe one simple approach to the management of coastal recreation. Nevertheless, coastal recreational managers will become or will need to work alongside coastal resource managers whose aim is to minimize conflict between different recreational uses and between recreation and other uses. In part the success or otherwise of the resource managers will help determine the recreational experience but, at the same time, providing opportunities which satisfy recreational demand will remain the key recreational management function.

Coastal Zone Management is an embracing concept which encompasses both resource management and the management of user enterprises such as recreation. In practice CZM is still in its infancy. The intensification of use in the marine and coastal environments has become remarkable only relatively recently. The use of land has a longer history, partly because human survival on land is easier than the marine equivalent. The institutions which govern land use and conflict resolution are well developed and relatively easy to monitor and control. The same is manifestly not the case in the marine and coastal environments. The institutions governing use are relatively sparse and weak. We have, therefore, to develop new approaches and institutional support to manage the marine and coastal environment effectively, efficiently, and above all in a manner which does not permit these environments to be officially degraded. Much needs to be done to translate international intentions into national policy and practical solutions. As part of such a process good coastal recreational managers need to understand the environment within which they are working and the operation of the activities which they seek to manage. An awareness of current management solutions and their implementation is also important. The remainder of this book provides information to help further that end.

Ultimately good management is delivered by perceptive managers.

REFERENCES

Adair, J. (1982) *Action Centred Leadership*, Gower, Aldershot.
Agenda 21 (1992) *Chapter 17 – Protection of the Oceans, All Kinds of Seas, including Enclosed and Semi-Enclosed Seas and Coastal Areas and the Protection, Rational Use and Development of their Living Resources*, United Nations Conference on Environment and Development.
Bromley, P. (1990) *Countryside Management*, E & FN Spon, London.
Cole, G. A. (1993) *Management Theory and Practice*, 4th edn, DP Publications, London.
Dower, M. (1965) *The Challenge of Leisure: the Fourth Wave*, Civic Trust.
DoE (1992) *The UK Environment*, HMSO, London.
DoE (1993) *Coastal Planning and Management: A Review*, HMSO, London.
DoE/Welsh Office (1992) *Coastal Planning*, PPG20, HMSO, London.
Drucker, P. (1955) *The Practice of Management*, Pan Books, London.
EC (1992) *Towards Sustainability Fifth Environmental Action Programme*, COM (92) 93.

Gubbay, S. (1990) *A Future for the Coast?: Proposals for a UK Coastal Zone Management Plan*, Report for the World Wide Fund for Nature from the Marine Conservation Society, Ross on Wye.

Gubbay, S. (1992) *Role of Coastal Groups in Coastal Zone Management*, Marine Conservation Society/World Wide Fund for Nature Discussion Paper CZM/4.

House of Commons Environment Committee: Second Report (1992) *Coastal Zone Protection and Planning*, HMSO, London.

Kerr, S. (1994) *Scottish Regional Planning*, RICS Workshop, Surveying at Sea: Business opportunities in the coastal zone, Cardiff, 30 September 1994.

Mannion, A. and Bowlby, S. (1992) *Environmental Issues in the 1990's*, Wiley, Chichester.

Mullard, S. (1994) *Towards an EU Strategy for Integrated Coastal Zone Management*, IEEP London, Background Briefing No. 1.

OECD (1993) *Coastal Zone Management Integrated Policies*, Paris, Organisation for Economic Cooperation and Development.

Ratcliffe, T. (1992) Responsibility for water sports management and development, *Ocean and Coastal Management*, 18, 259–68.

Seabrooke, W. and Miles, C. (1992) *Recreational Land Management*, E & FN Spon, London.

Selman, P. (1992) *Environmental Planning: The Conservation and Development of Biophysical Resources*, Paul Chapman Publishing Ltd, London.

Torkildsen, G. (1986) *Leisure and Recreation Management*, E & FN Spon, London.

Torrington, D. and Weightman, J. (1994) *Effective Management People and Organisation*, 2nd edn, Prentice Hall International, Hemel Hempstead.

World Coast 2000 (1993) *Preparing to meet the Coastal Challenges of the 21st Century*, Conference Statement, Noordwijk, The Netherlands, 5 November 1993.

World Commission on Environment and Development (1987) *Our Common Future*, Oxford University Press, Oxford.

PART TWO
The Coastal Recreation Environment

Working with Change: Wind, Waves and Tides

3

3.1 INTRODUCTION

The coastal zone of the United Kingdom has been quantified as 15 000 km (9500 miles) of coast line and one-third of a million square kilometres (125 000 square miles) of territorial waters (House of Commons Environment Committee, 1992). It includes over 160 estuaries and harbours ranging from wide expanses, such as Morecombe Bay and Lyme Bay, to the relatively protected Solent or the enclosed narrow waters of the Dart.

These waters offer considerable choice for coastal recreation, from swimming and jet skiing to racing 'round the cans' in £100 000 yachts. The vagaries of wind, weather and waves add to these varied venues to provide infinite possibilities for coastal recreational experiences. However not all experiences are pleasant ones. In October 1987 many yachts, pontoons and marinas were devastated by storm force winds. In August 1986 a balmy Sunday became a stormy August Bank Holiday Monday when ex tropical storm Charley hit the south coast of the UK.

How often does one hear 'I had not seen the chart' or 'I missed the 0555 forecast' uttered in the sailing club after a particularly difficult sail? The aftermath of a sunny sail at the start of the season is often a severe case of sunburn! Many accidents could be avoided if leisure users took more notice of the factors that conspire to make their environment hostile. Never before has such a large amount of information been available to advise the user of the likely weather up to a week ahead throughout the whole world. Ignorance is not a valid excuse when winched into the SAR (search and rescue) helicopter!

The physical processes involved in creating this environment are complex and have been the subject of many texts such as Barry and Chorley (1992). It is not within the scope of this book to repeat these explanations, rather to provide the maritime leisure manager with an

Coastal Recreation Management Edited by Tim Goodhead and David Johnson. Published in 1996 by E & FN Spon, London. ISBN 0 419 20360 5

appreciation of the environment so that operations will become more safe and enjoyable.

This chapter therefore draws out aspects of weather information that are most appropriate to marine leisure operators, managers and watersport enthusiasts. A global overview of wind, weather and currents is considered which is relevant to the ocean yachtsman and developers considering setting up overseas, followed by a more detailed appraisal for UK-based centres.

3.2 GLOBAL WEATHER

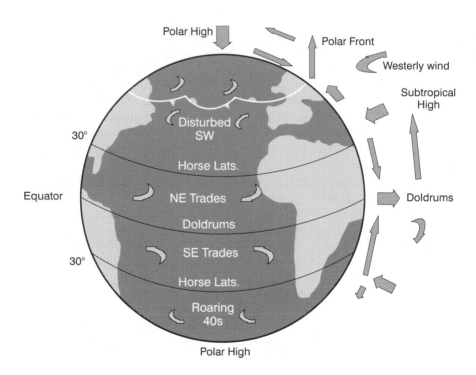

Figure 3.1 General atmospheric circulation. © WITMR 1155 pt.3

Variations in surface temperature and subsequently air temperature are the driving forces behind the weather systems. Solar energy is the major factor in directing these forces with the distribution of land and sea playing an important role.

3.2.1 DOLDRUMS

Due to the earth's shape more heat energy from the sun strikes the earth at the tropics than at the poles. Thus the surface of the earth is relatively hotter in the tropics than in higher latitudes, causing the air in contact to be warmed, expand, rise and form cloud. This area is known as the 'doldrums'. The air is hot and humid, with light surface winds or flat calm for days on end. Often heavy rainfall occurs with a sudden increase of wind (squalls).

3.2.2 TRADE WINDS

The air rising in the doldrums is replaced by air from the regions of approximately 30° N and 30° S. Due to the earth's rotation these winds are turned towards the right in the Northern Hemisphere and towards the left in the Southern to produce the North East and South East Trade Winds respectively. The wind is relatively steady (between 15 and 25 knots), and the weather is predominantly fair with cumulus cloud, good visibility and a long swell. For yachtsmen tradewind sailing is the ultimate experience and for tropical islands situated in the trade wind latitudes sailing conditions are superb. Hawaii, Barbados and the Canaries have become magnets for watersport enthusiasts.

3.2.3 SUBTROPICAL HIGH PRESSURE AREAS

At around 30° N and S are the Horse Latitudes. The air subsides and is dominated by high pressure. Winds are light and variable with little rainfall. All the major deserts lie close to this latitude. The name Horse latitudes is derived from stories of sailing ships becoming becalmed so that traders were forced to pitch their horses overboard in a desperate attempt to conserve fresh water. In the North Atlantic this area is normally referred to as the Azores High due to the position of the 'Arquipélago dos Açôres'. The extensions or ridges from this area produce UK 'heat wave' conditions in the summer. Water-based recreation can be good in these latitudes because of the dry, warm and sunny conditions. However, the light gradient winds mean that wind-powered sports must rely on winds caused by temperature differences between the land and sea to produce sea breezes, a rather precarious commercial situation which requires much local knowledge. Developers should therefore research a site fully before making any commitments. In summer the Mediterranean lies under the influence of these anti-cyclonic conditions, and excellent sea breeze conditions can be found. Vassiliki Bay on the Greek island of Lefkas, once a sleepy fishing village, is an example of where such conditions prevail, thus providing excellent windsurfing and catamaran sailing conditions. Up to 1000 craft can now be seen at this venue in the height of the season.

3.2.4 SEASONAL MOVEMENT

The doldrums and subtropical highs move only slightly north and south with the seasons over the Atlantic and Pacific due to the relatively slow take-up of heat by the water. But over large land masses the heating effect is more noticeable. In the Northern Hemisphere winter the sun is directly above the Tropic of Capricorn and heat lows are formed over Brazil, Southern Africa and Australia. In the summer these migrate north to cover Southern Asia (causing the SW monsoons), Central Africa – particularly the area of Ghana, Nigeria, etc. and the Southern Caribbean. In the summer/early autumn of each hemisphere the heated water may provide the driving force for the Tropical Storms or Cyclones which cause havoc in areas such as the Caribbean.

3.2.5 POLAR HIGH PRESSURE AREAS

At the poles the surface of the earth is cold and the air in contact, cools, contracts and becomes relatively dense. Thus vast areas of high pressure are produced with values as high as 1070 millibars (hectoPascals). These so called 'Polar Highs' dominate the poles throughout the year and Siberia in winter, producing cold but dry conditions.

3.2.6 TEMPERATE LATITUDES

Between the Polar High and the Subtropical High pressure areas are the temperate latitudes, and air from either of these can dominate the British Isles. Air from the Azores begins its journey in a warm moist region and is known as Tropical Maritime Air Mass in UK. As it travels north it is deflected to the right by the Coriolis effect to become a south-west wind. Also the sea surface cools the air, making it more stable and causing low cloud and hill fog on the coast particularly in spring when the water is at its coldest. If the sea surface temperature is within ½°C of the dew point of the air then 'sea fog' can be expected. Sea fog or 'advection' fog patches can be produced which can dramatically turn a warm, sunny and pleasant cruise into a cold and frightening experience.

Air from the poles is cold, as it moves across a warmer surface it is warmed, and becomes 'unstable'. The air in contact rises, cools and any moisture condenses to form cumulus cloud. In the UK this is known as

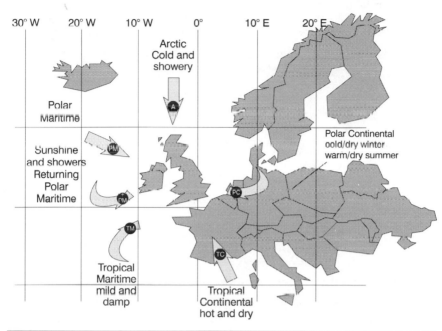

Figure 3.2 Air masses affecting UK. © WITMR 1155 pt.5

Name	Direction	Origin/track	General	Summer	Winter
Polar Continental Pc	NE or E	Eastern Europe	Picks up moisture if crosses North Sea	Low cloud, fog (Haar/Fret) on east coast	Very cold. Snow flurries on east coast
Polar Maritime Pm	NW or W	Canada and Greenland/N Atlantic	Unstable, sunshine and showers, good visibility	Possible hail and thunder	Wintry showers particularly in the west
Returning Polar Maritime rPm	SW	Canada and Greenland/N Atlantic	Warmed then cooled, i.e. unstable then stable	Heated again, giving sunshine and showers (hail and thunder!)	Remains stable, low cloud, mod/poor visibility
Tropical Arctic Northerly A	N	Arctic/Norwegian Sea	Very unstable	Does not normally occur	Snow/sleet showers, Polar Low can make snow prolonged/heavy
Tropical Continental Tc	S or SE	Sahara or SE Europe	Stable, brings industrial pollution and haze	Heat wave	Indian summer!
Tropical Maritime Tm	SW	Azores High/ N Atlantic	Mild drizzly weather, possibility of fog	Hot land breaks up cloud inland	Low cloud, mod/poor visibility

'polar maritime air'. This gives cool, clear conditions with excellent visibility. However once the cloud becomes large enough showers of rain can be produced from cumulonimbus clouds. These conditions are particularly dangerous for the yachtsman as they can deteriorate rapidly — visibility reduces, the wind increases in a gust or squall, occasionally hail, thunder and lightning are also present. A summary of these and the other air masses affecting the UK are shown in Figure 3.2.

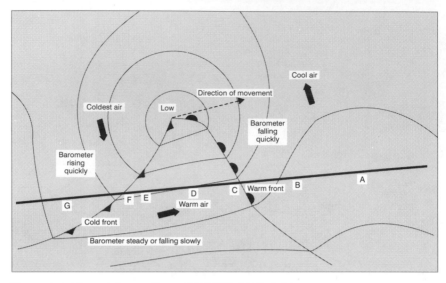

Figure 3.3 Frontal depressions. © WITMR 1155 pt.15

Where two masses of air meet defines the 'polar front'. The collision causes the wet and windy weather that often conspires to affect a UK-based holiday. In the Northern Hemisphere the warm tropical maritime south-west winds meet the cold winds from the pole, this causes an anticlockwise spin and the commensurate low-pressure areas of frontal depressions. In summer the North Pole is in perpetual daylight, the polar air is therefore not as cold making gales less likely. At the autumnal equinox (21 September) night descends at the North Pole (for six months) and gales become commonplace throughout the winter. The 'equinoctial gale' is therefore a foretaste of the winter gales and not as is often thought any more severe.

The movement of these depressions and passage of polar fronts, are summarized in Figures 3.3 and 3.4.

It is imperative that the leisure operator/user is able to identify these features and to interpret the weather charts and forecasts available, a list of which is given in Figure 3.5. It is also necessary to monitor local conditions to ascertain whether these forecasts are correct. Many a professional forecaster has been 'caught out' by not 'looking out of the window'!

3.2.7 LOCAL EFFECTS

Perhaps equally important to the leisure operators are the smaller scale effects such as diurnal (day/night) temperatures changes, land/sea temperature differences and effects caused by topographic features.

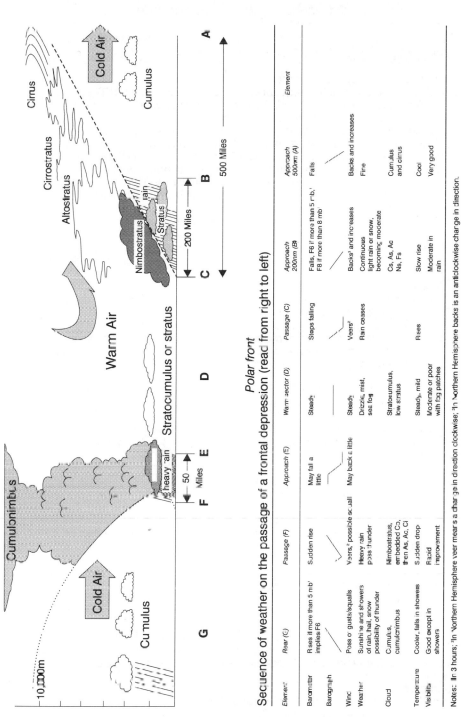

Polar front

Sequence of weather on the passage of a frontal depression (read from right to left)

Element	Rear (G)	Passage (F)	Approach (E)	Warm sector (D)	Passage (C)	Approach 200mm (B)	Approach 500mm (A)	Element
Barometer	Rises if more than 5 mb¹ implies F6	Sudden rise	May fall a little	Steady	Stops falling	Falls, F6 if more than 5 mb,¹ F8 if more than 8 mb¹	Falls	
Barograph								
Wind	Poss or gusts/squalls	Veers², possible squall	May back a little	Steady	Veers²	Backs² and increases	Backs and increases	
Weather	Sunshine and showers of rain, hail, snow possibility of thunder	Heavy rain poss thunder		Drizzle, mist, sea fog	Rain ceases	Continuous light rain or snow, becoming moderate	Fine	
Cloud	Cumulus, cumulonimbus	Nimbostratus, embedded Cb, then As, Ac, Ci		Stratocumulus, low stratus		Cs, As, Ns, Fs	Cumulus and cirrus	
Temperature	Cooler, falls in showers	Sudden drop		Steady, mild	Rises	Slow rise	Cool	
Visibility	Good except in showers	Rapid improvement		Moderate or poor with fog patches		Moderate in rain	Very good	Element

Notes: In 3 hours; ²In Northern Hemisphere veer means a change in direction clockwise; ¹In Northern Hemisphere backs is an anticlockwise change in direction.

Figure 3.4 Passage of Polar fronts. © WTMR I155 pt.14

Weather information for coastal areas can be obtained from the following sources:

BBC Radio 4 Shipping Forecast
198 kHz, and on local MF frequencies at 0045, 0555, 1355 and 1750
The 0045 hrs forecast is followed by a forecast for coastal waters up to 12 nautical miles offshore, valid until 1800 hrs.
The bulletins include a summary of gale warnings in force; a general synopsis of the weather for the next 24 hours and expected changes within that period; forecasts for each sea area for the next 24 hours giving wind direction and speed, weather and visibility; and the latest reports from coastal stations for which wind strength and direction, weather, visibility and sea level pressure are given. Coastal stations are marked on the chart by their initial letters.
BBC Inshore Waters Forecast
Gives forecasts for inshore water up to 12 nm offshore on Radio 4 at 0048 after the shipping forecast and on Radio 3 (91.0–92.3 MHz) at 0655 daily.
Local radio stations
Give a variety of forecasts at various times, some of which are more detailed than others.
Special forecasts for ships at sea
Forecasts for areas bounded by 65°N and 35°N and 40°W and the coast of Europe including the Mediterranean may be obtained by yachtsmen by contacting the Met Office Central Forecast Office by telephone (0344) 854913 (link calls are free) or by direct request to the nearest UK coast radio station. Weather centres provide a range of services and may be contacted direct to arrange a service.
Marine Call
Recorded Met office forecasts updated at least twice daily (three times in summer) cover up to 12 nm offshore including Channel and Irish Sea crossings.
In each case, dial 0891 500 and then the three figure number of the area required (e.g: 0891 500 457 for Lyme Regis to Selsey Bill) – good, but can be expensive!
Marine Weatherfax
Weather maps and forecasts are avilable by facsimile. A whole range of different options are available, listings may be found in the Nautical Almanac.
NAVTEX
This aid is an automatic teleprinter system used by ships but also accessible for recreation users in many maritime pubs giving shipping forecast and gale warnings.
Press forecasts
The delay between time of issue and the time they are avilable next day make them of limited value to seafarers.
TV forecasts
Can be a useful guide to the weather situation at the start of the passage.
Coast radio stations
BT Coast Radio Stations broadcast weather information on MF and VHF twice daily at 0733 and 1933 UT. The forecasts originate from the Met Office shipping forecasts. After an initial announcement on Channel 16 they will transmit on a specific frequency.
Inmarsat
Satellite communications offers similar services to the terrestrial networks.
Finally, Harbour Masters, Marina Operators and sailing clubs usually post the latest weather forecast to inform their customers!

Figure 3.5 Sources of weather information

3.2.8 SEA BREEZE

Differential heating of the sea and land can cause major variations in the weather over a 24-hour period, particularly on clear days. The sea temperature changes only slightly – it always feels cold sailing on the English Channel even in summer! However, over the land changes are significant. In the morning after sunrise the land heats up, the air in contact warms and rises causing air to be drawn in from the sea, thus setting up a 'sea breeze' in the late morning and afternoon. The force of this breeze in general is about force 3–4 (7–15 kns) and reaches its maximum at about 3 p.m. local time. These breezes give ideal sailing conditions but they quickly die away in the late afternoon, when the land cools. Also in some areas a 'hole' can occur. For example, in the Solent a south-west wind may act in the west, south-east in the east where these meet off Cowes yachts can be left becalmed.

3.2.9 LAND BREEZE

Just as the sea breeze sets in when the land warms a 'land breeze' occurs when it cools. In the early hours cold air from the land sinks and moves out to sea where it rises and a cycle is set up. It rarely reaches more than force 3. However, if the coast is sloping, very cold air on the hill tops will sink quickly and reinforce the land breeze (known as Katabatic reinforcement).

If a river or similar valley is present then funnelling can occur and winds can reach great strengths. These are most evident in the Mediterranean where the Mistral and Bora are good examples of such winds. A similar effect occurs around headlands, where the strength is particularly strong off the headlands. In the lee shelter is provided, but with many 'back eddies'.

It must be emphasized that the direction of wind relative to the coastline is also important. The sea breeze sets in at right angles to the coast, but as the day progresses 'Coriolis' takes effect and the direction changes to the right in the Northern Hemisphere (veers) so that it can blow parallel to the coast as the afternoon progresses.

3.2.10 OFFSHORE WINDS

Coastline topography exerts a strong influence over the consistency of offshore winds particularly in the immediate inshore zone. In built-up, tree-lined or hilly areas, offshore winds can be extremely gusty up to 2–3 miles offshore. Inshore sea conditions are generally calm even in quite strong offshore winds due to insufficient fetch for wave build-up. The

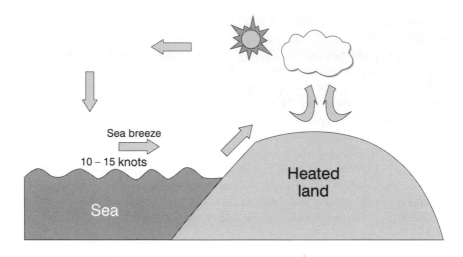

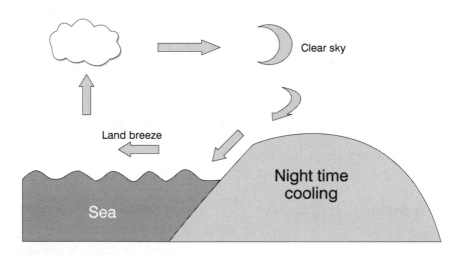

Figure 3.6 Sea breeze and land breeze. © WITMR 1155 pt.6 and 7

further off the coast one goes the more consistent the wind and the bigger the waves become. Despite the false sense of security given by the calm waters most watersports are not recommended in offshore winds. The risk of drifting away from the land and therefore encountering more extreme conditions and a worsening problem is too great. For beginners, sailing courses in gusty wind conditions should be avoided. The sudden changes in strength and direction will confuse and unnerve students. In the case of a lake location, where the wind is often gusty, organizers should study the conditions carefully before selecting the operating location. Often it is possible to find clean wind conditions simply by moving a little way from the launch site. But powerboating and waterskiing are two activities for which offshore winds are favourable due to the flat sea surface.

3.2.11 ONSHORE WINDS

Although the knowledge that a disabled craft would be returned to shore by an onshore breeze seems reassuring, it is very often a false sense of security. In light winds and calm sea conditions onshore winds are perfectly safe. However in winds above Beaufort force 3 sea conditions quickly become difficult, especially if the water is shallow, and there is a high risk of being swept onto a lee shore. Sailing instructors should always study the forecast and consider tidal conditions when operating in onshore conditions and be prepared to move to a new location quickly if conditions change.

Onshore winds generally give rise to rough inshore sea conditions and can make boating both uncomfortable and dangerous. If the coastline is gradually shelving the sea conditions in strong onshore winds will be quite severe with a lot of breaking white water. In the case of a steeply shelving coastline there will be a very severe shorebreak making launching of equipment a difficult and potentially costly affair. In addition to difficult sea conditions the wind may be gusty as it negotiates the frictional transition from sea to land (especially if the land is hilly).

3.2.12 SIDESHORE WINDS

Sideshore winds offer the best compromise for boating. Sea conditions are generally good and winds are not too gusty. Watersports facility developers should look out for prevailing sideshore winds when selecting a site.

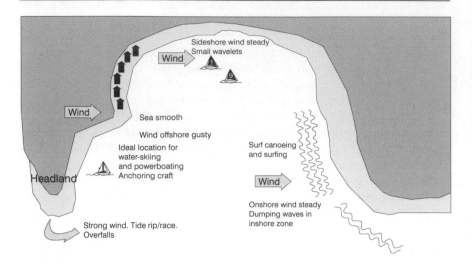

Figure 3.7 Wind direction and associated sea conditions. © WITMR 1155 pt.2

3.2.13 WIND AGAINST TIDE CONDITIONS

When wind and tidal stream oppose one another there is an increase in relative windspeed and thus an increase in wave frequency and height. Wind against tide sea conditions are characterized by short sharp chop making sailing exciting but difficult. Inexperienced sailors often get into great difficulties in these conditions. For experienced sailors and windsurfers, who are aware of the conditions and their own limitations, wind against tide conditions can be exciting and offer the opportunity to practise lots of downwind sailing and gybing without having to fight back upwind. Instructors should be aware when setting out in wind against tide conditions that as the tidal stream increases so will the relative wind and boats may quickly become overpowered. It is as well to err on the side of caution and reef boats down heavily.

3.3 WAVES

Waves also offer tremendous adventure playgrounds for the recreational water enthusiast. But they can cause treacherous conditions and an understanding and respect for them is of the utmost importance. The main cause of waves is the strength of the wind. They are also generated by the tide, other boats and undersea earthquakes known as Tsunami and (somewhat erroneously) tidal waves. If the wind is blowing offshore small waves are soon generated, but a relatively large distance (or fetch) is required before a state of equilibrium occurs and a 'fully arisen' sea ensues, where the wave height is then directly related to the wind speed. The Beaufort scale is used to identify wind and waves and a summary of this for waterbased users is shown in Figure 3.8.

This 'sea' will travel in a direction close to that of the generating wind. However it will then travel to another area where it becomes known as a 'swell' wave. These swells can travel hundreds of miles until they reach a shallow area or coastline where they form 'surf', break and lose their energy.

In the UK, Cornwall, South Wales and the west coast of Scotland have the best surf conditions due to their uninterrupted westerly fetch. If a residual swell remains in calm conditions and a new wind impinges on it the new wave pattern will interfere with the old one. At times the wave crests associated with the new wind will coincide with those of the residual swell giving rise to a bigger wave. This is known as 'constructive interference'. At other times a wave crest will coincide with a wave trough causing a flatspot. This is 'destructive interference'. It is interference which gives rise to the phenomenon of 'wave sets' (groups of larger and smaller waves) and the 'seventh wave theory' (every seventh wave is a larger one).

As waves enter shallow water the front of the wave slows down due to friction with the seabed. The back of the wave catches up causing the wave height to increase until it becomes unstable whereupon the wave will break. The depth at which the wave starts to 'feel bottom' and therefore increase in height is estimated to be approximately equal to the wavelength (up to 100 m in heavy weather). The speed at which the base of the wave is slowed determines the nature of the breaking wave and is itself determined by the steepness of the seabed. If the seabed is gradually shelving the waves build up and break slowly. If on the other hand the seabed is steep the waves will 'dump' or 'close out' giving an abrupt shore-break.

The state of the tide often affects the nature of the breaking waves as the inshore seabed profile may be very different at high water from that at low water. Generally in the UK shore-breaks occur at high water and the best 'surfing' waves occur mid to low tide. It is important to note, however, that breaking patterns are constantly changing as sands shift and water depth changes with the tide.

In the tropics, where the water is warm enough for coral to grow, the swell generally breaks on offshore fringing reefs giving a protected inshore lagoon free from surf. Reefs come in all shapes and sizes and, as a result, so do the waves that break on them. In the UK most of the swells break direct on to the beach and the beaches, although constantly changing, have certain characteristics in common. Figure 3.9 shows a typical UK south coast beach break.

Force	Description	Specification on land	mph	Speed kph	Knots	Sea state	Recreational use	Wave height (m)	Sea state
0	Calm	Smoke rises vertically	less	than	1	Sea like a mirror	Swimming	0	Calm
1	Light air	Direction of wind shown by smoke drift	1–3	1–5	1–3	Ripples with appearance of scales	Water skiing	0.1	Calm
2	Light breeze	Wind felt on face, wind vane moved by wind	4–7	6–11	4–6	Small wavelets, crests with glassy appearance	Jet skiing canoeing	0.2	Smooth
3	Gentle breeze	Leaves and small twigs in constant motion	8–12	12–19	7–10	Large wavelets, crests begin to break. Glassy looking foam, occasional white horses	Wind surfing dinghy sailing	0.6	Smooth
4	Moderate breeze	Small branches move	13–18	20–29	11–16	Small waves becoming longer, frequent white horses	Intermediate wind surfers and dinghy sailors, cruising yachts	1.0	Slight
5	Fresh breeze	Small trees start to sway	19–24	30–39	17–21	Moderate waves of pronounced long form. Many white horses, some spray		2.0	Moderate
6	Strong breeze	Large branches in motion, umbrellas used with difficulty	25–31	40–50	22–27	Some large waves, extensive white foam crests, some spray	Advanced windsurfers, racing dinghy sailors and yachtsmen	3.0	Rough
7	Near gale	Whole trees in motion, inconvenient to walk against the wind	32–38	51–61	28–33	Sea heaped up, white foam from breaking waves blowing in streaks with the wind	Expert wind surfers	4.0	Very rough
8	Gale	Twigs break from trees, difficult to walk	39–46	62–74	34–40	Moderately high and long waves. Crests break into spin drift, blowing foam in well marked streaks		5.5	High
9	Srong gale	Slight structural damage occurs	47–54	75–87	41–47	High waves, dense foam streaks in wind, wave crests topple, tumble and roll over. Spray reduces visibility		7.0	Very high
10	Storm	Trees uprooted, considerable structural damage	55–63	88–101	48–55	Very high waves with long overhanging crests. Dense blowing foam, sea surface appears white. Heavy tumbling of the sea. Poor visibility		9.0	Very high
11	Violent storm	Widespread damage	64–73	102–117	56–63	Exceptionally high waves, sometimes concealing small and medium sized ships. Sea completely covered with long white patches of foam. Edges of wave crests blown into froth. Poor visibility		11.5	Phenomenal
12	Hurricane	Widespread damage	>73	>117	>63	Air filled with foam and spray, sea white with . driving spray. Visibility bad		14.0	Phenomenal

Figure 3.8 The Beaufort Scale

Rips are wave-induced pressure gradient currents that flow offshore providing a path by which water, thrown up the beach by breaking waves, can return downhill to the sea. Rips are easily identified by a trained eye. They manifest themselves as a river within the breaking waves. Rips can be very strong (9 knots was recorded at a recent surfing contest in La Torche on the west coast of Brittany) and extend up to 1 mile offshore. For the highly skilled watersports professional they can be a useful way of getting offshore in severe wave conditions. Surfers use them to get behind the wave-break quickly and Australian surf lifesavers use the rips to access deep water in their rescue craft. For the unskilled, rips are potentially extremely dangerous and have been responsible for many drownings. Generally speaking the bigger the waves the stronger the associated rips. When waves approach a coastline at an oblique angle, as is the case with most beaches on the south coast of England, they will refract and align themselves to the coastline giving rise to long-shore currents. In addition all the waves will break in the same direction away from the shore. Surfers commonly refer to wave breaks as 'Right-handers' or 'Left-handers'; this describes the direction in which the wave breaks when facing the beach. Beach breaks with long-shore currents often have groynes on them. These are designed to limit long-shore sediment transport. As a general rule when strong winds are forecast in the open sea waves may be expected in any exposed areas. In the UK deep depressions centred out in the Atlantic will give rise to good surf conditions in all areas with an uninterrupted fetch to the depression.

3.4 TIDES, TIDAL STREAMS AND CURRENTS

The movement of the water both horizontally (tidal streams and currents) and vertically (tide) can also be used to advantage by the water based user. Just like the wind-tides, tidal streams and currents can be good servants but bad masters. The inconvenience of waiting for hours for sufficient water to enter a marina or trying to beat a 3 knot tidal stream entering a harbour can in most instances be avoided by a few calculations before sailing. The depth of water available can be calculated weeks ahead using tide tables, or even years ahead using computer programs (Tidecalc NP158) and for this only a rudimentary understanding of the tide is required.

It is well chronicled (*Admiralty Manual of Navigation*, Vol. 1, 1987) that the gravitational pull of the moon and to a lesser extent the sun

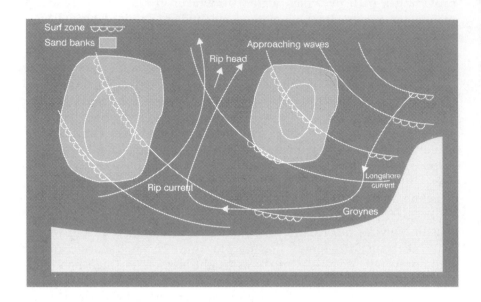

Figure 3.9 A typical UK south coast beach break. © WITMR 1155 pt.8

(approximately 45% of moon's effect) generates the tide. Hence these 'tide-raising forces' will only be discussed here in very general terms.

The moon's orbit around the earth is an ellipse and takes approximately 27⅓ days, so that at perigee (moon closest to the earth) the force is greater than at apogee (Figure 3.10a). Also the earth orbits the sun in 365¼ days (Figure 3.10b). The two orbits combine such that the moon will be overhead the same longitude on average every 24 hours 50 minutes (Lunar Day), also the moon will be on the same meridian as the sun (New Moon) every 29½ days (Lunar Month). The effect of the lunar day is to produce a tidal cycle of 12 hrs 25 mins (Figure 3.11), while the lunar month causes the fortnightly cycle of springs and neaps (Figure 3.12).

Due to these forces the water in the oceans, channels etc., resonates in a similar way to water in a bowl. How the water responds depends upon the size, shape and depth of the bowls with the tide wave moving around in an anticlockwise direction. Indeed the North

Atlantic almost acts as a single basin, the North Sea reacts as though made up of three and the English channel apparently acts as half a basin with its theoretical centre on Salisbury Plain! In the centre of each basin there is little rise or fall of tide, this is called the Nodal or Amphidromic Point.

The North Atlantic resonates to produce High Waters approximately 12 hours apart and therefore has a semi diurnal (½ day) tide. Most of the Pacific has a resonant frequency closer to 1 day and diurnal tides ensue (1 HW, 1 LW per day). The Baltic and Mediterranean hardly respond at all with ranges normally less than 1 m. At the other extreme the Severn Estuary responds particularly well so that ranges of 10 m are common. The position of the port is also important. Nearer the centre (amphidromic point) ranges will be smaller, e.g. Eastern North Sea, Portland in Dorset; further away ranges will be greater e.g. St Helier in Jersey. Also, as this 'tidal wave' progresses the Coriolis effect tends to deflect the water to the right thus producing larger tides on the French coast of the channel than the English side of the North Sea.

A further complication is the effect of shallow water compared with tidal wave. Just as a normal wave breaks because the trough is retarded, the tidal wave is similarly effected. This is most evident in the English channel where the rise of tide at Portsmouth takes 7 hrs, but the fall less than 5 hrs. Even more complicated distortions may occur, i.e. Portland, Swanage, Southampton and Holland. This can clearly be seen by reference to Figure 3.14.

Basin geomorphology is thus a major factor in determining the tide at a particular place. The major astronomical factors are as follows.

1. Perigee (once per orbit)
2. Springs (Full/New Moon)
3. For semi-diurnal ports, e.g. North Atlantic
    (a) Moon close to equator (twice per orbit, i.e. small declination)
    (b) Sun close to equator – equinoctial tides (Mar. and Sept.)
4. For diurnal ports, e.g. parts of Pacific
    (a) Moon at maximum declination – twice per orbit
    (b) Sun at max declination (June/Dec.)

When all these act together the height of tide will be close to HAT (Highest Astronomical Tide) and LAT (Lowest Astronomical Tide). It

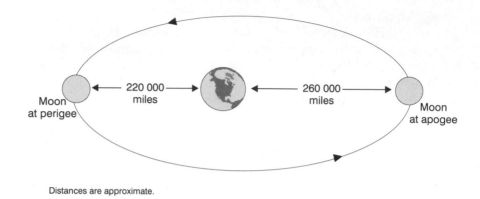

Distances are approximate.

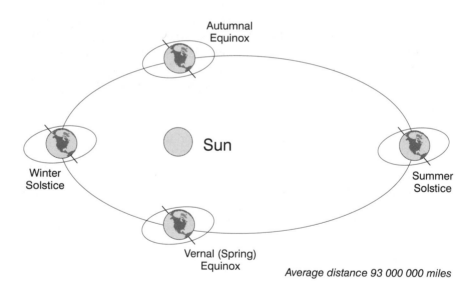

Average distance 93 000 000 miles

Figure 3.10 Orbits of the Moon and Earth. © WITMR 1155

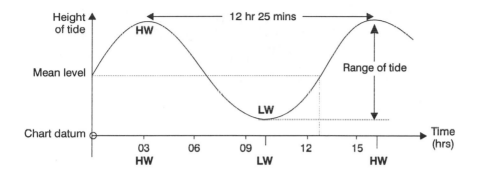

Figure 3.11 Tidal cycle. © WITMR 1155 pt.10

should also be noted that it takes time for the forces to take effect, e.g. in Portsmouth spring tides occur two days after New/Full Moon.

These forces cause the water level to rise and fall above and below its mean value (Mean Sea Level) and in areas where the tide is negligible (e.g. Baltic) this level is used on charts. However, on most charts a different level is used, known as 'chart datum'. This is approximately equivalent to the lowest astronomic tide (LAT). Areas that cover and uncover with the tide are shaded green on modern metric charts. The figures on the chart are called 'drying heights'. They are underlined and must be subtracted from the height of tide to obtain the depth. It should be noted that the height of objects on the land, e.g. lighthouses, hills and bridges, are usually measured above Mean High Water Springs not chart datum on Admiralty charts, whereas on maps these heights are given above Ordnance Datum.

The global wind pattern acts upon the water causing the ocean surface water currents. As a result the paths of these currents closely reflect those of the atmospheric circulation. The Gulf stream and N. Atlantic Drift bringing the warmer water that produces our milder climate. The cold Labrador current on the other hand conveys Icebergs to 40° N in July and produces dense fog banks off Nova Scotia. The wind-driven currents around the British Isles are variable in direction and of little significance to leisure users. But of great importance are the

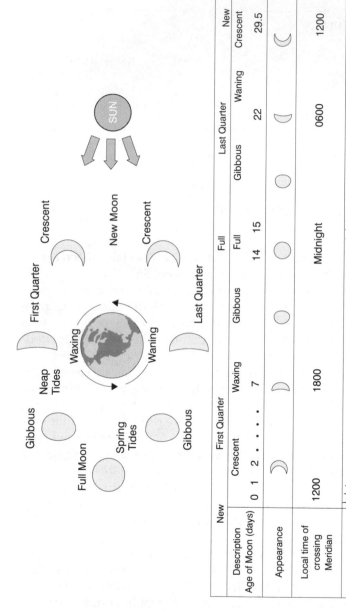

Figure 3.12 Lunar tides. © WITMR 1155 pt.11

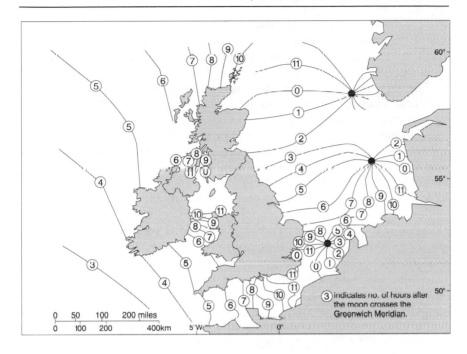

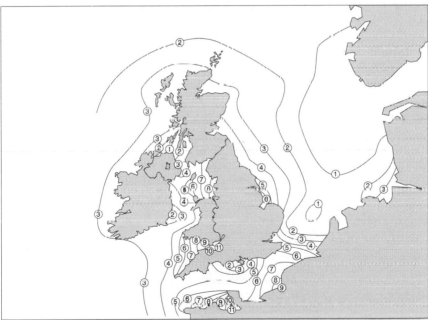

Figure 3.13 Tides around the UK

tidal streams caused by the tide-raising forces. This horizontal movement can reach over 9 knots in constricted waters such as Alderney Races at spring tides. An understanding of these is therefore vital to waterborne users.

The tidal streams tend to run along channels, and are called Flood and Ebb. They are also constricted by headlands where the stream can reach large proportions, e.g. off Portland Bill. Also the surface can be very disturbed if the depth shallows quickly. An 'overfall' is thus caused by the deeper water being forced to rise and disrupt the flow of the surface water. Close to the shore where the water is shallow the stream is much reduced and indeed there are occasions when 'back eddies' can give a yacht a considerable advantage. Similarly in shallow bays and out of deep channels the streams run less strongly.

Around the UK these streams are calculated by reference to a major port, e.g. Dover, Portsmouth, Sheerness etc. The data is given on the charts for each hour either side of HW, it includes the direction of the flow and the rates for both springs and neaps. By determining the percentage of the range between neaps and springs the value of a particular day is obtained.

The tidal stream atlas is particularly useful in giving an overview of the stream for a passage. A separate page is provided for each hour either side of HW giving both a graphical display – the boldness of the

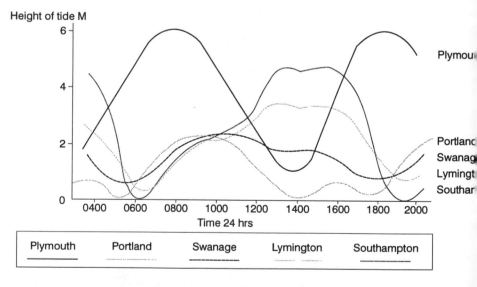

Figure 3.14 (a) The south coast channel tides. © WITMR 1155 pt.12

Data	17 May 1995	17 May 1995	17 May 1995	17 May 1995	17 May 1995	17 May 1995	17 May 1995	17 May 1995	10 May 1995
	Plymouth	Portland	St Helier	Swanage	Lymington	Southampton	Portsmouth	Dover	Portsmouth Neaps
Time	Height	Height	Height	Height	Height	Height	Height	Height	Height
0400	1.77	0.26	0.62	1.24	2.74	4.35	4.08	4.95	2.31
0500	3.26	-0.02 LW	1.99	0.66	1.87	2.9	2.72	3.64	2.68
0600	4.32	0.24	4.67	0.44	0.76	0.74	1	2.48	3.16
0700	4.98	1.12	7.83	0.87	0.44 LW	0 LW	0.39 LW	1.37	3.6
0800	5.42 HW	1.9	10.53	1.49	1.05	0.89	1.01	0.68	3.79 HW
0900	5.42 HW	2.15 HW	11.36 HW	1.83	1.64	1.78	1.69	0.52 LW	3.75
1000	4.94	2.13	10.82	1.95	1.77	1.9	1.98	1.05	3.5
1100	4.03	1.95	9.07	2 HW	1.97	2.15	2.49	2.87	2.91
1200	2.8	1.48	6.77	1.9	2.5	3.36	3.56	5.33	2.2
1300	1.56	0.57	4.51	1.65	2.88 HW	4.49	4.54	6.65	1.71
1400	0.73	0.13 LW	2.65	1.55	2.87	4.56 HW	4.83 HW	6.75 HW	1.6 LW
1500	0.59 LW	0.31	1.55	HW	2.89	4.46	4.71	6.36	1.85
1600	1.38	0.49	0.9 LW	1.49	2.94 HW	4.61 HW	4.46	5.42	2.13
1700	2.85	0.26	1.71	0.98	2.41	3.83	3.53	4.11	2.49
1800	4.15	0.27	3.51	0.6 LW	1.3	1.72	1.81	2.93	2.99
1900	4.94	0.92	6.52	0.82	0.61 LW	0.31 LW	0.67 LW	1.81	3.54
2000	5.46	1.76	9.68	1.43	0.92	0.74	0.9	0.91	3.97

OBTAINED FROM COMPUTER PROGRAM 'TIDECALC' NP158, Crown Copyright

Note: Full moon occurred on 14 May 1995

Figure 3.14b The variation in the tide

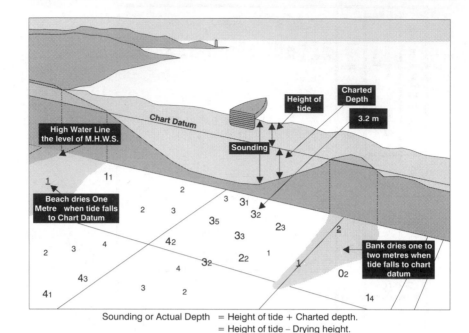

Sounding or Actual Depth = Height of tide + Charted depth.
= Height of tide − Drying height.

Figure 3.15 Cross-section showing charted depths and surroundings. © WITMR 1155 pt.13

arrow indicates the strength of the stream, and the values of the neap and spring rates. A graph is also provided inside the front cover to interpolate using the range of the particular day.

3.5 CONCLUSION

A good understanding of the weather, wind and tide and the corresponding sea conditions not only makes the sea a safer place but enables sensible choices to be made regarding the best time and locations at which to pursue water-based leisure interests.

Technological improvements have profoundly influenced the scope, accuracy, and level of detail of environmental information available to coastal recreation managers. Judicious use of this data, coupled with an understanding of the key principles, is an essential element of providing a safe and exhilarating recreational experience.

REFERENCES

Admiralty Manual of Navigation, Vol. 1 (1987), HMSO, London.
Barry and Chorley (1992) *Atmosphere Weather and Climate*, 6th edn, Routledge, London.
Houghton (1991) *Weather at Sea*, Fernhurst Books, Brighton.
House of Commons Environment Committee: Second Report (1992) *Coastal Zone Protection and Planning*, HMSO, London.
Royal Yachting Association (1989) *Shore Based Course Notes*, Publisher The Royal Yachting Association, Eastleigh.
Tidecalc – NP158, Hydrographic Office, Taunton.

Limitations for Coastal Recreation

4

4.1 INTRODUCTION

This chapter considers the constraints faced by coastal water-based leisure activities. Constraints are reflected in the desire, but inability, to participate in new activities; the inability to maintain desired levels of recreation; problems of access to leisure services; and insufficient enjoyment of current activities (Jackson, 1991). To this list are added constraints imposed by the concept of sustainable leisure.

The chapter considers these themes through the physical constraints on leisure, the provision of opportunity, the quality of the leisure experience, institutional constraints and issues of sustainability. The latter focuses on conservation of the natural resource and recreational pressure on that resource, although social impacts on the local community and issues of equal opportunity also feature in the discussion.

The chapter will be dealing with **structural** constraints as distinct from **intra-** or **interpersonal** constraints: the individual psychological states and attributes that inhibit an individual taking part in leisure and inhibiting factors associated with joint participation and relationships between participants.

4.2 PHYSICAL CONSTRAINTS ON LEISURE

Access for leisure in terms of its physical attributes and the contribution they make to the leisure experience is a function of coastal form and the characteristics of the leisure activity. Coastal landforms predetermine the suitability of site access, modified by human developments such as ports and roads. Many leisure activities require vehicular access, as with dinghy sailing and jet skiing for which cliff forms and extensive mudflats can pose a serious constraint. Coastal structures determine the

Coastal Recreation Management Edited by Tim Goodhead and David Johnson. Published in 1996 by E & FN Spon, London. ISBN 0 419 20360 5

shelter and exposure of the site and the area of water available. The continuation of form below the low water line determines bed type, water depths, current and turbulence which can either facilitate or constrain an activity. In relation to man's influence, it can also determine water quality by the flushing characteristics of an area of water.

In terms of the physical requirements for a leisure activity, many of the needs of individual sports are readily apparent. Sailing requires an area of land at the water's edge sufficient for a club house and boat storage with as gentle a slope to the water's edge as possible. Moorings and launching facilities should ideally be located on a lee shore to afford relatively sheltered water. The orientation of the stretch of water to be used and the geographical features of the area will govern the exposure, shelter and the rapidity or violence of weather changes and thereby the suitability and risks posed by the site. Dinghy sailing requires light to moderate winds, fairly consistent in direction during training. Rowing is a sport particularly fussy in its water conditions. Areas where large waves are likely to build up will be inappropriate. The proximity of suitable water conditions to suitable launch sites is also a consideration, as are the proliferation of submerged obstructions.

In recreational terms, coastal landforms can be classified as sand and shingle beaches, tidal forms such as mudflats and salt marshes, estuaries, cliffs and shore platforms. Each landform has implications for access to the waterline. In the following sections, only a brief insight can be given to the geomorphological complexities of coastal forms, the intention being to indicate the relationship between form and leisure.

In geomorphological terms, beaches are accumulations of sediments deposited by waves and currents in the shore zone, typically sand or pebbles, although silt beaches can be found on sheltered coastlines. The smaller the grain size the gentler the slope of the beach and the more compact the sediments. It may even be possible to drive a car across a fine sand beach and also launch and recover a powerboat, but it is often difficult. Suitability for launching reflects the firmness of the shore, the slope of the beach, the available depth of water and the strength and direction of the wind. A strong wave regime will almost always prevent a launch. The material comprising the beach is related to the nature of the material brought to the coast by rivers, eroded from adjacent cliffs or brought inshore by offshore or alongshore waves and currents.

A number of particular beach forms feature in the provision and sustainability of leisure. Prominent among them are marine barriers and sand dunes. Marine barriers, extensions of sand and shingle beaches, can provide an important source of shelter for inshore leisure activities such as dinghy sailing, canoeing and rowing. Often of ancient origin

(Chesil Beach originating during the Holocene) such features can appear relatively stable. The shoreward movement of sediment which formed Chesil Beach continues today, but without the addition of new shingle. Storms continue to sweep sediment over the ridge and into the lagoon (the Fleet) behind, gradually decreasing the water area. In contrast, other barriers continue to evolve with the addition of new sediments. The water areas behind barriers can become completely enclosed. However, large tidal ranges with their typically strong ebb and flow currents are likely to maintain gaps in the barrier for access to open water. Such strong currents will make conditions very dangerous for swimming and sub-aqua diving. Turbulence also reduces the visibility required for immersion sports.

Coastal dunes are essentially a feature of temperate and arid tropical zones, inhibited elsewhere by a variety of natural processes. They are formed where sand deposited on the shore dries out and is blown back up the beach. Dune topographies can be formed where large tidal ranges expose expanses of sand at low water to be blown inshore, as on the Atlantic coasts of Devon and Cornwall, or where wave action drives sand high up the beach. Extensive and complicated dune sequences can originate from as early as the Pleistocene. Dunes are built up at the back of a beach or on the crest of a beach ridge of sand or shingle where dune grasses colonize and start to trap blown sand. Continual accretion leads to dune growth. Patterns of ridges may develop as sand continues to move inshore and new material is blown up the beach.

Along low-lying coasts, dunes and marine barriers can form important defences from the sea, protecting properties and agricultural land. Recreation can place these defences at risk, trampling over dunes destabilizes the vegetation holding them together, opening the dune to erosion. At popular access points the dunes can be completely flattened, placing the land behind at risk as well as the ecosystem based on the dunes. The large expanses of sand which accommodate dune development can limit access to the water around low tide with the shallow shelving of the beach providing insufficient depths of water for craft launching or sub-aqua. Soft sand structures can also make conditions very dangerous, particularly for swimmers and surfers who are unaware of the structures' ability to change in a very short space of time.

Beaches, dunes and spits characterize the open coast where weather conditions and sea states restrict the use of coastal waters for considerable parts of the year. An absence of inlets, estuaries and natural harbours limits suitability for larger leisure craft which require sheltered water for mooring and havens in bad weather. Purpose built marinas will not necessarily solve these problems, as the conditions outside the marina will determine its accessibility, both at certain stages of the tide and during certain weather conditions, and the suitability of the wider area for recreation. Sailing, water-skiing, jet-skiing and rowing are examples of sports constrained by an absence of sheltered water.

In contrast to the open coast, coastal embayments and estuaries are characterized by tidal mudflats and salt marshes formed in sheltered areas by fine-grained silts and clays, originating from rivers, the seabed and erosion from adjacent coastlines. The sediments are worked by large to medium tidal ranges (i.e. greater than 3 m), with the flood and ebb tides carrying sediment within the estuary to create an ever changing pattern of channels and banks. Spits and barriers can be formed across the mouths of estuaries creating relatively sheltered water behind them. The areal extent of sheltered water will determine the distribution of activities and pressure within an estuary, provided there is suitable access. Space limitations can seriously constrain leisure opportunities. Canoeing requires sheltered water, for racing covering an area of 100 m by 35 m and for marathons, a corridor of 6–20 km (Quaife, 1993). Other watersports can have similarly demanding water specifications.

Vegetation is important in shaping the depositional features within and on the shores of the estuary. Algae (e.g. *Enteromorpha*) and marine grass wrack (*Zostera*) assist in the stabilization of sediments on the tidal flats, with salt-tolerant plants doing an equivalent job around the shores. Initial colonizers provide an environment for other plants to colonize (e.g. *Spartina*, *Salicornia* and *Juncus maritimus*) and for the gradual evolution of a salt marsh. The vegetation traps sediment brought in by the tide, slowly decreasing the water area of the estuary until the tide and recreation are confined into channels where the tidal force halts the accretion.

In estuaries access to the water can be a serious constraint. Soft saltings and marshes generally prohibit access to the water, although, narrow stretches may permit the use of artificial structures for launching. The construction of such structures, however, will depend on the sub-soil conditions, the tidal range and wave action, which together will determine its carrying capacity. There is inevitable congestion at those points where access is possible. The soft bed and high silt content in the water make estuaries generally unsuitable for swimming, surfing and sub aqua diving. They are more suited to sailing and power boating. The large tidal ranges of many estuaries can generate strong currents and their uneven bed topography, unpredictable turbulence. The tidal range also reduces access to recreation to certain states of the tide and determines the capacity of the site in terms of moorings. A large tidal range either requires marina developments or swinging moorings; the latter expensive in terms of the space required for a boat's head warps.

Another important coastal form is the cliffed coast, where marine and sub-aerial processes erode away the stable landmass to leave an exposed near-vertical surface. The rate of erosion reflects the durability of the rock formations, structural weaknesses, the configuration of the coastline, solubility of the rock, height of the cliff, vegetation cover and the nature of attack. Cliffed coasts can pose an exposed and impenetrable continuous barrier or harbour sheltered bays and inlets.

There are a large variety of cliff morphologies, reflecting the relative importance of the forces acting on the feature and the local geology. Marine forces attacking the base of the cliff, undermining its structure and leading to collapse, include corrosion through chemical weathering by salt water; corrasion through mechanical weathering by sediments within the water column; hydraulic action; and quarrying by wave action pulling away loose rock. Sub-aerial processes include weathering, ice-wedging and rain wash. Humans also feature in the picture, from erosion through tramping to mass movement due to construction works (Pethick, 1984). The more resistant coastal rock formations evolve into headlands, rocky stacks and offshore islands while the weaker rock formations surrounding them are cut away, forming coves, caves and embayments.

The material eroded from the face of the cliff accumulates at the base of the slope to be worked and removed by marine processes, leaving a break of slope. The slope will depend on the rate of supply relative to the rate of removal, with a vertical cliff face typifying greater rates of removal than supply. The accumulation of fallen rock or deposited beach material at the base of a cliff serves to protect the cliff from marine erosion, dissipating wave and storm energy. The removal of this natural barrier can accentuate the rate of erosion. A beach frontage opens up a cliffed coast to recreational opportunity, provided that access is available. Along many coastlines in the United Kingdom coastal erosion accounts for the loss of miles of coastal and cliff path each year. Access for craft is limited to inlets and coves with gentler features permitting road access and space for parking adjacent to the water's edge. A single lane boat launch can require 2–3 acres adjacent to the launch point. For certain soft coasts and cliffed coasts the only access to the adjacent water area will be from the sea and harbours further along the coast.

As the cliff recedes, a portion of the rock formation, lying below the lowest level of erosion, may remain, generating a shore platform. The shape of this platform can vary greatly, although in northern hemispheres the platforms tend to be wide, gently sloping and linear in profile (Pethick, 1984). Many of the processes which shape cliff forms also shape the adjacent shore platform. The seabed off a cliffed coastline can provide much of interest to sub-aqua divers and relatively clear waters, although, close inshore, conditions can be dangerous with violent wave action against the cliff face and generally exposed conditions. Care must be taken sailing close inshore. Submerged obstacles can pose a significant hazard.

It is possible to find a mix of geomorphological features along a stretch of coast. On steep and rocky coasts, sand and shingle beaches may be found in shallow bays, heads, coves and inlets, often poorly accessible if at all. Beach sediments can also form a frontage to cliff forms.

4.3 PROVISION OF OPPORTUNITY

Leisure and its component activities have numerous variations with specific requirements of the resource and facilities. Different sites meet these requirements to different extents and as such limit access to different degrees. In terms of facilities, pontoons, jetties and ramps will often be needed to facilitate access and site suitability. Other basic facilities could include buoyage to mark racing courses and mooring facilities (either swinging moorings or a purpose-built facility). While smaller boats can be trailed to and from the water, larger boats require to be in situ. For canoeing, landing stages or pontoons with a deck 300 mm above water level or slipways (with a maximum gradient of 30 ft) are quoted as requirements, although a sand or shingle foreshore can be used (Quaife, 1993).

The level of use of existing facilities is an important determinant of opportunity. Facilities for the launching, recovery and storage of boats and trailers will require careful planning if they are not to adversely constrain the level of opportunity at peak times. The number of slipways and their widths should reflect the maximum demand and should bear a relationship both to the size of the parking area and how concentrated the demand will be. Allowance should be made for boat passing and trolley widths. Once in the water, the boats must have room to rig and moor without obstructing the slipway. On the shore, issues of congestion can equally constrain opportunity. Appropriate access and parking provision needs to be accompanied by a good traffic flow system to avoid risks of injury and damage to pedestrians, cars and trolleys.

The requirements of recreation are more stringent for access by the disabled to leisure activities. If not specifically designed for, a large portion of the population is affected: the blind and sight impaired, the deaf or hard of hearing, wheelchair users or people with restricted mobility and those with learning difficulties. Each disability has certain requirements.

For example, in terms of fishing opportunities for wheelchair users, access requires:

- a car park adjacent to the shoreline with sufficient parking space width to allow for a wheelchair to be placed by the car;
- wheelchair access to the shoreline: a smooth firm surface of minimum width 1.35 m (with passing points of 1.8 m) and gentle, if any, slope;
- a level and stable fishing platform with an absence of obstructions including dense vegetation; and
- facilities designed with a chairbound person in mind in terms of door widths and handles.

Such requirements are common to a number of other disabled sports, for example, canoeing and rowing require the same car park and wheelchair access with a hard bank clear of vegetation at the water's edge allowing for easy entry into the craft. Steps, distances, uneven surfaces, an absence of hand rails and difficult handles and latches can constrain access for the ambulant disabled, while poor visual communication and lighting (for lip reading) will constrain opportunities for the hard of hearing. The sight impaired require an obstruction free environment and tactile information and guidance systems (Thomson, 1993).

One of the fundamental constraints on opportunity in terms of access and provision rests with property rights. Unless publicly provided, opportunities are constrained by the extent of private provision (Curry, 1994). Access across the foreshore around much of Great Britain is purely tolerated, there is no legal right of access. Under common law, the foreshore is owned by the Crown, with certain exceptions: where the Crown granted land to such as the Duke of Cornwall and the Church Commissioners. In terms of access, the status of the foreshore is one of private ownership. However, under the public common law rights of fishery and navigation there are ancillary rights including the crossing of the foreshore to fish or navigate in the sea or tidal waters. This is permitted where access has been statutorily appropriated for the purpose or where a legal right has been acquired by custom and long usage. These rights of access do not extend to a right to bathe or to allow recreation automatically on the foreshore, inclusive of wildfowling. While the Crown or the grantees of the foreshore hold that land for the benefit of the public, these activities are not considered to be part of this definition. Certain local authorities, however, have acquired leases from the Crown for the purposes of public recreation. There is also a right of access for owners of adjacent land for the purposes of navigation. Access for marine recreation is, as a result, not only constrained by the physical environment but also by the need for permission and provision by private landowners and the resultant potential for a mismatch of access and suitability of the location for leisure.

Access to much of the foreshore and waters around the United Kingdom is through the existence of public rights of way which may be defined in terms of the times they may be used and in the purpose and mode of use, or unlimited. The rights held by the public over rights of way are those conveyed at their dedication or creation by statute (Highways Act 1980) or through proven long use (20 years) (*ibid*.). Access by footpaths is only permitted on foot; bridleways by foot, bicycle and horseback. Vehicular access is only permitted on rights of ways dedicated as carriageways. It is only a right to pass and repass for legitimate travel, although there are legitimate ancillary acts determined on the grounds of reasonableness, such as a right to pause and admire the view. While a landowner is under a duty to maintain a right of way (Highways Act 1980), access can often be effectively impaired by vegetation and other obstacles interfering with passage. In using a public right of way, individuals must not interfere with any other persons with the same right of way. In order to prevent congestion unlimited public access might not be possible.

Unless the owner or occupier of land has a specific, often financial, interest in the provision of leisure, there are a number of disadvantages to private provision, counting against the granting of a right of access. Irrespective of any interference that access may cause with the activities of the landowner, under The Occupiers Liability Acts 1957 (s. 2) and 1984 (s. 1) and the Health and Safety at Work etc. Act 1974 the occupier has a duty of care for the health and safety of persons on his land, invited or otherwise (Scott, 1993). This would include visitors to a recreational site. This responsibility extends to persons beyond the boundaries of the site under a common law duty to take reasonable care that the use of the premises does not cause injury to persons outside or commit nuisance (public or private). The impact is not confined to the leisure participant or other users of the water space. Problems of noise, traffic congestion and disturbance extend to the local community. Personal watercraft are a frequently cited example, evoking great extremes of emotion among local residents. A common law action in nuisance, for an injunction or damages, can be brought by local residents if an activity can be shown to interfere unreasonably with a neighbour's enjoyment. An action can be brought against the persons

directly responsible for the disturbance or against the site operators
(Scott, 1993). In addition, any restrictive covenants attached to land
could well hinder the way that recreation can take place.

In addition to the ownership of access, rights to undertake certain
forms of recreation, for example, wildfowling fall within private
ownership, beyond the reach of public access. Certain rights can be
reserved by a vendor upon selling land and in some instances these
rights are capable of transfer to third parties. Among these is the right of
profit à prendre, a legal and equitable right to take from another's land
natural produce, inclusive of wild animals (albeit subject to statutory
restrictions under the Wildlife and Countryside Act 1981, as amended).
Such rights can also be conveyed by licence. A profit in common can
extend these rights to a group of individuals by express grant or under
the Prescriptions Act 1832. Wildfowling rights are, as a result, often
monopolized by clubs and individuals, who as owners of interests in
land restrict access and can bring an action in nuisance against persons
affecting their enjoyment of their rights. Fishing rights and rights to
shellfish on the foreshore can also fall within private ownership,
although a public right (subject to statute law for the conservation of fish
stocks and sea fishery committees' bye-laws) exists for the greater part of
the coastline.

The constraints of foreshore ownership are manifest in the limited
number of public hards and slipways around the coast and the
predominance of club or privately operated facilities. Many public
launching hards are in good condition and well maintained, offering
excellent facilities (see also Chapter 12). There are, however, some that
are neglected, silted up and blocked with rubbish (White, 1991).

Club membership can often be a pre-requisite to access, with the
associated membership and launch fees. It may be possible for non-
members to use club launch facilities at a charge, in excess of those
charged to club members. Cost is a real and increasing constraint on
access to leisure, particularly those dependent on expensive equipment.
Allied in part to the cost of the equipment, but also to the character of
the activity, there can be a perceived exclusivity or cultural barrier
attached to an activity.

Cost and the economics of leisure also feature in the distance-
constraint placed on accessibility, along with the availability of
transportation and the time required for travel. Sites of closer proximity
to urban areas are considered to be more accessible than those further
away, assuming a uniformity in other criteria (Bovaird et al., 1984).
Distance, the availability of public transport and the position of the site
in relation to urban developments are also factors in the sociological

composition of those participating in leisure activities at the site, reflecting the characteristics of the catchment area. Issues of equal opportunity among ethnic minorities to leisure activities have received significant academic debate in recent years, along with gender, demographic and educational issues (Lyons, 1991; Mee, 1990). Elitism, culture, racism and the costs of participation in relation to disposable incomes are attributed as contributing to **unequal opportunity**. The provision of social equality of opportunity under the assumption that participation costs are a major obstacle to participation has led to subsidized or 'free' provision or 'recreational welfare' in the past. Constraints on local government finance and the introduction of Compulsory Competitive Tendering are likely to alter this situation, pressing for a reduction in subsidy (Coalter, 1993).

In addition to the availability, or otherwise, of facilities and attractions at a site and the suitability of the environment for recreation, opportunity can also be constrained by a lack of awareness of the site or its provisions. An absence of information and advertising can be a powerful constraint on the leisure opportunity (Bovaird *et al.*, 1984).

4.4 QUALITY OF THE LEISURE EXPERIENCE

In addition to physical and economic constraints on access there are constraints related to the quality of the leisure experience. Leisure is not only associated with partaking in a particular activity but also with psychological desires and experiences; the sense of freedom, happiness, relaxation, excitement, good humour and well-being that are sought by undertaking the activity (Seabrooke and Miles, 1993). There are a number of factors which can either provide for or inhibit the leisure experience.

Safety is one such factor and can be responsible for preventing a recreational activity altogether. The degree of personal safety can be a factor of the environment, man's influence on that environment, the influence of other activities utilizing an area and the individual's own behaviour and experience. As explained in Chapter 3, the unpredictability of the marine environment, typified by the rapid development of storm conditions and the existence of dangerous currents can be a temporal if not ongoing constraint on leisure activities, especially for the more inexperienced participant. The environmental criteria required by swimming include an absence of both marine obstacles and strong tidal and wave-induced currents, with a firm, gently sloping (preferably coarse sand or fine gravel) shore. Ideally a swimming area should have a uniform and gentle slope into a water depth of 6 ft. For children the slope should be of the order of 1:12/15. While a site may not meet these criteria, access may still be possible, although the quality of the experience may be affected.

The weather is a decision criterion not confined to issues of safety. Rain, sunshine (or absence thereof) and temperatures can be perceived as constraints depending on individual preferences and the activities to be pursued (Bovaird *et al.*, 1984).

In terms of man's influence on the environment, a critical consideration is water quality, not only important for immersion and wet sports but also sports directly exploiting the resource, such as fishing and wildfowling. Surfers and divers are regarded to be more at risk than swimmers due to greater periods of exposure. Although the risk from present levels of pollution is regarded as negligible, the incident of illness is a significant disincentive to immersion sports. A full discussion of this issue is given in Chapter 5.

The importance of water quality not only varies between different leisure activities but also between different forms of the same activity, such as canoeing. While canoeing is not an immersion sport, siting should take into account outfalls and pollution traps as some forms are wetter than others.

Marine vegetation can impact on water quality and the suitability of a site for recreation. At the lowest level in the marine food chain, phytoplankton can increase in such numbers so to make the water unsuitable for immersion sports. 'Algal blooms' are caused by a combination of a rise in temperature, increased radiant energy, reduced salinity and increased nutrient availability. In coastal areas sewage discharge and agricultural run-off exacerbate nutrient levels. Algal blooms can represent large populations of a few or a single species, indicative of their physiological suitability to specific environmental conditions. It is suggested that the red tide phenomena (a single species bloom) may well be associated with the release of substances which are self-stimulatory or toxic to other organisms. Red tides can occasionally cause the death of large numbers of fish and birds, principally through the existence of certain dinoflagellates, for example, *Gymnodinium brevis*, *Goniaulax polyedra*, *Exuviella baltica*. No connection with human health has been made, although blooms are associated with discolouration of the water, 'scum' on the water's surface and an unsavoury odour.

Submergent plant life of higher forms, either attached to the bottom or free floating, can again make immersion sports unpleasant and even hazardous. Other activities can encounter problems due to clogging, such as boating and water skiing. Fishing can be particularly frustrated.

Human influences on safety extend to the parallel use of water space for different activities. While many activities can coincide quite happily, some are mutually exclusive. Individuals immersed in the water are particularly vulnerable (e.g. swimmers and divers). While diving operations are often accompanied by boats displaying standard maritime signals, such as 'diver down' or 'man in water', these are not universally recognized by casual users. Issues of safety can often lead to initiatives to segregate different recreational activities. Even relatively compatible activities are facing a trend towards segregation. With the growing popularity in maritime leisure activities and greater numbers of participants concentrating around certain geomorphological features, such as estuaries and harbours, congestion is becoming a significant safety issue in certain areas. An issue for both the water and adjacent land areas. The wash of high-speed power boats can pose a hazard to other craft such as water-skiers and canoes and collision is an ongoing danger.

Not only is congestion leading to an increased risk of injury to persons and craft but also to a depreciation in the pleasure gained from an activity (Ashton and Chubb, 1972). Sites can be said to have a perceptual or social carrying capacity which relates to 'people's perceptions of other users and the extent to which this affects their enjoyment' (Curry, 1994), affecting the quality of their leisure experience. The type, numbers and speed of craft and the behaviour of their occupants in relation to the attributes of the leisure experience sought by an individual will determine that individual's perception of density and the carrying capacity of the site (Ashton and Chubb, 1972). Individuals seeking quiet enjoyment may similarly have the quality of their leisure experience affected by the shore-based by-products of water-based recreation, such as noise generated by radios, dogs and even children.

The pressure on the resource can result in a visual depreciation of the natural interest and attractiveness of the site and the ecological depreciation of, for example, the diving resource. The visual and natural interest of a site is a significant contribution to the quality of the leisure experience and the attraction to a site.

Depending on the criteria used by an individual to determine the quality of their leisure experience, limitations to achieving that quality can include an absence of facilities at a site and the quality of those facilities. At one extreme the absence of slipways and cranes to launch vessels will severely constrain access for certain activities. On the other hand, supporting facilities can significantly enhance the suitability of a site for a particular activity and enhance the users' enjoyment of the site.

Not only providing for the leisure experience, facilities serve to assist the sustainability of leisure, by utilizing the 'honey pot' concept; leisure activities are focused in specific areas facilitating greater management and the protection of more environmentally sensitive sites. Facilities such as dedicated car parks, for example, can prevent the destruction caused by off-road car parking to the backshore area. Support facilities could incorporate the provision of launching facilities, loading and off-loading facilities, boat storage, changing areas and parking, lifeguards and life-saving equipment, refuse collection and beach cleaning and information systems warning of hazardous conditions, tide times etc. The appropriate facilities will be determined by the particular activities being catered for.

4.5 INSTITUTIONAL CONSTRAINTS

Allied to facility provision and the close relationship between the land and opportunity for water-based leisure, one of the main categories of institutional constraints comes in the form of planning policies and the development controls operated by local authorities. The influence of the Town and Country Planning System is covered in detail in Chapter 6.

On the water the management institutions influencing leisure opportunities are varied as is their degree of influence and the management techniques open to them. In terms of water-based leisure, the principal institutions are those given below. Local authorities are responsible for the licensing of pleasure boats and boatmen to carry passengers, except where they fall within the scope of the Merchant Shipping Acts and bye-laws for the control of certain categories of recreation. The National Rivers Authority is responsible for amenity and recreation potential in inland and coastal waters under its control. Harbour authorities are responsible for recreational activity within their area of jurisdiction, albeit in many cases a by-product of their responsibilities for the good management of a commercial port and the safety of navigation. These institutions adopt a number of techniques to cater for such issues as safety, congestion and environmental protection.

A number of these techniques, such as information systems and wardening, predominantly enhance opportunity rather than constrain leisure, so will not be considered here. There are, however, five categories of techniques which either, by their nature or through their selection and design, constrain water-based leisure activities:

- zoning
- bye-laws
- charging

- the control of numbers
- enforcement

Provision for recreation is only one of a number of responsibilities held by these organizations, often a conflicting one and largely a secondary responsibility. This is reflected in resource allocation priorities. In relative terms, access to recreational opportunities, the quality of the leisure experience and its sustainability are potentially at risk from the multi-functional nature of the agencies responsible for its provision. Similarly, the extent to which opportunities can be provided are constrained by the mandates of the agencies concerned. An organization cannot exceed the powers conferred on it by statute.

Zoning and timetabling as management techniques are used to reduce the likelihood of conflict between different water-based activities, social side-effects on land, or damage to environmentally sensitive areas. They can also be used to provide a positive recreational opportunity and enhanced safety. Zoning and timetabling can be voluntary agreements with clubs or formal arrangements laid down by the managing authority. In the first instance, zoning restricts where a leisure activity can take place and timetabling, when it can take place. A good design should reflect the spatial, temporal and seasonal distribution of the activity and its preferences in terms of access and environmental conditions and the level of usage; the degree of restriction is relative to design. Timetabling can be a serious constraint, in that popular times tend to be popular for most recreational activities.

The factors affecting the suitability of a particular water area for sailing are, for example:

- depth of water (variations in depth owing to tide, water management and climatic conditions);
- shape and size of the water area;
- water characteristics;
- wind characteristics (it is generally easiest to launch a dinghy from a windward shore);
- other users;
- accessibility;
- environmental factors;
- conservation factors.

What the activity requires of these attributes will depend on the nature of the activity taking place, whether it is training, casual recreation or racing and the craft used, the attributes outlined under 'physical constraints' and 'provision of opportunity':

sailboards require a	1 m depth of water
dinghies	1.3 m
cruisers and keelboats	1.3–1.8 m and
ocean-going boats	4.5 m

(Wilson, 1993)

Where the design does not cater for these requirements, congestion, an enhanced risk of accidents and a depreciation in the quality of and opportunity for recreation can occur. While a general guide to the capacity of an area of water is 2.5–5 boats/ha, this capacity will reflect the size of boats, the skills of the helmsmen, the level of management and the occasion (i.e. a greater number of boats per hectare would be acceptable during a regatta and fewer during training).

Bye-laws are local laws operating over the area of an authority, made by the authority under power conferred by statute and confirmed by the appropriate Secretary of State. Bye-laws have in common the purpose of constraining undesirable behaviour, whether it be conflict, destruction of the resource or pollution prevention. The principal coastal authorities with powers to make bye-laws which affect marine leisure activities, include local authorities, the National Rivers Authority, local Sea Fisheries Committees and harbour authorities. Many of these bye-laws pertain to recreation, although, given the responsibilities and remit of the implementing authority, they are often directed primarily at other maritime activities, for example, the conservation of fish stocks. Local authorities have the power to regulate leisure activities either through the control of landward facilities, access and parking facilities for example, or through bye-laws for the control of leisure craft out to 1000 m from low water mark for the purposes of preventing dangerous navigation. This extends to water-skiing and the use of other powered craft (s. 76 Public Health Act, 1961). Bye-law making powers also extend to the regulation of public bathing, the designation of bathing areas and times of bathing (Public Health Act, 1936) (Scott, 1993). Local authorities are increasingly using their bye-law making powers in these areas. Within harbour authority areas, the adoption of speed limits and zoning are becoming increasingly common, along with the allocation of navigation channels to either commercial or recreational craft. In certain estuaries and harbours, speed limits have been imposed under bye-law making powers. In many cases this has been associated with a failure to provide for forms of recreation which require speeds in excess of the limit, rendering certain sports, such as water-skiing, impossible.

Leisure activities can be constrained around certain areas of the coast used for strategic purposes. Due to the relative remoteness of coastal areas and the potential to use the sea as a buffer zone and target area, the coast is used on a large scale for military exercises. The Military Lands Act 1892, as amended by the Military Lands Act 1990 and the Land Powers (Defence) Act 1958, conveys powers to the Secretary of State for Defence to make bye-laws for securing the public from danger either in relation to military exercises conducted on land, at sea or in tidal waters. 'Danger areas' are created for marine exercises independent of the shore for such activities as missile target practice and submarine exercises. Similar exclusion zones lie around oil rigs and, in terms of anchoring around submarine cables, gas lines and historic wrecks (Protection of Wrecks Act, 1973).

User charging can be used as a resource allocation mechanism, both temporally and spatially; as a discouragement to excessive levels of use; as a source of revenue to offset operational costs and provide for service improvements; or to establish a relationship between cost and benefit. Charges can be levied as an entrance or administrative charge (including launching and car park charges) or as a service charge. Experience in the use of charging has found no significant resistance to the payment of recreational fees, especially if management services are provided. It is, however, a disincentive to some. The extent to which user charging will constrain access reflects the ability and the willingness of the user to pay, which in turn will reflect the quality of the experience gained from the site, proximity to the user, the existence of substitute sites and whether a tradition of payment exists for the activity, along with the state of the economy and an individuals economic situation (Bovaird *et al.*, 1984).

The control of numbers involves the use of licences to control numbers of, for example, passenger carrying pleasure boats or, alternatively, the allocation of the sole use of a resource to a club which then limits numbers and controls behaviour through club mechanisms. This mechanism has been used to limit the number of water-skiers in several estuaries around the United Kingdom. Similar outcomes can be achieved by limiting the number of moorings or marina berths and the capacity of slipways and car parks on the shoreline.

Such management measures are accompanied by monitoring and enforcement mechanisms. Where resource priorities lie elsewhere, inadequate resources can jeopardize the effectiveness of those techniques, opening up opportunities for conflict and a depreciation in the quality of the leisure experience of the majority by the conflagrations of an irresponsible minority. Problems of craft identification for enforcement purposes has led to a few local craft registration initiatives, the recording of ownership against craft. As yet there are no national registration schemes.

In addition to the specific institutional framework of a site, leisure activities are constrained by certain national and international bodies of law, such as the International Regulations for Preventing Collisions at Sea 1972 and the associated 'rules of the road'. The constraint here purely pertains to unreasonable and dangerous behaviour. Similarly, save in an unavoidable emergency, a vessel must not tie up to channel buoys or lighthouses.

4.6 ENVIRONMENTAL DESIGNATIONS

The degree to which environmental designations constrain recreation and access for the same depends on the principles underpinning the designations and their status in law. There are many categories of designation, however, the main designations in respect of the coast include National Parks, Areas of Outstanding Natural Beauty and Heritage Coasts, Sites of Special Scientific Interest, Ramsar sites, Special Protection Areas and Special Areas for Conservation.

National Parks were established under the National Parks and Access to the Countryside Act 1949 to preserve characteristic landscape beauty, to protect wildlife, buildings and places of architectural and historic interest and to provide access and facilities for open air public enjoyment. Areas of Outstanding Natural Beauty, established under the same piece of legislation, were designated for the preservation and enhancement of their natural beauty. These two designations afford conservation interest a greater say in the deliberation of planning applications and the development of bye-laws and access agreements. Recreation is a secondary consideration. With similar effect, the definition of Heritage Coast affords the environment, but also in this case recreation, greater weight in development plans and planning consents.

Sites of Special Scientific Interest are sites designated under the Wildlife and Countryside Act 1981 (as amended 1985) as of special interest by reason of their flora and fauna or their geological or physiographical features. Of national significance, any operation deemed damaging to the particular interest of the site (which could well include leisure activities or access) is subject to the consent of, or provisions written into a management agreement by, the relevant nature conservancy, English Nature in England and Countryside Council for Wales. The local planning authority is also obliged to consult with the relevant nature conservancy prior to the deliberation of a planning application.

A further designation, Nature Reserves takes three forms in relation to the coast – National Nature Reserves, Local Nature Reserves and Marine Nature Reserves. Under the National Parks and Access to the Countryside Act 1949, National and Local Nature Reserves can be created through nature reserve agreements negotiated between the owners or occupiers of land or through the purchasing or leasing of land by the relevant nature conservancy. In the former instance management plans and bye-laws can be made to protect the reserve through restricting public access and prohibiting actions likely to disturb or damage the scientific interest of the reserve. This can extend to bye-laws prohibiting the launching and mooring of any boat within a reserve. Where the land is in public ownership and the overriding protection objectives are not endangered, recreation may be permitted. The third category, Marine Nature Reserves, are designated within an area of 'land covered (continuously or intermittently) by tidal waters or parts of the sea in or adjacent to Great Britain up to the seaward limits of territorial waters' for their nature conservation interest. There are only two MNRs designated to date. Bye-law making powers exist for the protection of the natural interest. These bye-laws can restrict the rights of entry and anchoring by pleasure boats during certain times of the year and in particular areas of the reserve. Fishing activities can also be restricted by bye-laws made by the local sea fisheries committee (Sea Fisheries Regulation Act, 1966). The killing and disturbance of animals and plants is also prohibited (Garner and Jones, 1991).

Special Protection Areas (SPAs) are one of a number of measures required by the EEC Directive 79/409 on the Conservation of Wild Birds to preserve, maintain or re-establish a sufficient diversity and area of habitat for threatened and vulnerable bird species and all regularly occurring migratory species. In the designation of these areas 'economic and recreational requirements must be considered only after ecological, scientific and cultural requirements' (Pritchard *et al.*, 1992, p. 6). Ramsar sites are wetlands of international importance designated under the Convention on Wetlands of International Importance especially as Waterfowl Habitat 1971. Within Great Britain, the protection required by SPAs and Ramsar sites is effected through designation as Sites of Special Scientific Interest.

While conservation designations often reflect habitats and concentrations of species of importance nationally and internationally and through their legal provisions constrain recreational opportunity, the concept of sustainability extends the constraints to the wider impacts of recreation on the natural environment.

Watersports can impact on the environment in a number of ways, potentially leading to the physical deterioration of the resource base. The impact and its significance depends on the vulnerability of the habitat and its species composition. Certain coastal ecosystems are particularly vulnerable. Estuaries and dune systems are considered to be especially sensitive, while cliff structures and their ecosystems less so (Sidaway, 1988). There is a measure of scale to be added here. While recreational impact may be locally devastating, it is not likely to threaten the survival of plant species and habitats. It certainly does not rank with issues such as deforestation and agriculture.

Facilities' development, their location, design and management can affect the landscape quality, destroy habitats and disturb or increase the stress levels felt by the wildlife. The use of a site as a recreational area will inevitably lead to changes in local ecosystems. Habitats will be destroyed and wildlife displaced to provide car parks and facilities. In terms of explicit provision, changes to the ecosystem will need to be made to withstand the intensity of use. It may be necessary to plant trees and shrubs able to withstand soil compaction and damage from vandalism. Dramatic examples of the consequences of facility development without due consideration for the environment include the 'proliferation of troublesome plants and animal species' (Edington and Edington 1986, p. 4), due to ill-designed organic waste disposal facilities, ultimately interfering with swimming and fishing and posing a risk to health. The poor design of access routes can lead to a widening of the 'pathway' or area affected by trampling, potentially to the point of creating a barrier to species' movement (Sidaway, 1993).

As craft numbers increase, a number of deleterious environmental impacts can arise: ecological damage, aesthetic changes and amenity quality changes (Adams, 1993). Boat induced propeller damage and wash disturb immersed plant life and mud in shallow water, increasing turbidity and reducing light penetration. Marine planktonic productivity and plant biomass can be adversely affected, potentially destroying spawning grounds and important food sources (Liddle and Scorgie, 1980). Jet powered craft have been associated with high mortality among incubating fish eggs (Sutherland and Ogle, 1975; Adams, 1993). Flora and fauna typically have narrow tolerance levels in respect of the environmental conditions they require for survival and health. Aquatic animals, for example, are sensitive to salinity, water movement, temperature and plant formations. Plants not only form an important part of the food chain, but also provide essential shelter and support (Edington and Edington, 1986).

The degree of impact on the natural interest of a site by different forms of recreation is still somewhat under debate. Arguments for the reconciliation of wildfowl and animals to the noise and visual stimuli generated by recreation are countered by arguments to the contrary. Motorized forms of recreation, wildfowling, bait digging and access across the foreshore at low tide are featured as sources of disturbance (Green, 1985). Even sailing has been associated with the displacement of waterfowl, by a number of studies. The degree of disturbance does, however, vary with the species. Pochard (*Aythya ferina*), tufted duck (*Aythya fuligula*), goosander (*Mergus merganser*) and mallard (*Anas platyrhynchos*) tolerate relatively close contact and return after the disturbance has passed (Edington and Edington, 1986). The temporary desertion of nest sites by such species, however, can open up opportunities for predation. Gulls are particularly adept of using such opportunities to steal eggs. Interruptions caused to attempts to secure mating and feeding territories and the bonding between parent and offspring can also lead to mortality. The degree of disturbance depends on the form of recreation and the composition and seasonal profile of populations at a site relative to patterns of recreational use (including duration spent in any one area) (see Table 4.1). Breeding and over-wintering wildlife are considered to be more vulnerable, as are populations under environmental stress. Disruption to feeding may be critical, for example, if combined with low food supplies and short feeding periods due to day length or tidal conditions (Sidaway, 1993). Speed and user behaviour are particularly important in determining the impact of recreation on the environment, contributing to the degree of unusual stimuli, wash and exhaust emissions. The spread of water-based recreation to previously remote locations, such as the breeding beaches of the little tern, has been associated with the actual decline of such species in Europe (Green, 1985).

Unconscious and unplanned effects are numerous. Tramping feet and vehicular wheels cause direct mechanical impact, soil compaction and erosion and indirect effects through altering drainage lines and soil stability in neighbouring areas. The burrows of animals and the interstices occupied by microscopic soil animals can be obliterated (Edington and Edington, 1986) and vegetation and trees bruised and destabilized. Reductions in species diversity and succession by trample-resistant species are a monitored outcome (Curry, 1994), with dune ecosystems particularly vulnerable to trampling, being highly unstable. Local impacts are widespread, although generalizations cannot be made as to the degree of impact (Selman, 1992). The picking, uprooting or destruction of wild plants can also have a significant local impact: a legal offence for some 60 listed species (Wildlife and Countryside Act, 1981 (as amended)).

Table 4.1 Recreational disturbance

Effects	Possible consequences
(a) Temporary disruption to feeding or breeding • less critical in late summer post-breeding season. • more critical when food supplies are restricted and daylight hours/feeding time reduced e.g.: over-wintering or winter migratory species.	Bird takes cover or flies to undisturbed area High energy loss compared to food supply: repeated disturbance leads to exhaustion and vulnerability to predators
(b) Effects on breeding adult: (i) disturbance when prospecting for suitable nesting sites (ii) disturbance during incubation period	Delay in breeding: loss of suitable site to other of similar species Exposure of eggs. Heat loss: non-incubation: risk of predation
(c) Effects on young: (i) if adult flushed from nest and/or delayed return (ii) if taking cover in response to alarm calls by parent bird	Exposure of chick: heat loss: loss of food: risk of predation Interruption to feeding and brooding (heat loss). Predators attracted by alarm call
(d) Effects on habitat from accidental fire	Loss of breeding cover; loss of food supply

Effects b(i) and d may affect size of breeding population: b(ii), c(i) and c(ii) may affect breeding success.
Source: Sidaway (1993).

In addition to unintentional impacts on the natural environment, certain recreational activities actively exploit the natural resource, as with fishing and wildfowling. While 'hunters' typically safeguard their quarry (subject to their knowledge of population dynamics), their activities can indirectly affect the natural balance of the ecosystem, altering the ratio of species (as through bait digging), manipulating the natural habitat and adding by-products to the environment such as spent lead shot and fishing tackle (Edington and Edington, 1986).

Each site will have an ecological carrying capacity, a maximum level of recreational use that can be sustained without the above impacts causing unacceptable or irreversible damage to a site. Attracting much academic debate, 'unacceptable' and 'irreversible damage' are still difficult to determine, although, the precautionary principle is a commonly utilized aid to definition. Modes of behaviour, patterns of activity and the level of use in relation to the natural environment will determine the constraint imposed by the concept of environmental sustainability in the recreational context.

The limitations imposed by the concept of sustainability and the need to maintain the natural interest of a site need not be absolute. There are a number of technological developments which provide scope for reducing the impact of leisure on the environment, for example, shallow-hulled boats and butane-powered boats. In the instance of shallow-hulled boats such introductions will need to be accompanied by management measures, with the potential for greater access to shallower areas, as with mud flats and salt-marshes.

4.7 CONCLUSION

The degree of constraint felt by the participants in leisure activities today is largely relative. The access to opportunity has increased significantly with such historical events as the coming of the railways, the growth in car ownership and the increase in disposable incomes. Since the 1950s the growth in popularity of water-based sports has been matched by technological developments and an associated rise in recreational opportunities. The development of the fibre-glass hull, outboard motor and aqualungs have given rise to sports such as water-skiing, sub-aqua and jet skiing. Opportunities are today available to a wider sector of the population than they have been in the past.

REFERENCES

Adams, C. E. (1993) Boat traffic loading on inland waterways, *Leisure Studies*, **12**, 71–9.
Ashton, P. G. and Chubb, M. (1972) A preliminary study for evaluating the capacity of waters for recreational boating. *Water Resources Bulletin*, **8**, 571–7.
Bovaird, A. G., Tricker, M. G. and Stoakes, R. (1984) *Recreation Management and Pricing*, Gower.
Chmura, G. L. and Ross, N. W. (1978) *The Environmental Impact of Marinas and their Boats*, Narragansett: University of Rhode Island, Department of Environmental Management Marine Advisory Service.
Coalter, F. (1993) Sports participation: price or priorities?, *Leisure Studies*, **12**, 171–82.
Curry, N. (1994) *Countryside Recreation, Access and Land Use Planning*, London: E & FN Spon.
Edington, J. M. and Edington, M. A. (1986) *Ecology, Recreation and Tourism*, Cambridge: Cambridge University Press.
Garner, J. F. and Jones, B. L. (1991) *Countryside Law*, London: Shaw & Sons.
Green, B. H. (1985) *Countryside Conservation*, London: E & FN Spon.
Jackson, E. L. (1991) Leisure constraints/constrained leisure: special issue introduction, *Journal of Leisure Research*, **23**(4), 279–85.
Liddle, M. J. and Scorgie, H. R. A. (1980) The effects of recreation on freshwater plants and animals – a review, *Biological Conservation*, **17**, 183–206.

Lyons, A. (1991) Participation patterns, *Sport and Leisure*, **32**(5), 19.

Mee, P. (1990) Outdoor activities: getting the balance right, *Sport and Leisure*, **31**(4), 15–17.

Pethick, J. (1984) *An Introduction to Coastal Geomorphology*, London: Edward Arnold.

Pritchard, D. E., Housden, S. D., Mudge, G. P., Galbraith, C. A. and Pienkowski, M. W. (1992) *Important Bird Areas in the United Kingdom including the Channel Islands and the Isle of Man*, Sandy, Bedfordshire: Royal Society for the Protection of Birds.

Quaife, C. (1993) Canoeing. In John Graint and Kit Campbell (eds), *Outdoor Sports: Handbook of Sports and Recreational Building Design*, Vol. 1, Oxford: Butterworths Architecture, 151–3.

Scott, M. (1993) *Leisure Services Law*, 2nd edn, London: Sweet & Maxwell.

Seabrooke, W. and Miles, C. W. N. (1993) *Recreation Land Management*, London: E & FN Spon.

Selman, P. H. (1992) *Environmental Planning: The Conservation and Development of Biophysical Resources*, London: Paul Chapman.

Sidaway, R. (1988) *Sport, Recreation and Nature Conservation*, Study 32. London: Sports Council.

Sidaway, R. (1993) Sport, recreation and nature conservation: developing good conservation practice. In S. Glyptis (ed.), *Leisure and the Environment: Essays in Honour of Professor J.A. Patmore*, London: Belhaven Press.

Sutherland, A. J. and Ogle, D. G. (1975) Effects of jet boats on salmon eggs, *New Zealand Journal of Marine and Freshwater Research*, **9**, 273–82.

Thompson, N. (1993) Facilities for people with disabilities. In John Graint and Kit Campbell (eds), *Outdoor Sports: Handbook of Sports and Recreational Building Design*, Oxford: Butterworths Architecture, 9–11.

White, P. (1991) *Powerboating – A Guide to Sports Boat Handling*, Brighton: Fenhurst Books.

Wilson, R. (1993) Sailing. In John Graint and Kit Campbell (eds), *Outdoor Sports: Handbook of Sports and Recreational Building Design*, Oxford: Butterworths Architecture, 136–50.

Water Quality and Pollution

5

5.1 INTRODUCTION

The coastal waters around the UK, as well as being used for leisure and recreation, are used for transport, food, mineral and energy resources and as a repository for the country's sewage and industrial waste. Such a variety of different activities are not always complementary. Apart from health and aesthetic effects affecting those of us that wish to use the coast for recreation, pollution of these waters may have effects on the biota and the marine environment itself. However, in this particular section our prime concern is how water quality interacts with leisure activities.

Swimming and other water-based recreational activities began to increase in popularity around the UK's coastline in Victorian times (Chapter 1). Before this, water had always been recognized as a key component in both health and disease. The health-promoting effects of a dip in saltwater were – and still are promoted with enthusiasm. Sea water was once considered as an alternative medicinal treatment to spa water, often drunk by the glassful. Latterly the practice of drinking sea water has become far less fashionable, particularly as research indicates that ingestion of sea waters around our coast can have markedly adverse effects on human health. All the indications are that water-based recreation will continue to increase. This means that the health hazards facing the recreators will also continue to gain prominence. Indeed, as more and more people participate in high-exposure activities such as surfing and windsurfing, diving and sailing, the relative importance of the hazards associated with recreational waters will increase.

A range of substances that exert a variety of polluting effects enter coastal waters via a number of sources. These include landborne sources – discharges via rivers, streams, drains, pipes and run-off; shipborne and

Coastal Recreation Management Edited by Tim Goodhead and David Johnson. Published in 1996 by E & FN Spon, London. ISBN 0 419 20360 5

maritime industrial sources – accidental, deliberate or operational; regulated dumping of material at sea (radioactive waste, sewage sludge etc); 'environmental' sources such as atmospheric deposition. However, in terms of impact on the coastal environment the key sources of pollutants are riverine inputs of industrial, agricultural and domestic effluents and the coastal sewage discharges serving the population of 12.5 million who live on the coast. For these reasons, this account will thus focus on the effects that sewage contaminated sea water may have on recreation. The effects that chemical and radioactive pollution and other anthropogenic inputs may have are discussed elsewhere.

5.2 SEWAGE DISCHARGES

Sadly for the marine environment, the Victorian interest in marine recreation coincided with the development of their preferred method of sewage disposal – untreated discharges through sea-outfalls. The engineers responsible for developing the sewerage system had total faith in the infinite dilution and disinfection capacity of the seas surrounding the UK. Thus, not only was the raw sewage discharged direct to sea, but the route chosen was via short outfalls which often discharged directly on to beaches.

In 1970 a working party of the then Ministry of Housing and Local Government conducted an inquiry into the disposal of sewage to sea (Working Party on Sewage Disposal, 1970). The working party concluded that sewage should only be disposed of to sea after it had been screened, comminuted and through long sea-outfalls – not through the then current practice of short sea-outfalls. This policy was not actively pursued until the EU introduced its directive concerning the quality of bathing water (CEC, 1976). Currently around 1500 million litres of sewage are discharged into UK coastal waters every day. The bulk of this material is untreated.

Sewage treatment involves a number of discrete stages. Preliminary treatment involves passing the effluent through screens to remove larger solids (including plastics) and may be accompanied by maceration. Preliminary treatment has little effect on the microbial loadings of the effluent. Primary treatment involves settlement and sedimentation of the effluent to remove the bulk of solids – resulting in approximately 50% reduction in microbial loadings. Secondary treatment involves biological treatment of primary treatment effluent. Its purpose is to reduce the effluent's ability to deplete the oxygen content of the receiving water. Secondary treatment reduces bacterial content of the effluent by up to 99%, but as (i) the original bacterial concentrations are extremely high and (ii) viruses are far less effectively removed during this stage, the resulting effluent is still loaded with microbes. Tertiary treatment involves polishing secondary treated effluent to remove nutrients or microorganisms – ultra-violet sterilization is a form of tertiary treatment.

Apart from routine discharges through short and long sea-outfalls, periodic discharges occur through storm water and overflow outfalls. These are designed to deal with the excess flow generated during storms and heavy rainfall, when raw sewage is diverted from the regular treatment works. Such outfalls often discharge completely untreated sewage directly on to beaches above low water mark. This problem was highlighted when the owner of a private beach at Croyde Bay in North Devon sought redress through the courts for offensive deposits of sewage solids on the beach of his holiday complex. He claimed that it was directly affecting his livelihood by disaffecting visitors and was also concerned for his position should a visitor to the complex become ill. The action was brought against South West Water who eventually settled out of court, effectively meeting the demands of the plaintiff to prevent the nuisance continuing.

A thousand outfalls are estimated to be actively discharging sewage around the UK coastline, around half of which can be classified as major. In 1989 a WRC survey of 620 of these outfalls indicated that 60% discharged raw sewage and a further 8% were only subject to preliminary treatment – a rather grand term for screening. Of the 250 or so outfalls to coastal waters serving summer populations of 10 000 or more, around 80% currently receive only preliminary or no treatment (HCEC, 1990). Approximately 40 long sea-outfalls are in commission around the UK, with more under construction or planned as components of major capital projects. This begins to define the scale of the pressure on our coastal waters. In the following sections the regulatory mechanisms governing sewage discharge to sea, the potential hazards posed by sewage discharges to recreators and the latest information on quantification of risks encountered will be discussed.

5.3 REGULATORY CONTROLS ON QUALITY OF MARINE WATERS

There is a range of legislation currently in place to regulate marine pollution. However, with direct reference to sewage pollution, there are three key measures – the UK Water Resources Act (1991) and two European Union (EU) directives – one on the Quality of Bathing Waters (CEC, 1976) and one on Urban Waste Water Treatment (CEC, 1991).

The Water Resources Act (1991) empowers the National Rivers Authority (NRA) to regulate the sewage discharges that the water companies may make to coastal waters. The NRA set consents limits on such discharges which are designed to protect the waters into which the sewage is discharged. This system is, however, manifestly flawed and many coastal discharges either do not have numerical consents or regularly breach whatever consents may have been set.

The Urban Waste Water Treatment Directive (CEC, 1991) is designed to ensure that urban waste water entering collection systems is subject to secondary treatment or its equivalent before its discharge to receiving waters. This directive also makes provision for tertiary treatment where it is necessary to meet more stringent environmental criteria – so called 'sensitive' areas. The directive is designed to be applied to coastal sewage discharges that serve populations in excess of 10 000 and estuarial discharges serving populations in excess of 2000. Largely as a response to this directive the UK Government will cease all discharges of raw sewage to coastal waters by 1998. On the face of it this directive will go a long way to protect the marine environment and recreators by securing more effective sewage treatment. However, sceptics may suggest that the loopholes in the directive will be used to maintain the status quo. Many small outfalls are not covered by the directive and primary treatment alone will be sufficient if the sewage discharges into so called 'less sensitive areas'. Water companies may claim that the vast majority of outfalls discharge into less sensitive areas and will thus only require primary treatment. This argument may be further backtracked to claim that preliminary treatment rather than primary treatment may be sufficient if the discharge is via a long sea outfall. This would both reduce costs to the water companies and reduce the amount of sewage sludge to be disposed of.

The EU adopted the Directive on the Quality of Bathing Water in 1975 (CEC, 1976) with the dual aims of protecting the environment and public health. This directive sets minimum standards which bathing water must meet. It is only concerned with water used for bathing and not for any other recreational use such as surfing, windsurfing, diving or sailing. The increasing popularity of such activities coupled with more effective wet and dry suits, has extended the areas used for water-based recreation well beyond the traditional bathing beaches. Thus no monitoring of the quality of sea water used by large numbers of water recreators is currently being undertaken. It seems that the interests of this sector of the leisure community are not being served. The scope of the bathing water directive, although limited to traditional bathing waters, is worthy of consideration as it is the only model that we currently have that aims to protect the health of those undertaking their leisure in coastal waters.

5.3.1 THE CURRENT EU BATHING WATER DIRECTIVE

The quality of bathing waters is currently assessed according to this directive and judged as pass or fail – there are no other grades. The NRA has the primary responsibility for the monitoring of bathing waters, assessing the quality of designated waters throughout the season and presenting the results to the local authority (NRA, 1994). The local authority in turn publish the results on noticeboards at the beaches. In the UK the bathing season is considered to extend from May to September. Samples are taken at least 20 times during this period, at approximately fortnightly intervals. The directive sets quality standards that must be achieved in such waters. A range of 19 physico-chemical, bacteriological and aesthetic determinants are specified at either Imperative (I) or Guideline (G) values.

The standards on which the UK (and other EU states) currently base their compliance are the total and faecal coliform I standards. These are basically used as microbiological indices of sanitary quality. The most widely used index organisms are the coliform group of bacteria – including total coliforms (originating from both human and environmental sources) and those coliforms that originate from human and animal guts (faecal coliforms).

The target faecal coliform is *E. coli*, a bacterium that is found in massive numbers in human (and other animal) faeces. In recent years a further faecal index bacterial group – faecal streptococci – has gathered support as a more appropriate index of sanitary quality of recreational waters (Rees, 1993, 1994).

The characteristics of an index organism can be summarized thus:

- present when pathogens are likely to be present;
- indicates an imminent risk;
- present in greater numbers than pathogens;
- resistant to environmental stresses;
- easily cultivated in the laboratory;
- easily identified;
- randomly distributed;
- growth in culture independent of other organisms.

For the purpose of compliance assessment, the NRA's monitoring begins in May, two weeks before the start of the bathing season and continues through to the end of September. In accordance with the directive, samples are collected in approximately 1 m depth of water 30 cm below the surface and should be taken at places where the daily average density of bathers is highest.

At any sample point water quality will be affected by the following factors:

- **temporal** – seasonal, tidal, diurnal, sewage discharge patterns, etc.;
- **spatial** – position along the shore, off the shore, etc.;
- **variable** – adverse weather conditions, irregular events and discharges, etc.

The samples should be collected from a standardized position, stored in lightproof containers and analysed as soon as possible. Direct sunlight will cause a tenfold reduction in bacterial numbers in a sample bottle within 30 minutes. Any period of storage will affect bacterial numbers, although such changes can be minimized by cooling.

Once collected, other aspects of sample processing can affect microbial counts, including analytical procedures such as sample dilution, incubation conditions (resuscitation, culture media, temperature) and counting of colonies. There are two methods of quantifying index bacteria in water samples – multiple tube fermentation (MPN) and membrane filtration (MF). Either method is recommended in the EU Directive. However, both methods produce inaccurate estimates of index numbers, particularly in the case of marginally polluted waters (Fleisher, 1990).

Microorganisms released into sea water from waste water discharges are diluted, dispersed, sediment out and die. Such factors are used to justify the practice of discharging sewage to coastal waters. They also contribute to the extreme variations in estimates of bacterial numbers made on the same bathing water on different occasions in the monitoring programme. Thus, for example, if the results for a particular determinant over the monitoring season are examined, they can vary from zero per 100 mls up to several thousands per 100 mls. The anomalies can readily be highlighted when one compares the situation which arises when other organizations (such as local authorities) undertake monitoring programmes in tandem with the NRA.

The inherent variability in estimating bacterial numbers coupled with the vagaries of sampling coastal bathing waters suggest that the published data are at best speculative snapshots rather than accurate quality assessments. Therefore it seems logical to assume that whether a bathing water passes or fails the criteria of the EU Directive depends rather more on the time and way the sample is collected than any other factor.

The other microbial determinants – salmonella, enteroviruses and faecal streptococci – are effectively ignored. There is growing support for the theory that faecal streptococci are a more appropriate indicator of sewage contamination than are the coliforms and faecal coliforms (Rees, 1993, 1994). Faecal streptococci are more resistant to environmental stresses than are faecal coliforms and thus survive longer. They are rarely found in an unpolluted environment and are a better indicator for the potential presence of viruses which cause the majority of health problems for people bathing in sewage polluted waters (section 6.4).

5.3.2 PROPOSED AMENDMENTS TO THE EU BATHING WATER DIRECTIVE

The EU bathing water directive has long been considered inappropriate and in need of review. Early in 1994 proposals to amend the directive were issued for comment. These proposals have addressed some of the critical issues but flaws still remain. The 1994 proposals to amend the directive vary most importantly in the microbiological determinants. One determinand, total coliforms, has been dropped. The previous and largely ignored G standard for faecal streptococci has been hardened into an I standard. It is proposed that the I and G standards for faecal coliforms be maintained at the same numerical values, but more discretely defined as *Escherichia coli*. The controversial zero standard for enteroviruses is proposed to be maintained in a somewhat amended format. The amended proposal recommends that samples be analysed monthly for the presence of enterovirus during the bathing season. Waters should only be exempted from these monthly enterovirus estimations if they met the G standard for *E. coli* and the I standard for faecal streptococci in the previous two bathing seasons. Under these conditions the enterovirus level in the bathing water must be measured once more during the bathing season.

These amendments have begun to address the issue of the most appropriate indicator of recreational water quality. The inclusion of faecal streptococci in determining compliance does extend the value of the directive. The longer lived faecal streptococci are far better mirrors of viral contamination than are the shorter lived *E. coli*. However, enteroviruses are not an index organism but a discrete group of potentially pathogenic viruses. They are extremely difficult to isolate and identify consistently. Certainly there are relatively few laboratories that can successfully undertake enterovirus determinations on a sufficiently large scale in the UK. The situation concerning analytical capabilities for this determinant is considerably reduced in all member states.

Further, a zero standard for this determinant is quite unrealistic as it may be opportunistically present in a sample due to a number of external sources – animal droppings, run-off etc. Theoretically only one such event could lead to a bathing water failing the directive. If a viral standard is to be set, then it must be an attainable one.

The suggestion that a bacteriophage should be included at some subsequent stage is most encouraging. Although they are viruses and possess all the properties of that group, phages are relatively easy to isolate and enumerate. There are a number of bacteriophage candidates – the F-specific RNA phage, the somatic coliphages and the *Bacteroides fragilis* phage. Current research indicates that the F-specific RNA phage may be the most appropriate model of human enteric viruses in the recreational water environment (Havelaar *et al.*, 1993).

The reader is further referred to the report of the House of Lords Select Committee on the European Communities (HLSCEC, 1994) for a full and reasoned analysis of the issues surrounding the proposed amendments to the bathing water directive.

5.4 DISEASES AND MICROORGANISMS

Recreational water users always expose themselves to a certain health risk – water is an alien environment to humans (Cartwright, 1991). The pathogenic microorganisms that may be found in sea waters have a wide range of sources, including sewage pollution, but also include organisms naturally found in the marine environment. Some hazardous organisms, then, are not associated with sewage discharges. These include leptospires (causative organisms of leptospirosis), *Trichobilharzia ocellata* (a protozoan that can cause the complaint known as swimmers itch), free-living amoebae, *Vibrio* **spp** (cholera and gastrointestinal illnesses) etc. (Philipp, 1991). Additionally there is a degree of spread of pathogenic microorganisms, particularly viruses, in good-quality bathing waters via person to person transmission. Thus such organisms and the diseases they can cause are not expressly controlled by the existing EU bathing water directive (or the proposed amendments to the current directive).

Both the EU bathing water directive and the EU urban waste water treatment directive are aiming primarily at the control of systematic faecal pollution and eutrophication. These directives only regulate a part of the overall health risk encountered in recreational waters. The EU bathing water directive is further limited in its scope when one considers that no waters other than designated bathing waters are monitored. What leads to a bathing water being designated is open to question – they are generally popular resort beaches with various facilities used by a large number of bathers. Therefore large sections of marine recreators can expect no protection from this directive – particularly those active offshore. However, it is obvious that the control of sewage discharges will contribute enormously to the reduction in the health risks encountered by immersing oneself in the marine environment.

Sewage contains a particularly unhealthy cocktail of both harmless and pathogenic microorganisms. The largest component is organisms that are only pathogenic under exceptional circumstances – characterized by *E. coli* and faecal streptococci. These are the indicator bacteria referred to in the preceding sections. Presence of these index organisms is taken as a sign of potential pathogen presence. The infectious hazards posed by sewage are considerable. The health risk from recreational exposure to sewage contaminated waters is generally considered to be less than that posed by drinking sewage contaminated waters. However, bathers are estimated to ingest between 10 and 15 mls of sea water each time they bathe, thereby compounding any health risk (Rees, 1993). Additionally, exposure to breaks in the protective skin barrier and mucous membranes may serve as additional access points for pathogens. The main hazards associated with recreational use of waters are infection, physical injury through accidents and drowning (Cartwright, 1991). This account deals only with the infectious risks that recreators are exposed to.

The main microbiological hazards arising from exposure to recreational waters include a range of infections caused by viruses, bacteria (including blue-green algae), protozoans (including *Cryptosporidium* **spp** and *Giardia* **spp**) and microalgae (Philipp, 1991). Bacterial diseases transmitted via water include bacillary dysentery, typhoid, cholera and a range of milder gastrointestinal illnesses. However, such diseases are usually associated with the ingestion of very large numbers of bacteria, thus the particular pathogen usually has to be present in enormous numbers to cause the disease. For this reason, where sewage contamination has occurred or is suspected, virus borne gastrointestinal infections are of particular concern, including those caused by enteroviruses (a group which includes coxsackieviruses groups A and B, echoviruses, polioviruses and hepatitis A virus), Norwalk virus, small round viruses and small round structured viruses. With these viral complaints the infectious dose required to manifest the disease is largely unknown and may be as little as one viral particle.

A number of eye, ear, nose and throat infections may be caused by organisms such as waterborne adenoviruses and parvoviruses. Skin complaints have been associated with bacteria such as *Staphylococcus* **spp** and *Pseudomonas* **spp** and a range of yeasts including *Candida albicans* (causative organism of thrush). Skin irritation and contact dermatitis have been associated with exposure to blue-green algae and dinoflagellates.

Several studies worldwide have demonstrated that a range of minor symptomatic illnesses have been associated with the recreational use of water (for example, Dufour, 1984; Cabelli, 1983: Cabelli *et al.*, 1982; Seyfried *et al*, 1985a, 1985b; Balarajan *et al.*, 1991; Jones *et al.*, 1991; Kay *et al.*, 1994). Thus the association between 'minor' illnesses and sewage contaminated sea water has been accepted. However the link between more serious infections such as meningitis, poliomyelitis and hepatitis A and recreational waters is more difficult to determine. The viruses responsible for those infections have been isolated from sewage polluted waters but there have been no substantiated cases of either poliomyelitis or meningitis acquired through this milieu. Only two outbreaks of hepatitis A have been attributed to recreational water activities (Bryan *et al.*, 1974; Philipp *et al.*, 1989). In such illnesses the source of infection is difficult to determine – retrospective sampling of the water body is obviously impossible and the disease may have an incubation period of several weeks. All that is possible is to assemble circumstantial evidence to point to the likely source of infection. This leads to what are generally referred to as anecdotal instances of serious infections that may be attributable to recreational water exposure. Such instances are generally dismissed as unsubstantiated by the regulators and the water industry, much to the displeasure of interest groups such as Surfers Against Sewage.

What is obvious is that bathers in sewage polluted waters may face an increased risk of minor morbidity such as gastrointestinal, skin and upper respiratory tract ailments due to the presence of infectious organisms in that water. The risk factor is further compounded with recreators who increase their degree of exposure by participating in high-contact activities such as surfing and diving.

5.5 HEALTH EFFECTS

The first investigation into the health effects of bathing in coastal waters around the UK was undertaken by the Public Health Laboratory Service (PHLS). This report concluded that the risk to health from bathing in sewage contaminated waters could be ignored, with the possible exception of a few aesthetically revolting beaches (PHLS, 1959). This observation shaped the UK government's regulatory response to sewage discharge to sea until the 1980s. Cabelli and co-workers (Cabelli *et al.*, 1982; Cabelli, 1983) were the first to use a survey of beach visitors with a follow-up questionnaire in an attempt to link health effects with water-based recreation. This work led to the demonstration of a statistically significant bathing related incidence of gastrointestinal symptoms indexed to the level of faecal streptococci in the water. Similar beach studies have been undertaken in a number of countries and the so-called Cabelli approach has been endorsed by the World Health Organisation (WHO), the United Nations Environment Programme (UNEP) and the US Environmental Protection Agency (WHO, 1992).

Although the results of these various studies have not always been entirely consistent, a general trend is obvious. Thus all studies have demonstrated that bathers exhibit a higher incidence of symptomatic illness after they have been exposed to sea water than do non-bathers. The commonest relationship demonstrated is that between water quality and gastrointestinal symptoms, although other commonly reported symptoms relate to the eye, ear and upper respiratory tract.

A number of criticisms were made relating to the original Cabelli methodology (Lightfoot, 1989; Fleisher, 1990, 1991). This led the UK to adopt a dual approach in its major studies to establish the relationship between water quality and risk to bathers' health (Pike, 1990, 1991, 1992, 1994). This study was jointly funded by the UK Departments of Environment and Health, the NRA and the Welsh Office. The final report of this UK national study into the health effects of sea bathing was issued in January 1994 (Pike, 1994). It describes the two test methodologies used and the results obtained in the final Phase III component of the study. During the complete study, almost 18 000 people were assessed on 13 different beaches. The Phase III studies comprised 10 of those beaches. The study involved two methods – a survey to determine symptoms reported by individuals undertaking a range of bathing-related activities at beaches varying widely in water quality and a study using healthy adult volunteers randomly split into those who bathed and those who did not bathe in waters of good quality.

The key conclusions in the report can be summarized thus:

- bathers reported symptoms more frequently than did non-bathers;
- the degree of water contact was related to the rate of reporting symptoms – more contact, more symptoms;
- 15–24-year-olds reported symptoms more frequently than did other age groups;

- relative increases in frequencies of diarrhoea symptoms in bathers were related to levels of total coliform bacteria and enteroviruses, but this link only became significant at the *I* level for these determinants.

Closer examination of the report indicates that there are several features which may cloud the generally upbeat line that accompanied its launch. Thus it is interesting to note that the healthy volunteer method is largely relegated from the final conclusions, described rather more as an epidemiological refinement than a method to determine the health effects of sea bathing. This is somewhat surprising when one considers that one of the report's final conclusions states that 'the only consistent relationship between water quality and the rates of gastrointestinal symptoms occurred with faecal streptococci when measured at chest depth and when counts exceeded 35–40 per 100 mls' (Pike, 1994). This conclusion is further detailed in a subsequent paper (Kay *et al*, 1994), indicating that a key component of the healthy volunteer research had been virtually overlooked.

The more widely applied beach survey method provides the bulk of the concluding remarks. The line taken in the interim report (Pike, 1992) is somewhat softened in the final report. The four beaches of poorer water quality consistently reported higher rates of illness than did the four beaches of better water quality. The lack of statistically significant correlations with the other indicators and with waters with dubious rather than outright poor quality is taken as sufficient evidence on which to maintain the current standards. The report also notes that the sampling strategy in the beach survey was such that correlations would indeed be difficult to establish. The flaws in the sampling strategy were unavoidable, particularly given the beaches chosen. One would expect the key correlations to arise in the bathing waters of poorer quality. However, the four beaches of poorer water quality in the Phase III study all had extensive tidal ranges and supported short sewage outfalls. At low tide bathers would have to walk for up to 1 km before being able to bathe, when coincidentally water quality would be poorest. Thus sampling at low water – which regularly occurred – would reflect conditions where exposure to risk was minimized as bathers were nonexistent. In reality the conditions where bathers would be active would coincide with the best water quality. It is also interesting to note that in the 1992 component of the survey, in the two poor quality bathing waters (Instow and Cleethorpes) bathers were only recorded at the time of sampling on two or three days out of the 30 or so sampled at each beach. Furthermore, as sampling took place (in line with the EU Directive) at 30 cm depth in 1 m of water, the water to which the majority of water users would have been exposed would not have been assessed. This is particularly salient when one considers the correlations between 35 faecal streptococci per 100 ml sea water and gastrointestinal symptoms when sampled at chest depth in the cohort component of the study (Kay et al., 1994).

Considering these factors it is hardly surprising that correlations between indicators and symptoms do not reach statistical significance. That they exhibit the consistent trend that they do is remarkable. Consistently the dirtier beaches reported higher rates of illness than did the clean beaches. The report thus indicates that as water quality decreases the likelihood of contracting a range of symptomatic illnesses increases. It is generally acknowledged that the analysis of the beach survey published in the final report is only a preliminary one. The microbiological determinands were averaged over the study period and then related back to health effects – thus the actual microbiological conditions encountered by bathers has yet to be related to health effects.

In summary, then, the UK Health Effects of Sea Bathing report produced a confused set of conclusions. The beach survey data should be re-examined and related to tidal and sewage discharge patterns. Due credence should also be given to the findings of the cohort study where a link between a level of faecal streptococci ten times lower than that suggested as the new *I* level and gastrointestinal symptoms was demonstrated. Caution should be exercised in giving a clean bill of health to current standards based on these data as they stand.

5.6 THE IMPACT OF LEISURE ACTIVITIES ON WATER QUALITY

With one or two notable exceptions, very little is published on the effects of water-based recreation on the quality of water. There is much conjecture that many sports are polluting the water system, but these claims have very little scientific work supporting them. This does not mean to say that leisure activities are non-polluting, but only that they contribute so little when compared with other sources of aquatic pollution that they appear inconsequential. However, most of the effects of pollution from recreational sources will have a local effect and/or a cumulative effect and therefore should not be ignored. Often water sports take place in enclosed waterways or estuarine systems. Pollution in these systems is exaggerated due to the concentrating nature of an enclosed system and the adsorption and accumulation of pollutants by sediment.

In many cases those that participate in watersports are environmentally aware. The nature of many sports, swimming, diving, sailing, for example, means that they take place in environmentally important areas and the participants tend to be educated to good environmental practice. This education occurs not only through the personal interests of the participants but also through the dissemination of information by sports authorities, other leisure bodies and pressure groups, e.g. RYA, surfers against sewage, Solent Protection Society. Other sports such as powerboating and jet skiing are not so environmentally sympathetic, and conflict can occur in areas where these sports take place. Conflict may also occur between local and visiting participants, with locals being more aware of regional environmental issues and the consequences of damage to that area. Visitors can often pollute with impunity as they do not have to live with the consequences. When looking regionally, it must be remembered that leisure may be the major industry of the area and therefore a balance must be struck between watersports and the environment.

The major sources of pollution attritutable to watersports are as follows:

5.6.1 MARINE SANITATION POLLUTION

The past few years has seen a debate into the regulation of discharge from boats. Many have looked for regulations that would stop the discharge from marine toilets. This would require the use of holding tanks and onshore disposal facilities, as required in the United States and some restricted waters in the UK, e.g. the Lakes and inland waterways. With the exception of completely enclosed water areas where there is no flushing e.g. lakes, the effect of discharge from leisure craft is actually quite small when compared with what is pumped from outfall pipes. More rigorous EU bathing water standards will however make it imperative to improve the water quality by whatever means.

5.6.2 OIL AND PETROCHEMICALS

Oil-based pollution from water-borne activities can enter the aquatic system by many different means. Most obviously diesel, petrol and oil can be spilt at fuelling barges. Bilge water can also be a source of oil pollution. It may be that these small amounts may be negligible compared with oil terminal spills and the illegal flushing of tanks from large ships. However, one recent source suggests that amount of oil equivalent to 15 Exxon Valdez oil spills is introduced into US waters every year from 8 m-plus two-stroke outboard engines (Mele, 1994). In addition these small spills will be occurring in rivers estuaries etc, which are environmentally very sensitive areas. Unfortunately, the fuels used commonly in the boating industry are highly toxic. Diesel is used as it perceived as a safe fuel, but due to its high aromatic content, is in fact highly toxic and more damaging than many other fuels (Clark, 1989). Oil and petrochemicals affect aquatic organisms in various ways. Heavy oil products act physically by smothering organisms; clogging gills of fish, arthropods and molluscs; or matting the feathers of birds or fur of mammals. In addition, these heavy, but more importantly the lighter oil products are highly toxic to animals and plants with petroleum residues concentrating in fish, birds and mammals (GESAMP, 1991). Generally the lighter fractions of oil tend to be more volatile, which means that they disperse or evaporate more quickly, but their mobility means that they are more easily absorbed by wildlife.

It is not only the fuel itself that can be damaging environmentally, but also engine emissions. The marine industry has called for the EU to set emission standards for Europe. Two-stroke engines are thought by Mele (1994) to be 80 times more polluting than car engines. Exhaust from marine engines, particularly the oil/petrol mix used by outboard engines, is a source of tainting. Tainting causes the loss of commercial fishing due to the oily taste of the meat of some fish and shell fish (Clark, 1989).

5.6.3 PLASTIC LITTER

Plastic litter which can get into the water system (although not exclusively) by means of water-based sports. Plastic packaging, bottles and beer-can collars do not chemically alter the water, but are a physical source of pollution. It is easy for them to be discarded overboard or at the water's edge. In addition fishing gear in the form of lines and polypropylene is often discarded into the water. Plastic litter is buoyant and persistent. Animals get snared in it and ingest it. For air breathing animals, getting trapped in line or plastic sheeting can cause suffocation. The ingestion of litter can cause intestinal blockages for many animals. Small birds and fish have been known to get stuck fast in plastic beer can collars (Clark, 1989; GESAMP, 1991).

5.6.4 ANTIFOULING

Antifouling paints are used on the hulls of pleasure craft and some installations such as piling in an attempt to prevent or slow the growth of aquatic organisms that might otherwise settle on the surface. A great deal is known about fouling in the marine environment where it is a considerable problem. Fouling in freshwater systems is a more complex issue. The nature of the fouling varies with different environmental conditions, e.g. hardness of water (Callow, 1993), but generally the numbers of nuisance species are less than in the marine environment.

By nature antifouling compounds, in common use, are toxic and thus constitute a pollution problem in the marine environment. The active biocides usually target juvenile stages of the organisms and act to inhibit settlement and/or growth. The use of paints in the leisure industry is still very small compared with the amounts used in the commercial area. However, the issue of antifouling paints and harm to the environment has proved to be a most controversial debate in the past years. It is possibly the only pollution issue where the leisure industry can be shown to have had a dramatic and widespread impact on the environment and legislation has been rushed through the British Parliament and other countries to effect a ban on the use of a substance. Alzieu and Portmann (1984) were the first workers to consider the adverse effects of antifouling paint on commercial fisheries. Their findings led to a more widespread look at the effects on the marine environment at large. These workers considered that three factors have contributed to the adverse effects on fisheries in the past 25 years. Firstly, the major expansion in the boating as a leisure pursuit in Europe during the 1970s and '80s. Secondly, the increased cultivation of the Pacific Oyster, *Crassostrea gigas,* a species of oyster, grown in place of the European native oyster, *Ostrea edulis,* and found particularly sensitive to some antifouling compounds. Thirdly, the introduction of tributyl tin (TBT) as an antifouling agent (Alzieu and Portmann, 1984).

The active biocidal ingredients are combined into a paint base. The more traditional so-called 'hard coatings' release the toxin in a relatively uncontrolled way, with a high release of toxin soon after the application of the paint and a slowing down of release as the coating ages and eventually becomes ineffective as an antifouling. The more recent and commonly used copolymer paints are more effective as they release the biocide at a more constant rate over a longer period of time. This allows the use of lower levels of the toxin in the paint and thus is judged a more environmentally acceptable paint base. The copolymer paints also have a self-polishing property, whereby the movement of water over the painted surface, e.g. a boat hull, helps the surface layer of the paint to continually wear away, thus removing any surface growth and exposing a new layer of toxin. It is claimed that this self-polishing property, which is dependent on water movement, reduces the amount of toxin that is released into the environment when a boat is on its moorings. The two commonly found antifouling active ingredients are copper and TBT.

Copper

Copper is a heavy metal and although many animals and plants require it in trace amounts, at higher levels it is toxic to many physiological systems. Many crustaceans, molluscs and fish are particularly sensitive to copper. Because of its toxicity it has been and is now used extensively in antifouling paints. Copper was very common in the period leading up to the advent of tributyl tin and has been reintroduced subsequent to the TBT ban. The amount of copper released into the aquatic environment from antifouling paints is negligible compared with other industrial sources. In the pre-TBT era it was estimated that 180 t yr^{-1} was released in the area between Santa Barbara and San Diego, California (Clark, 1989). The levels of copper in the post-TBT ban show increases in some areas and this is now a cause for concern. Examples of such areas are the Arachon basin (Claisse and Alzieu, 1993) and the California coast (Stephenson and Leonard, 1994).

S-triazines

The use of s triazines as biocides in antifouling paints is a recent development. their use represents the need for biocidal ingredients that may also be environmentally more acceptable than copper.

Although their use as antifouling agents is quite recent, the triazines have been used as herbicides for a number of years. They are known to be toxic to algae (Lewey, 1992). Apart from these few algae, little is known about the toxicity of these compounds to marine organisms (Gough et al., 1994). These authors have reported that significant levels of s-triazines have been detected in areas of high boating activity and in particular around marinas.

Tributyl tin (TBT) – a case study

When TBT was introduced as an antifouling agent in the 1980s it was considered to be an ideal compound. It was highly toxic to target species, it was very long lasting, thought to be degraded rapidly in the environment, and it could be incorporated into a copolymer paint, thus reducing the leaching of toxin when the boat was moored. These technical factors combined with marketing features, such as low maintenance and the range of colours available made TBT paint extremely popular.

In 1982 the French government imposed a partial ban on TBT paints, following evidence from the bay of Archacon where oyster cultivation failed in areas in close proximity to moored yachts. This temporary ban was later made permanent.

Following the French ban and evidence of high levels of TBT in some estuaries and after the failure of commercial oysters, the UK government set up a consultative period and gave the paint industry six months to investigate the problem and search for alternatives. During the consultative period, the Royal Yachting Association (RYA) and professional bodies from the industry, e.g. the Paintmakers Association, lobbied hard to oppose what looked like an increasing likelihood of a ban. Initially the scientific evidence was not strong. Much of the evidence concerning the failure of oyster fisheries in the UK was not supported. Increasingly it appeared that the Ministry of Agriculture Fisheries and Food (MAFF) were supporting the oyster fisherman who had been encouraged to farm Pacific oysters after the earlier failure of native oyster beds due to a combination of circumstances. Two months into the six-month moratorium, in 1986, the use of TBT-based paint on yachts under 25 metres long was imposed under the Control of Pollution Act (1974). What triggered this precipitous ban is unclear. There was certainly an increased body of scientific evidence concerning the toxicity of TBT to molluscan species and in particular, oysters, mussels and dogwhelks. This evidence was now not only being gathered in Europe, but also from the USA. It is interesting to note, however, that to that date, the government in power had no environmental legislation in place and this certainly looked like an ideal political opportunity.

Further consideration should be given to why, accepting that TBT is one of the most toxic substances known, the ban was only imposed on craft under 25 metres and excluding all commercial shipping. It was argued that the problem was restricted to inshore waters and estuaries and therefore was only pertinent to craft capable of moving in those waters, i.e. yachts under 25 metres. One look at an estuary such as Southampton Water is enough to disavow anyone of this idea. Large container ships, tankers and liners constantly enter and moor in the city docks, and oil tankers use the estuary's oil terminals. To this day these ships are antifouled with TBT-based paints. It was argued that the commercial ports used by shipping were in areas with little or no environmental value. Again a look at ports such as Portsmouth and Southampton reveal that these important ports are in close proximity to extensive marine Sites of Special Scientific Interest (SSSI) which have been designated as such for their extensive and ecologically important intertidal mudflats. The ban of this efficient antifouling compound would cost a great deal to the shipping companies and the navies of the

Western world. Edward Goldberg of Scripps Institution of Oceanography considers that the US navy calculated a 15% saving in fuel consumption leading to annual savings of 150 million dollars on the entire US fleet. One is led to believe that the continued use of TBT antifouling on the British fleets was also a political and economic decision.

In 1986 the UK ban of TBT became permanent under the Food and Environmental Protection Act (1985). This ban was on the use of TBT on all craft under 25 metres, except those with aluminium hulls and was applied to all copolymer paints with more than 7.5% TBT and other (free association) paints with more than 2.5% TBT. The ban was aimed at reduced TBT levels in coastal waters to an acceptable level MAFF recommended 20 ppt). Dalley (1989) reviewed the legislation in the UK and other countries and to date most countries in the developed world have implemented some form of TBT ban.

In 1994 the International Maritime Organisation (IMO) suggested that the 25 metre ban should be raised to craft over 50 metres. Any environmental argument for the continued use of TBT must take into consideration the gains in savings of fossil fuels and a subsequent reduction in fossil fuel contamination in coastal waters.

In 1993 Claisse and Alzieu published another paper concerning antifouling and the environment (see above, p. 109). Their research showed an increase in the copper content of oysters near marinas and moorings in the Archacon basin. They speculated that the ban on TBT-based paints led to an increased use of copper-based antifoulings which may lead to yet another environmental problem associated with the leisure industry.

5.7 BOAT WASH

While not strictly being a water quality issue, physical disturbance by boat wash and propellers certainly needs consideration. Wash can play a major part in the erosion of riverbanks. This disturbance not only has long-term effects on the bank and erosion/deposition cycles but can also be detrimental to bankside vegetation and bird-nesting sites. In response to this and other safety concerns, there is a proposed ban of fast motor boating on Lake Windermere. Also continued propeller action leads to increased oxygenation of the water that in turn can lead to an upset of microflora which leads to the disruption of entire ecosystems. Increased levels of oxygenation by propellers led to deterioration problems in the lagoons and canals of Venice.

5.8 CONCLUSION

Water quality can have adverse affects on recreational activities in the marine environment. In particular the practice of discharging vast quantities of untreated sewage to our coastal waters may well cause recreators to become ill. There are measures in train designed to protect the health of bathers (the EU bathing water directive), but these measures do not extend to other recreational users or to areas other than those designated as bathing waters.

The EU has proposed amendments to the bathing water directive, reflecting concerns expressed through the life of the directive. These go some way to relate the standards to more accurate determinants of the sanitary quality of the water. However, the fundamental concerns about the precision of sampling strategies and analytical methods available remain to be addressed.

The UK study into the health effects of bathing in sea water affected by sewage discharges was an extensive attempt to correlate health risks to water quality. It remains a very good piece of work, but the ready acceptance of the inconclusive nature of the links between water quality and illness is inappropriate. The data demands further analysis before accepting the most expedient outcome. What is undeniable is, however, that those enjoying their leisure in coastal waters may become ill if those waters receive sewage discharges.

Many of the concerns regarding the impact of boating on the environment are being addressed by the British Marine Industries Federation (BMIF) in the BMIF environment initiative.

This initiative includes the Poole Environment Project which will lead to the development of a code of practice for the marine industry.

Responsible behaviour by the industry is not enough: the users must also show commitment to the environment. BMIF have published a guide for boat users and many sporting bodies, e.g. British Canoe Union, RYA publish codes of conduct for watersport enthusiasts (for more details see Chapter 14).

REFERENCES

Alzieu and Portmann (1984) The effect of tributyltin on the culture of Crussostrea Gigas and other species, *Proc. Ann. Shelf Conf.* **15**, 87–100.
Balarajan, R., Soni Raleigh, V., Yuen, P., Wheeler, D., Machin, D. and Cartwright, R. (1991) Health risks associated with bathing in water, *British Medical Journal*, **303**, 1444–5.
Bryan, J. A., Lehmann, J. D., Setiady, I. F. and Hatch, M. H. (1974) An outbreak of hepatitis A associated with recreational lake water, *American Journal of Epidemiology*, **99**, 145–54.

Cabelli, V. J. (1983) *Health Effects Criteria for Marine Recreational Waters*, EPA-600/1-80-031, US Environmental Protection Agency, Health Effects Research Laboratory, Triangle Park, North Carolina 27711, 98 pp.

Cabelli, V. J., Dufour, A.P., McCabe, L. J. and Levin, M. A. (1982) Swimming associated gastroenteritis and water quality, *American Journal of Epidemiology*, **115**, 606–16.

Callow, M. E. (1993) A review of fouling in freshwaters, *Biofouling*, **1**(4), 313–28.

Cartwright, R. Y. (1991) Recreational waters: a health risk for the nineties? Keynote paper to Symposium, *Health Related Water Microbiology*, International Association of Water Pollution Control and Research, Glasgow, 3–5 September 1991 (R. Morris, L. M. Alexander, P. Wyn-Jones and J. Sellwood, eds), 1–10.

Claisse, D. and Alzieu, Cl. (1993) Copper contamination as a result of antifouling paint regulations?, *Marine Pollution Bulletin*, **26**(7), 395–7.

Clark, R. B. (1989) *Marine Pollution*, Oxford: Clarendon Press.

Council of European Communities (1976) *Directive Concerning the Quality of Bathing Water* (76/160/EEC), Official Journal L31/1, 1976.

Council of European Communities (1991) *Directive Concerning Urban Wastewater Treatment* (91/271/EEC), Official Journal L135/40, 1991.

Dalley, R. (1989) Legislation affecting tributyltin antifoulings, *Bio fouling*, **1**(4), 363–6.

Dufour, A. P. (1984). *Health Effects Criteria for Fresh Recreational Waters*, EPA 600/1-84-004. US Environmental Protection Agency, Cincinnati, Ohio 452658.

Fleisher, J. M. (1990) Conducting recreational water quality surveys: some problems and suggested remedies, *Marine Pollution Bulletin*, **21**, (12), 562–7.

Fleisher, J. M. (1991) A re-analysis of data supporting the US Federal bacteriological water quality criteria governing marine recreational waters, *Research Journal, Water Pollution Control Federation*, **63**, 259–64.

GESAMP (1991) *The State of the Marine Environment*, Oxford: Blackwell Scientific Press.

Gough, M., Fothergill, J. and Hendine J. (1994) *Mar. Poll. Bull.*, **28**(10), 613–20.

Havelaar, A. H., Van Olphen, M. and Drost, Y. C. (1993) F-specific RNA bacteriophages are adequate model organisms for enteric viruses in fresh water, *Applied and Environmental Microbiology*, **59**, 2956–62.

HCEC (1990) House of Commons Session 1989–90, Environment Committee, Fourth Report, *Pollution of Beaches. Volume I*. Report with Appendix together with the Proceedings of the Committee relating to the Report, 11 July 1990, Her Majesty's Stationery Office, London.

HLSCEC (1994) House of Lords Session 1994–95, Select Committee on the European Communities, *Bathing Water. First Report*. Report with Appendices together with the Proceedings of the Committee relating to the Report, 6 December 1994, Her Majesty's Stationery Office, London.

Jones, F., Kay, D., Stanwell-Smith, R., and Wyer, M. (1991) Results of the first pilot-scale controlled cohort epidemiological investigation into the possible health effects of bathing in seawater at Langland Bay, Swansea, *Journal of the Institution of Water and Environmental Management*, **5**, 91–8.

Kay, D., Fleisher, J. M., Salmon, R. L., Wyer, M. D., Godfree, A. F., Zelenauch-Jacquotte, Z. and Shore, R. (1994) Predicting likelihood of gastroenteritis from sea bathing: results from randomised exposure, *Lancet*, **344**, 905–9.

114 Water Quality and Pollution

Lewey, S. A. (1992) *Physiological Studies on the Brown Alga* Sargassum muticum *(Yeudo) Feusholt*, PhD thesis, University of Portsmouth.
Lightfoot, N. E. (1989) *A Prospective Study of Swimming-related Illness at Six Freshwater Beaches in Southern Ontario*, PhD thesis, University of Toronto.
Mele, A. (1994) *Polluting for Pleasure*, London: W. W. Norton.
National Rivers Authority (1994) *Bathing Water Quality in England and Wales – 1993*, Water Quality Series No. 12, National Rivers Authority.
Philipp, R. (1991) Risk assessment and microbiological hazards associated with recreational water sports, *Reviews in Medical Microbiology*, **2**, 208–14.
Philipp, R., Waitkins, S., Caul, O., Roome, A., McMahon, S. and Enticott, R. (1989) Leptospiral and hepatitis A antibodies among windsurfers and waterskiers in Bristol City docks, *Public Health*, **103**, 123–9.
PHLS (1959) Sewage contamination of coastal bathing waters in England and Wales. A bacteriological and epidemiological study. By the Committee on Bathing Beach Contamination of the Public Health Laboratory Service, *Journal of Hygiene, Cambridge*, **57**, 435–72.
Pike, E. B. (1990) *Health Effects of Sea Bathing (ET 9511 SLG). Phase I-Pilot Studies at Langland Bay, 1989*, WRc Report DoE 2518-M, WRc plc, Medmenham, 109 pp. + 2 appendices.
Pike, E. B. (1991) *Health Effects of Sea Bathing (EM 9511). Phase II Studies at Ramsgate and Moreton, 1990*, WRc Report DoE 2738-M, WRc plc, Medmenham, 89 pp. + 3 appendices.
Pike, E. B. (1992) *Health Effects of Sea Bathing (EH 9021). Phase III Studies in 1991*, WRc Report DoE 3164 (P), WRc plc, Medmenham.
Pike, E. B. (1994). *Health Effects of Sea Bathing (WMI 9021). Phase III. Final report to the Department of the Environment*, WRc Report DoE 3412 (P), WRc plc, Medmenham.
Rees, G. (1993) Health implications of sewage in coastal waters – the British case, *Marine Pollution Bulletin*, **26**(1), 14–19.
Rees, G. (1994) Epidemiology of diseases associated with bathing waters, *Marine Environmental Management Review of Events in 1993 and Future Trends*, **1**, 41–4.
Seyfried, P. L., Tobin, R. S., Brown, N. E. and Ness, P. F. (1985a) A prospective study of swimming-related illness I. Swimming-associated health risk, *American Journal of Public Health*, **75**, 1068–71.
Seyfried, P. L., Tobin, R. S., Brown, N. E. and Ness, P. F. (1985b) A prospective study of swimming-related illness II. Morbidity and the microbiological quality of water, *American Journal of Public Health*, **75**, 1071–5.
Stephenson, M. D. and Leonard G. H. (1994) Evidence for the decline of silver and lead, and the increase of copper in the coastal marine waters of California, *Mar. Poll. Bull.*, **28**(3), 148–53
Working Party on Sewage Disposal (1970) *Taken for Granted. Report of the Working Party on Sewage Disposal*, Ministry of Housing and Local Government, Welsh Office, Her Majesty's Stationery Office, London.
World Health Organisation (1992) *Consultation on Health Risks from Bathing in Marine Waters* (WHO/UNEP Joint Project, MED POL Phase II), Athens, 15–18 May 1991. EUR/ICP/CEH 103, WHO, Regional Office for Europe, Copenhagen 1992.

Planning and the Provision of Marine Recreation Facilities

6

6.1 INTRODUCTION

Recreational use of marine waters requires the provision and subsequent management of specialist facilities. To undertake this development requires understanding the complex organizational structure operating in coastal areas and, particularly, understanding the town and country planning system. This section, therefore, deals with the legal context in which the development of recreation facilities takes place, concentrating particularly on the planning system in England and Wales. It is not concerned with the management of recreational facilities.

Recreational use of marine areas relies on access to the water from nearby land and, usually, facilities located on the land. Thus, the provision of marine recreation involves considering both land and water areas in an integrated way. Where water areas are suitable for recreation use and such use can be encouraged, appropriate land-based provision of access, parking and facilities should be provided. Conversely, where recreation use is not appropriate, for example, because of nature conservation constraints, lack of provision of land based facilities should prevent recreational use which would threaten wildlife.

6.2 THE LEGAL FRAMEWORK

Marine recreation facilities may be provided by public bodies, like local authorities, or private bodies, like sailing clubs, private owners or business organizations. They must have a sufficient interest in the land (which may include under the water) to be able to implement their proposals. There are a range of legal interests over land (Burn, 1988):

Coastal Recreation Management Edited by Tim Goodhead and David Johnson. Published in 1996 by E & FN Spon, London. ISBN 0 419 20360 5

- freehold interest or ownership in fee simple absolute;
- leasehold; and
- other interests.

The Law of Property Act 1925 provides the modern legislative framework concerning land. A freeholder or owner in fee simple absolute has greatest freedom of action over his/her land or property and can keep or sell it or give it away during life or after death. He/she is entitled to rent or profit generated by that land.

A leasehold interest is a lesser interest in land or property, created by an agreement or lease between a freeholder or lessor and a lessee. As stated in the lease, it allows the lessee the freedom of the land or property for a period of time in return for payment. At the end of the stated time, the property reverts to the freeholder or lessor. On any land or property there can be a series of leases but each will be subordinate to a superior lease and provide for the enjoyment of fewer freedoms.

Other legal interests include covenants and easements, both of which allow or restrict stated activities, and profits *à prendre* which allow certain natural products to be taken from land. Licences are personal permissions to access, use or take things from land or property.

In the context of providing marine recreation facilities, the first two are most important. For example, to provide slipways or launch parks or to develop a marina, the provider or developer must either own the land or have a leasehold interest where the proposed work will not conflict with any restrictive covenants in the lease. Additionally, both developing and managing the recreation facility is likely to require the negotiating and effecting of a range of other legal interests in the land or property.

Current ownership patterns on the coast are complex with different systems affecting the three elements of the coastal zone: the land; the inter-tidal area; and the water. This is a critical consideration in the development of certain recreation facilities, like marinas, which may span all three.

On the land there is a myriad of public and private ownerships. Major public sector coastal land owners include port and harbour authorities, the Ministry of Defence and local authorities. Private-sector owners include the National Trust, conservation bodies like the Royal Society for the Protection of Birds, major estates and tourist and recreation businesses. There are many small-scale private landowners and occupiers of homes and business accommodation on the coast.

The intertidal zone or foreshore and the seabed, including the tidal parts of river estuaries[1] (Pickering, 1993), generally, is considered to be owned by the Crown. It is managed by the Crown Estate Commissioners (CEC) who now seldom dispose of such land. Interests must be acquired by lease or by licence.

Water areas are subject to various public rights: for example, fishery and navigation. The latter gives rights to wander and to anchor in tidal areas.

While it is possible, though complicated, to acquire the legal interests to develop marine recreation facilities, neither the freehold ownership nor a leasehold interest is sufficient to guarantee that the required facility may be provided. Both interests allow only for the continuing existing use of that land or property, assuming that use is legal. This is because of the responsibilities given to public bodies to protect the public or community interest where the intentions of individuals would threaten it. Town and country planning is probably the best known of these activities, but others operating on the coast concern coastal defence, water quality, wildlife conservation, public access, marine minerals and fish stocks. Each activity has its own legislative and organizational framework and the areas of jurisdiction vary, making the task of undertaking any development in the coastal zone complex. For example, the local authority has duties in relation to town and country planning and to coast protection but its jurisdiction extends only to low water mark (unless in a harbour or estuary). The jurisdiction of the National Rivers Authority (NRA) (to be integrated into the proposed Environment Agency) for water quality extends to a three mile limit. The responsibilities of CEC for exploitation of the seabed begin only at low water mark but extend over the territorial sea to 12 miles. The Ministry of Agriculture, Fisheries and Food (MAFF) has powers that extend over the Exclusive Economic Zone, i.e. to 200 miles. This complex organizational structure is summarized in Figure 6.1 (Gubbay, 1992). It represents the *ad hoc* evolution of an institutional system with no integrated assessment of requirements or integrated approach to the development and management of the coast, whether for recreation or other uses.

6.3 TOWN AND COUNTRY PLANNING

The point was made earlier that marine recreation is dependent on land-based access and facilities. This makes town and country planning a very important regulatory mechanism affecting the provision of new marine recreational facilities. This represents the main governmental interference in the use and development of land and property in Britain. The Government has stated (SoS, *et al.*, 1990) that the aim of the town and country planning system is to 'secure the most efficient and effective use of land in the public interest'. It is intended that development will be sustainable and that the cumulation of decisions will retain the best of the country's environment for future generations (DOE/WO, 1992a). New development must fit harmoniously with its surroundings and spoilt environments must be improved.

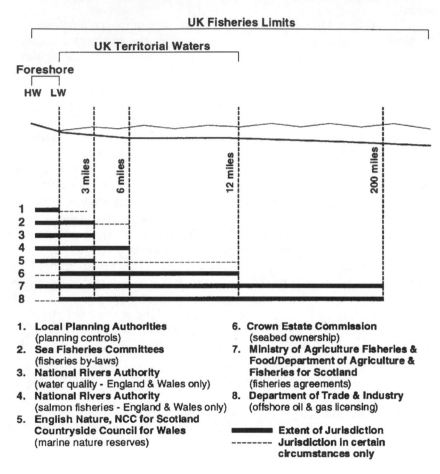

1. **Local Planning Authorities**
    (planning controls)
2. **Sea Fisheries Committees**
    (fisheries by-laws)
3. **National Rivers Authority**
    (water quality - England & Wales only)
4. **National Rivers Authority**
    (salmon fisheries - England & Wales only)
5. **English Nature, NCC for Scotland**
    Countryside Council for Wales
    (marine nature reserves)

6. **Crown Estate Commission**
    (seabed ownership)
7. **Ministry of Agriculture Fisheries &**
    Food/Department of Agriculture &
    Fisheries for Scotland
    (fisheries agreements)
8. **Department of Trade & Industry**
    (offshore oil & gas licensing)

———— **Extent of Jurisdiction**
-------- **Jurisdiction in certain**
    circumstances only

Figure 6.1 The extent of jurisdiction of some coastal organizations

To achieve its aim, the planning system must ensure that adequate new development for the community may be built and that infrastructure and services, like roads and sewers, are provided while also ensuring that land of important landscape, wildlife, historic or architectural quality is not spoilt. It has, therefore, both a positive role in steering new development to appropriate locations and a regulatory role in controlling inappropriate development.

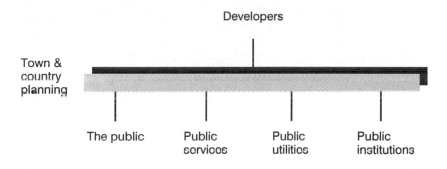

Figure 6.2 Planning at the interface between different interest groups

Deciding where new development should be located or the extent of areas to be protected from development, clearly, has implications for the land owners, occupiers, residents, businesses and other users of an area as well as public bodies which provide goods and services to an area. Any planning decision, whether on the allocation in a plan of a new sports facility or in the determination of a planning application for a new sailing school, will create a range of benefits to certain groups while resulting in costs, or negative benefits or externalities, to other groups. Town and country planning, therefore, is a highly political activity. It operates at the interface between the developer and the wide range of other bodies/groups which contribute to 'the public interest', as shown in Figure 6.2, and has been described as an activity to resolve conflicting interests in the development and use of land/water and property.

6.3.1 THE TOWN AND COUNTRY PLANNING SYSTEM

The principal act establishing the legislative framework for the planning system in England and Wales is the Town and Country Planning Act 1990 (TCP Act 1990), substantially amended by the Planning and Compensation Act 1991. This legislation covers the three main elements of the planning system in England and Wales:

1. forward planning;
2. development control; and
3. compulsory purchase.

The most widely known element of the planning system is development control. This is the process by which permission must be sought for, and be made on, development proposals. It represents the nationalization of private rights to develop and use land and property, vesting that right in the community in the role of the local planning authority (LPA).

Each planning application is determined on its merits. To determine each planning application in isolation would be *ad hoc* and could result in an irrational pattern of development. It is necessary for there to exist an overall strategy or plan establishing the future 'shape' of development in an area. The forward planning element, therefore, involves the preparation of policy and plans which provide the basis for development control decision-making. To enable local authorities to acquire land for development required by the community but stymied by private ownership, the third element of the planning system is compulsory purchase. This allows local authorities to purchase land compulsorily. While it is currently favoured neither by central or local government bodies, it remains a power available to, and used by, LPAs.

6.3.2 THE OPERATION OF THE PLANNING SYSTEM

The town and country planning system in England and Wales is determined by central government and established through national legislation though, increasingly, it is influenced by decisions of the European Community (EC). While central government retains controlling and advisory interests in the operation and administration of planning, day to day work is undertaken by LPAs.

LPAs in metropolitan areas are metropolitan districts and London boroughs and in non-metropolitan areas are counties and districts. Additionally, national parks have their own planning authorities and most urban development corporations have substantial planning powers. The area over which each LPA operates is restricted to its administrative area as defined by legislation. Most local authority boundaries extend seaward only to low water mark, the exceptions being where there is an estuary or harbour and the boundary is taken across the entrance. Clearly, this creates problems to LPAs seeking to establish coastal recreational policies.

A second problem is caused by the location of certain boundaries. Rivers traditionally differentiate ownerships or administrations. In estuaries and harbours, the split of planning responsibility between authorities may be divisive where the objectives of the authorities differ: one may promote maximum commercial or recreational use of the estuary; the other, conservation interests. Clearly, neighbouring authorities should liaise, consult and produce joint policies for the whole estuary. While frequently this happens, administrative boundaries hamper integrated policy and decision-making in estuary and harbour areas.

6.3.3 THE ROLE OF CENTRAL GOVERNMENT

The Secretary of State for the Environment in England and the Secretary of State for Wales in Wales (described as 'the Secretary of State' below) hold overall responsibility for the administration of town and country planning in England and Wales respectively (Heap, 1991). Their role includes ensuring that the policy and execution of planning is consistent and continuous throughout England and Wales. To this end, the legislative framework for planning created by Acts of Parliament is supported by regulations and advice. Advice is published mainly in circulars and the newer policy guidance. Policy guidance comes in several forms: planning (PPG); minerals; and regional or strategic planning guidance.

The Secretary of State retains a wide range of powers over planning matters (GB, 1990). He can create statutory instruments (see below) which set the effective level of planning control, 'call-in' development plans for his approval, give directions requiring planning applications to be determined by him in the first instance and overrule the decision by a LPA on a planning application if an appeal is made to him by an applicant. He has powers to direct that LPAs act in particular ways and retains a range of 'default' powers where LPAs fail to fulfil duties and responsibilities. He is supported by senior civil servants and the Planning Inspectorate. Inspectors have powers to make decisions on his behalf (Telling and Duxbury, 1993).

6.4 PLANNING AT THE LOCAL LEVEL

6.4.1 FORWARD PLANNING

Forward planning relates to the preparation of policies and proposals for the future use and development of land and property in their area by LPAs. Particularly important are the statutorily required (GB, 1990) development plans. These are supported by non-statutory plans and policy, i.e. supplementary planning guidance. This can provide detailed design or site specific information or be used where policy matters extend beyond normal planning matters, for example, where a partnership or management agreement between a developer and an authority is sought, or for cross boundary policy. Recreation matters are frequently covered by such non-statutory mechanisms because authorities' roles extend beyond the control of recreation development to its provision and management. It is also appropriate for marine recreation especially where it needs to be managed in an area with a sensitive environment (Chapter 13). Such non-statutory plans 'should complement and be consistent with development plans' (DOE/WO, 1992b).

The term 'development plan' has different connotations in different types of administrative area. In non-metropolitan areas, the development plan comprises a structure plan and a local plan. Each county planning authority has to prepare, and normally adopts, a structure plan for its administrative area (GB, 1990) setting out the long-term, strategic policy for the use and development of land in its area. The strategy must have regard to national and regional planning guidance and will have a time horizon of at least 15 years. Structure plans have been required since 1968 and all counties have them and are rolling them forward, altering or amending them as necessary. As local plans must conform to structure plans, these plans secure consistency in local plans prepared for the area.

A local plan must be prepared by each district planning authority and national park planning authority for the whole of its administrative area (GB, 1990). An appropriate time horizon for such plans is 10 years. Local plans must conform to the general policies of structure plans and interpret them for the local area, showing detailed proposals for the use and development of land and setting out policies for the control of development. In any matter of conflict between structure and local plans, the local plan prevails (GB, 1990).

Local plans are not new. However, until 1991, their preparation was discretionary so some districts have full coverage, others partial and some no coverage at all. Since 1991, district wide local plans have been statutorily required and will be completed over the next few years.

The development plan for a metropolitan area is a unitary development plan (UDP), normally adopted by the authority and covering the whole of its administrative area (GB, 1990). It has two parts produced in the same volume. Part I, which must have regard to national and regional guidance, is general and strategic and relates to the long term. Part II is detailed and specific with a shorter time horizon.

Development plans must be limited to land-use planning matters, i.e. to things that can be controlled by the planning system (see sections

6.5.1 and 6.5.2 below on development control and the definition of development) though policies can be justified on social or economic grounds. The implication of this is that some matters on which LPAs might wish to express policy, for example, the management and use of land to influence recreation activity, must be contained in non-statutory plans unless they are clearly land-use planning matters.

All development plans comprise a written statement, illustrative material (diagrammatic for structure plans and UDP Part Is and on an Ordnance Survey base for local plans and UDP Part IIs) and the notice of adoption by the LPA (or, exceptionally the notice of approval by the Secretary of State). The written statement includes the policies and proposals of the authority, supported by an explanatory memorandum or reasoned justification. Topics covered in development plans include: population and housing; the local economy; transport and traffic management; the conservation and enhancement of the natural and man made environment; minerals; waste; land reclamation; tourism, leisure and recreation; and energy generation. Policies must be compatible with the Government's overall objective of achieving sustainable development (DOE, 1992a).

6.4.2 THE SIGNIFICANCE OF DEVELOPMENT PLANS IN RECREATION PROVISION

Development plans are of great significance to owners, occupiers and prospective developers of land and property because of their legal role in development control (Taussik, 1992a). Section S54A of the TCP Act 1990 states:

> Where, in making any determination under the planning Acts, regard is to be made to the development plan, the determination shall be made in accordance with the plan unless material considerations indicate otherwise.

Decisions about coastal recreation, therefore, will be based on policies contained in plans, particularly local plans and UDP Part IIs. Anyone seeking to undertake such development, therefore, should consult the development plan before committing resources to pursuing proposals. The development plan will demonstrate the general attitude of the planning authority to different types of recreation and indicate the areas to be protected from development. Local plans and UDP Part IIs are most useful because they are site specific. However, until all such plans exist, the structure plan may be all that is available. While LPAs may be generally supportive of recreation provision, policy statements in plans may be such that it is inappropriate to pursue particular development proposals in particular locations.

Development plans are intended to reflect the way the community of an area wishes to see that area developed. The contents of plans have substantial impact on the use and, therefore, the value of land and property in an area. For these reasons, it is important that there is public debate about their contents. The regulations require LPAs to undertake consultations before they embark on the process of adopting a plan. Statutory consultees include the NRA, the Countryside Commission and the Nature Conservancy Council for England (NCCE) or Countryside Council for Wales (CCW) as well as the Secretaries of State for the Environment and Transport or for Wales and planning authorities in or adjacent to the plan area. Additionally, authorities are advised to consult bodies including the Sports Council and the Regional Council for Sport and Recreation (DOE, 1992a). All representations must be considered by authorities in preparing their plans. This provides an opportunity for a range of public interests to be involved in policy formulation.

In addition, there are opportunities for public involvement (Taussik, 1993a) and research has demonstrated that such involvement can be effective in achieving amendments to the plan (Adams and May, 1990). Most LPAs invite informal comments when a draft plan is prepared. Before the plan can be adopted there are formal opportunities to make representations. LPAs are required to consider any representations that are made to them and may amend the plan in response to them but, if they do not, they must explain why.

Anyone owning or wanting to develop land for recreational facilities or managing recreation should seek to influence development plans in order to have the most favourable planning policy context in which to operate. While the most logical plan to be involved with is the local plan or UDP Part II, the context for these will be set by structure plans and UDP Part Is, suggesting that involvement in them may also be necessary. The Sports Council devotes considerable resources to ensuring the best possible policy context for sport and recreation.

6.5 THE CASCADE OF POLICY

The combination of Government and LPA policy creates a cascade of planning policy, as much for the provision of recreation as for other uses of land and property. Figure 6.3 shows the policies at higher levels being incorporated in the lower levels of plan making but, also, policy feeding upwards from the local level.

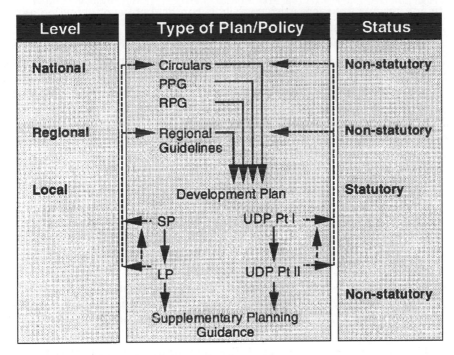

Figure 6.3 The hierarchy of plan and policy making

The Government's general attitude to development is set out in PPG1 *General Policy and Principles*. There is a general presumption in favour of development which conforms to the development plan. This applies as much to recreational development as to other development although there are certain areas liable to coastal erosion or landslide where there may be local presumptions against development.

Recreation merits attention in several circulars and PPGs, but the main sources of guidance relevant to marine recreation are PPG17 *Sport and Recreation* (DOE/WO, 1991a) and PPG20 *Coastal Planning* (DOE/WO, 1992b). Guidance is limited by the extent of the administrative control of the planning system.

PPG17 *Sport and Recreation* states that adequate land and water resources must be allocated for organized sport and for informal recreation and makes specific reference to the provision in local plans of policies for boating facilities. It acknowledges that there is a widespread shortage of mooring facilities for boats, both on inland waters and on the coast, and suggests that the re-use of redundant docks may provide extensive new moorings without undue detriment to the environment. National parks and heritage coasts provide scope for recreation use but, in any case where there is irreconcilable conflict between recreation and conservation, conservation must prevail.

PPG20 *Coastal Planning* states that the coast, particularly the undeveloped coast, is seldom the most appropriate location for development and development which does not require such a location is to be discouraged. Recreation is recognized as requiring a coastal location. The aim should be to balance and reconcile recreation with landscape and wildlife conservation interests and contain the impact of recreation through appropriate management measures. Policies for the provision of facilities for marine recreation should be based on local environmental capacity. This guidance also draws attention to the recreational re-use of redundant docks.

The undeveloped coast, therefore, is likely to be severely constrained for marine recreation facilities of any scale, not only because of this advice but also because much of the undeveloped coast is protected for its wildlife and landscape quality (Taussik, 1993b). Neither are areas at risk from flooding, erosion or land slip suitable for development though developers may be able to demonstrate that they can overcome these problems. The developed coast, on the other hand, offers opportunities for developments requiring such locations although much work may be needed to improve the area.

Coastal matters have received little attention in regional or strategic planning guidance though this may change following the publication of the London and South East Regional Planning Conference's 'Coastal Planning Guidelines for the South East' (SERPLAN, 1993). This reiterates that protection should be given to the undeveloped coast and suggests that development needing a coastal location should normally be located in the developed coast (more detail is given in Chapter 12).

Recreation is the most frequently occurring type of policy related to the coast to be found in development plans (Taussik, 1995). However, a considerable amount of the policy relates to land-based, rather than marine, recreation, reflecting the scope of planning and its administrative area of operation. Government policy constraining development in the undeveloped coast is restated at the local level, complemented by policies positively supporting the retention of existing and the provision of new facilities, like marinas, in coastal settlements on the developed coast. It is clear that some authorities perceive marina development as a focal point in the regeneration of their dock and harbour areas. However, LPA attitudes reflect local circumstances. Several authorities on the south coast which experience congestion in some areas (Bell, 1992) are unwilling to consider favourably development proposals which will result in unacceptable congestion of the water. In this, structure plan policies are reflected by the contents of local plans.

Some local plans include policies for particular types of water recreation, for example, to concentrate sailboarding in particular locations or to minimize the effects of noisy watersports. However, the limitation of planning to deal with such issues is highlighted by reference in some plans to the need for relevant bye-laws.

6.5.1 DEVELOPMENT CONTROL

Section 57 of the TCP Act 1990 states that 'planning permission is required for the carrying out of any development of land'. This is the legal requirement for the control of development. Most development control is undertaken by district planning authorities though national park planning authorities undertake their own development control, as do most urban development corporations.

The control of development is a necessary element of the planning system. Without it, the preparation of development plans would be meaningless. The purpose of development control is to allow appropriate development to be undertaken while stopping inappropriate development. Hence the presumption, in PPG1, in favour of development which conforms to the development plan.

6.5.2 THE MEANING OF 'DEVELOPMENT'

Only 'development' requires planning permission, making its definition very significant. Section 55 of TCP Act 1990 states that development is:

> the carrying out of building, engineering, mining or other operations in, on, over or under land, or the making of any material change in the use of buildings or other land.

This is a sweeping definition covering anything that could materially affect the character or appearance of land or buildings. It leaves little besides the planting and removal of vegetation to the discretion of owners and occupiers of land and property. It includes any development of land or buildings that results in physical change of the property: building operations include building new property and demolishing, extending, altering or rebuilding existing property; engineering operations include works that affect the physical nature of an area like constructing or removing embankments, providing moorings on the seabed or dredging channels. Development also includes changing the use of land or building although that may not result in any change to its appearance. The provision of facilities for marine recreation, therefore, will almost undoubtedly constitute development.

If every small change of use or building operation was subject to control, the planning system would be too overburdened to operate. Therefore, both the legislation itself and supplementary legislation clarify the position and remove certain activities from the meaning of the term 'development' or provide a general grant of planning permission for it. For example, Section 55 (2)(a–g)) of TCP Act 1990 states that works internal to a building and changing the use of buildings or land to another use that is in the same class of use are not development. Therefore, they are not subject to planning control. The second of these allows considerable flexibility in the use of land and property. The classes of use are set out in the Use Classes Order (GB, 1987), a statutory instrument prepared by the Secretary of State. Each class has been designed to contain only uses which generate similar effects on the environment in terms of location, operation, pollution, traffic generation, parking and so on, so changes of use within that class will generate few problems. Changes between classes or to/from a use not in a class are subject to planning control.

The classes of use include: shops; food and drink; business; and hotels and hostels. Of most significance to recreational managers is Class D2, Assembly and Leisure, which, as well as a range of leisure uses like cinema and concert hall, swimming bath, skating rink and gymnasium includes areas for indoor or outdoor sport or recreation, as long as they do not involve motor vehicles or firearms. Subject to the limitations of building design, changes of use which are within this class can be made without any interference from the planning system.

6.5.3 PLANNING PERMISSION

A general grant of planning permission has been provided by the Secretary of State through the General Permitted Development Order (GPDO) (GB, 1995a). Article 3 grants planning permission for all the types of development listed as 'Permitted Development' in Schedule 2 of the Order though this is reduced in national parks, areas of outstanding natural beauty and conservation areas.

While there are classes of development relevant to recreation (Part 4, temporary buildings and uses; Part 5, caravan sites; Part 27, use by recreational organizations), the most substantial developments, including those on the coast, which benefit from these permitted development rights are major developments subject to Acts or Orders of Parliament or Orders under section 14 or 16 of the Harbours Act 1964. Such developments are likely to be substantial in scale and effect and can include developments which extend over and beyond the foreshore as, for example, the Cardiff Bay barrage scheme with its enormous implications for water-based recreation in the area.

Although the display of advertisements is not itself development, the erection of a structure or the use of a building to display advertisements is development. Consent must be obtained for the display of advertisements but those which conform to the Control of Advertisements Regulations are deemed to have planning consent (GB, 1990). This is relevant to recreation operators and managers with the need for signage for information and/or safety purposes.

Where development of operations or change of use which is not permitted development is proposed, planning permission must be sought by submitting a planning application to the LPA for their determination. Applications for operations may seek outline, rather than full, planning permission to establish the principle of a proposed development.

A planning application will include forms and plans, certificates and a fee. It may also include a statement of environmental assessment (EA). The procedures for dealing with applications are set out in the General Development Procedure Order (GDPO) (GB, 1995b). As decisions must reflect the public interest, public bodies are consulted and publicity to the general public is undertaken. Among the statutory consultees, the water authority and NCCE or CCW are particularly relevant to proposals for the development of marine recreation facilities. LPAs may undertake non-statutory consultations with, for example, the Countryside Commission in England (or CCW), the Sports Council, Regional Tourist Boards, Harbour Authorities and the NRA.

The basis of determining planning applications is that:

'applications for development should be allowed . . . unless the proposed development would cause demonstrable harm to interests of acknowledged importance. (DOE/WO, 1992a)

In determining any planning application:

the authority shall have regard to the provisions of the development plan, so far as material to the application and to any other material considerations. (GB, 1990)

The role of the development plan, therefore, is primary though it can be over-ruled by recent Government policy, by site specific information or by considerations identified through formal and informal consultations and representations.

Considerations pertinent to the determination of planning applications concerned with marine recreation depend on the nature, scale and location of the proposal. They include traffic generation and highway safety, parking provision, the environmental effect of new building, the effect of the proposed use on existing uses, the implications of recreational use on wildlife and safety and pollution effects. Special designations to protect landscape, wildlife or historical quality are significant and guidance is clear about the determination of applications in special protection areas and special areas of conservation (DOE, 1994).

Proposals for development can be permitted or refused by the LPA. Where planning permission is refused, the LPA must state its reasons. Where the negative effects of development proposals could be reduced by putting conditions on the development or its subsequent use, conditional permission can be granted though conditions cannot duplicate or conflict with the effect of other controls. They could be used, for example, to mitigate the threat of flooding (DOE *et al.*, 1992).

Proposals granted full planning permission or permission for reserved matters can be implemented immediately. Outline planning permission does not convey a right to implement the proposals as permission for the details, known as 'reserved matters', must be obtained first. Full planning permission lasts five years before lapsing. Applications for reserved matters must be made within three years of the grant of outline planning permission. Permission for reserved matters lasts two years, or five years from the grant of outline permission, whichever is later.

Where applicants are not satisfied by a refusal of, or conditions attached to, a planning permission, they can appeal to the Secretary of State. There is no appeal mechanism for anyone other than an applicant. Although LPAs make most decisions on planning applications, the Secretary of State can direct that planning applications are referred ('called in') to him for his determination in the first instance (not to be confused with appeals, where the Secretary of State or his inspector makes a second decision). These will be applications which are particularly contentious or concern matters of national importance, including threats to sites of international wildlife value (DOE, 1994).

Obtaining planning permission is an uncertain, delaying and expensive activity although full local plan coverage should reduce some of these problems. Potential developers or their agents should seek the LPA's advice before embarking on expensive work (Taussik, 1992b). Pre-application discussion can identify issues and modifications can be made to the proposal to make it more acceptable to the authority. However, the advice will be provided by officers of the authority and that is all that will be offered – advice. Potential developers should not rely on this advice. Planning committees do not always follow officers' recommendations when planning applications are determined.

Pre-application discussion can establish the need for environmental assessment (EA). The Town and Country Planning (Assessment of Environmental Effects) Regulations 1988 implement the requirements of EC Directive No. 85/337 on the assessment of the environmental effects of proposed development. They require that planning applications for certain developments are not determined until the LPA has considered an EA.

Developments to which this relates are set out in Schedules 1 and 2 of the Regulations. Several classes of Schedule 2 are relevant: the construction of a harbour or dam, a yacht marina or a holiday village. Such developments need EA when they are likely to have significant effects on the environment, for example, where a development location is particularly sensitive or vulnerable or where there are 'unusually complex and potentially adverse environmental effects'. Bearing in mind the protection given to substantial areas of the coast, the requirement for EA in areas of sensitivity and/or vulnerability is important.

Pre-application discussion can cover planning gain. This can be defined as 'a public benefit which is extrinsic to the particular development but which is provided by the developer at his own expense and tied to a grant of planning permission' (Alder, 1990) Planning gain is secured through planning obligations under Section 106 of TCP Act 1990. This allows LPAs and developers to make agreements about action that developers can take to secure the objectives of LPAs which cannot be met through conditions on planning permissions. Such planning agreements have been widely used to deal with the provision of infrastructure associated with new development and to secure such items as public open space and community facilities. Circular 16/91 'Planning obligations' Annex B suggests they have a role in the creation of nature reserves or other nature conservation benefits (Curry, 1993). It is also a method by which public access to the coast (DOE/WO, 1992b) or protection from flooding (DOE *et al.*, 1992) can be secured.

Where development is undertaken without planning permission or there is no or limited compliance with conditions attached to permissions, LPAs may take enforcement action against the breach of planning control. Enforcement mechanisms include planning contravention notices, breach of condition notices, injunctions to restrain the breach and enforcement and stop notices (Telling and Duxbury, 1993).

6.6 LIMITATIONS OF THE PLANNING SYSTEM

The planning system is a major influence on the way that land and property on the coast, as inland, may be used and developed. Not only does it establish plans and policy and ensure that they are implemented through development control, but it includes measures to enforce or secure the implementation of planning proposals. In spite of its complexity, planning has substantial limitations in contributing to coastal management and to coastal recreation in particular.

Planning can deal only with 'land use/planning matters'. Essentially this means with development, as defined by the planning acts. Anything which is **not** development cannot be controlled. Informal recreational use of the coast or of the water itself cannot be controlled through the planning system. Conflicts which arise between different recreation use groups must be managed by mechanisms other than planning.

The problem of local authority boundaries has been mentioned. Varying policies over water areas by adjacent authorities generate confusion for potential developers of marine recreation facilities as well as providing a source of conflict between the authorities. Recognition of the institutional complexity and increasing conflict in the exploitation of the coast has resulted in moves to engender more integrated approaches to coastal management. This may involve the establishment of fora or groups to disseminate information and broaden knowledge so that decision-making can be undertaken on a wider contextual understanding or it may be extended to the preparation of plans concerned with management in the coastal zone. Such plans include: coastal zone management plans and coastal strategies; shoreline strategies and management plans; estuary and harbour management plans; catchment management plans; and plans like heritage coast management plans or coastal recreation strategies. Each has a particular function but there is potential for considerable overlap between them. This must be minimized and the integration maximized, perhaps by the coastal zone management plan providing a strategic and integrative role. Unlike development plans (for which there is no marine equivalent), there is no statutory requirement for them and they lack the status of development plans. As a considerable amount of management of land and water areas may be achieved through the control of development on land, it is very important that appropriate policies from these management plans are incorporated as land use/planning policies in development plans. Development plans, in turn, provide input to these non-statutory plans. A number of these initiatives are considered in more detail in Chapters 12 and 13.

There are different control mechanisms for sea and land areas. Unlike on land, where the planning system integrates the considerations of a wide range of public interests, control of the use of sea areas is sectoral. Therefore, in addition to obtaining planning permission, the developer of marine recreation facilities must obtain several other permissions as well as negotiating a lease or licence from the Crown Estate or other owner.

The permissions required vary with the nature and location of the development and the following paragraphs are not intended to be comprehensive. Construction projects outside harbours normally require approval through an Order under the Transport and Works Act 1992 but that may come from the Secretary of State for Transport for transport projects or from the Secretary of State for the Environment or for Wales for, for example, recreation projects. Even if no such Order is required, consent from the Department of Transport (DOT) (GB, 1949) would be needed if there was a question of obstruction to, or reduction in, safety for navigation and a licence from MAFF would be required for the deposition of materials (including for construction) on the seabed (GB, 1985).

Where the construction project is within a harbour, regulation is by the DOT for navigation purposes and MAFF/Welsh Office for fisheries harbours (GB, 1964). Harbour Empowerment Orders and Harbour Revision Orders may be required for the construction for recreation of new harbours and for works within existing harbours, respectively. A Harbour Revision Order may also be required where dredging is needed that is not covered by existing harbour authority powers. Further permissions from MAFF and, perhaps, DOT may be required for dumping the dredged material. Consent from DOT and a licence from MAFF could also be required (see above).

Projects involving the provision of pontoons, moorings or other moored structures like diving platforms are likely to be subject to multiple consents. Where they are in estuaries, they may be subject to planning control, but they are also likely to require navigational consent from DOT, an environmental licence from MAFF and consent from the Harbour Authority if they are within a harbour.

It is clear that the development of facilities to provide for marine recreation raises substantial regulatory requirements for the developer. While those on land, concentrated in the planning system, may seem complex, such a developer must also understand the regulatory systems controlling use of water areas and the seabed. Here, the sectoral system of consents and licences means that permission must be obtained from different organizations. This is extremely complex and expert advice needs to be sought to ensure that permissions are sought where they are required but that time is not wasted and uncertainty created where they are not needed.

6.7 CONCLUSION

Providers and managers of coastal recreation facilities face a range of problems in undertaking development which straddles the land–sea divide which are above and beyond those experienced by their land-based colleagues. The legal and institutional framework is considerably more complex and, often, not logical from a marine perspective. The implications of this are that gaining all the permissions will be time-consuming and, therefore, expensive. The likely need to undertake an EA will increase that cost further. The level of uncertainty, already likely to be great in the context of the substantial environmental constraints on the coast, generated by the number of interested parties is likely to be very high. For any such developer, there is considerable advantage in identifying and pursuing opportunities for water-based recreational facilities that pursue proposals or conform to policies in the development plan.

Similar problems are faced by any developer operating in the coastal zone and across its three constituent elements. It has been suggested (H. of C., 1992) that the creation of a single coastal authority would allow existing duties, responsibilities and powers to be integrated. While this would provide a much clearer institutional framework for those operating in the coastal zone, it has been criticized for adding to the complexity of institutions and has not been favoured by the Government (DOE, 1992b).

An alternative suggestion has been for the extension, seawards, of land-based powers. In the context of regulating change which constitutes development, the planning system is well established and integrates a wide range of opinion (see Figure 6.1) both in preparing development plans and in making planning decisions. The latter has always required wide consideration of the externalities generated by development proposals and requirements for EA mean that potentially damaging proposals in sensitive areas are even more formally investigated.

The activities of forward planning and development control, unlike those concerned with the use of marine resources, are conducted on an open basis, with attention to public and third-party interests respectively. This would seem to offer advantages for coastal developers as a range of permissions which must be separately sought could be subsumed in the grant of the planning permission. For example, inland resources of the highest quality agricultural land are identified by MAFF and protected through development plan policies and development control decisions. Planning applications which are not in accordance with the development plan (departure applications) and which affect stated amounts of agricultural land have to be referred to MAFF. Negative opinion from MAFF is likely to be instrumental in the determination of applications. Similar processes exist for other public interests and could be equally effective for the marine environment.

While such an extension of planning control could improve the current regulatory framework in the coastal zone, it would not, as it does not on land, remove the need to seek other consents, for example, for the storage of hazardous materials or for potentially polluting activity or for building consent. Also, as on land, it would relate only to 'development' and would be of no use where activity involved no development. As on land, planning would remain limited in its ability to control informal use of water areas, especially if no land-based facilities are required.

In spite of the advantages that this could offer, the Government does not propose to extend the planning system seaward (DOE/WO, 1993). While it considers that the land use planning system has a number of strengths, it states that they 'may be more apparent than real' when compared with sectoral development controls. Other countries have perceived the benefit of extending planning in this way. For example, the Swedish Planning and Building Act of 1987 requires municipalities to plan the use of land **and water** areas. Water areas extend seawards for 12 nautical miles. Comprehensive plans (*översiktsplan*) must be prepared by each municipality and will include matters such as marine recreation, protection of fishery including of breeding grounds, navigation routes and wildlife protection areas. This allows topics like marine recreation to be considered in a more systematic way than is currently possible in England and Wales.

NOTE
[1] Ownership of the bed of the tidal parts of rivers differs from the ownership of the bed of the non-tidal parts of rivers where, normally, the riparian owners on either bank own the bed to the mid point.

ABBREVIATIONS

CEC – Crown Estate Commissioners
CCW – Countryside Council for Wales
DOE – Department of the Environment
DOE/WO – Department of the Environment and Welsh Office
EA – Environmental Assessment
GB – Great Britain
GDPO – General Development Procedure Order
GPDO – General Permitted Development Order
H. of C. – House of Commons Environment Select Committee
LPA – Local Planning Authority
MAFF – Ministry of Agriculture, Fisheries and Food
NCCE – Nature Conservancy Council for England (English Nature)
NRA – National Rivers Authority
SERPLAN – The London and South East Regional Planning Conference
SofS – Secretary of State for the Environment
TCP Act – Town and Country Planning Act
UDP – Unitary development plan

REFERENCES

Adams, D. and May, H. (1990) Land ownership and land use planning, *Planner*, **76**(38), 11–14.
Alder, John (1990) Planning agreements and planning powers, *Journal of Planning Law*, December, 880–9.
Bell, Peter (1992) Case Study 4: *The Solent in Coastal Planning and Management*. Proceedings of a Conference at The Castle, Winchester on 27 November 1992. Hampshire County Council, Winchester.
Burn, E.H. (1988) *Cheshire and Burn's Modern Law of Real Property*, 14th edn, Butterworths, London.
Curry, N. (1993) Negotiating gains for nature conservation in planning practice, *Planning Practice and Research*, **8**(2), 10–15.
Department of the Environment (1992a) *Development Plans and Regional Planning Guidance*, PPG12, HMSO, London.
Department of the Environment (1992b) *Coastal Zone Protection and Planning. The Government's response to the second report from the House of Commons' Select Committee on the Environment*, HMSO, London.
Department of the Environment (1994) *Nature Conservation*, PPG9, HMSO, London.
Department of the Environment, Ministry of Agriculture, Fisheries and Food and Welsh Office (1992) *Development and Flood Risk*, Circular 30/92 (Circular FD1/92 of MAFF and 68/92 of WO), HMSO, London.
Department of the Environment and Welsh Office (1991a) *Sport and Recreation*, PPG17, HMSO, London.
Department of the Environment and Welsh Office (1991b) Circular 16/91, *Planning Obligations*, HMSO, London.
Department of the Environment and Welsh Office (1992a) *General Policy and Principles*, PPG1, HMSO, London.

Department of the Environment and Welsh Office (1992b) *Coastal Planning*, PPG20, HMSO, London.
Department of the Environment and Welsh Office (1993) *Development below Low Water Mark. A Review of Regulation in England and Wales*, Department of the Environment, London.
Great Britain (1925) *Law of Property Act*, HMSO, London.
Great Britain (1949) *Coast Protection Act*, HMSO, London.
Great Britain (1964) *Harbours Act*, HMSO, London.
Great Britain (1985) *Food and Environment Protection Act*, HMSO, London.
Great Britain (1987) *The Town and Country Planning (Use Classes) Order*, Statutory Instrument 1987 No. 764, HMSO, London.
Great Britain (1988) *Town and Country Planning (Assessment of Environmental Effects) Regulations*, Statutory Instrument 1988 No. 1199, HMSO, London.
Great Britain (1990) *Town and Country Planning Act*, HMSO, London.
Great Britain (1991) *Planning and Compensation Act.* HMSO, London.
Great Britain (1992) *Transport and Works Act*, HMSO, London.
Great Britain (1995a) *Town and Country Planning (General Permitted Development) Order 1995*, Statutory Instrument 1995 No. 418, HMSO, London.
Great Britain (1995b) *Town and Country Planning (General Development Procedure) Order 1995*, Statutory Instrument 1995 No. 419, HMSO, London.
Gubbay, Susan (1992) Management for a crowded coast, *Landscape Design*, December/January, 10–12.
Heap, D. (1991) *An Outline of Planning Law*, 10th edn, Sweet & Maxwell, London.
House of Commons Environment Select Committee (1992) *Coastal Zone Protection and Planning*, HMSO, London.
The London and South East Regional Planning Conference (SERPLAN) (1993) *Coastal Planning Guidelines for the South East*, SERPLAN, London.
Pickering, H. (1993) *Property Rights in the Coastal Zone: England and Wales*, Working Papers in Coastal Zone Management No. 1, University of Portsmouth, Portsmouth.
Secretaries of State for Environment, Trade and Industry, Health, Education and Science, Scotland, Transport, Energy and Northern Ireland, the Minister of Agriculture, Fisheries and Food and the Secretaries of State for Employment and Wales (1990) *This Common Inheritance. Britain's Environmental Strategy*, Cmnd 1200, HMSO, London.
Taussik, J. (1992a) Development plans: implications of an enhanced status, *Estates Gazette*, 5 September, 106–7.
Taussik, J. (1992b) Surveyors and preapplication enquiries. *Estates Gazette*, 30 May, 96–100.
Taussik, J. (1993a) *Development Plans: Effective Involvement in Plan Preparation*, Department of Land and Construction Management Working Paper, University of Portsmouth, Portsmouth.
Taussik, J. (1993b) *The Town and Country Planning System in the Coastal Zone: England and Wales*, Working Papers in Coastal Zone Management No. 8, University of Portsmouth, Portsmouth.
Taussik, J. (1995) *Development Plans Coastal Areas.* Working Papers in Coastal Zone Management No. 13, University of Portsmouth, Portsmouth.
Telling A. E. and Duxbury, R. M. C. (1993) *Planning Law and Procedure*, 9th edn, Butterworths, London.

Additional sources

Rendel Geotechnics (1993) *Coastal Planning and Management: A Review*, HMSO: London.

PART THREE
Operation and Safety

Small Craft Equipment, Operation and Organizations

7

7.1 INTRODUCTION

Water-based recreation, like any leisure-related sector is constantly changing due to the pressures of supply and demand, marketing, commercialization and the impact of technology. The pace of change appears to be escalating, as more water-based opportunities are developed. These changes are particularly evident in those activities which rely on individual skill to compete against the physical water environment and/or other individuals.

This chapter explains some of the recent small craft trends and identifies what has caused the changes in user participation in this sector. Consideration is also given to the requirements that these changes are placing on coastal recreation providers and the specific facilities which are now required. Finally the problems of control, associated with these rapidly expanding and contracting watersports activities, and the various organizations which have developed to cater for their needs are examined.

7.2 BACKGROUND ISSUES

Before looking at the activities themselves it is important to explain some of the reasons why this sector is so prone to change. Traditionally small craft enthusiasts have been motivated by the challenge of the elements (e.g. riding the biggest wave) and the thrill of competition. Physical conditions (Chapter 3) are still extremely important for most of these sports. More recently however, three additional factors can be identified as follows.

7.2.1 THE BOUNDARIES OF NEW TECHNOLOGY

The types of material that manufacturers are able to use to produce water-based recreation equipment are changing, and so are the

Coastal Recreation Management Edited by Tim Goodhead and David Johnson. Published in 1996 by E & FN Spon, London. ISBN 0 419 20360 5

processes that are used for manufacture. If one looks at the racquet industry (tennis, squash, racquet ball, badminton etc,) the carbon fibre injection moulding process has not only revolutionized the weight, but also the shape of the product. Carbon fibre has also had a profound impact on water-based recreation. Not only has the raw material price dropped significantly in the 1990s but also the number of companies wanting to work in the recreation market has increased.

Some of these changes have been brought about by factors external to the leisure industry such as the decrease in the need for armaments. As the world has become safer, the defence industry has started looking for replacement markets. British Aerospace in Manchester, for example, have recently started a boatbuilding division, using their expertise in materials to manufacture in a new market.

7.2.2 MARKETING

All mainstream sports are trying to increase their market share as the demography of the UK population changes. Competition to attract the young participants of tomorrow has never been more fierce, particularly as older established participants move on to other activities and the total numbers in this age group decrease. Watersports have responded by developing new equipment (e.g. windsurfers) and introducing training schemes aimed specifically at a target age groups. The Royal Yachting Association (RYA) for example promoted a 'Year of Youth' initiative in 1993. Competition for market share is intense in an industry which includes not only other sports, but for example home computers, and home entertainment in a total leisure market worth an estimated £100 billion.

Within water-based recreation the impact of marketing appears to speed up product lifecycle, with new sports and products being produced at an alarming rate. Indeed, the RYA have expressed concern that as a result of marketing hype some sports equipment in this sector is perceived almost as a 'fashion accessory'.

7.2.3 AVAILABLE FREE TIME/INCOME

The predictions of the 1980s were for decreasing working weeks. In actual fact the trend has been in the opposite direction with 'jobs for life' disappearing and working weeks increasing. Many individuals will change jobs several times through their working career, as jobs are increasingly offered on short term contracts of three or five years. The net effect is one of personal insecurity and an underlying fear of being out of work.

As Barry Onions, ex chair of ILAM commented at the 1993 ILAM conference, 'we are developing a cash rich/time poor or time rich/cash poor society with its subsequent effect on leisure participation'. This factor particularly has directly affected participation in the small craft sector of water-based leisure. Developments in this sector have been generated in sports with a heavy reliance on equipment, geared towards the cash rich/time poor participant, the 'yuppie' of the mid 1980s.

7.3 SMALL CRAFT EQUIPMENT

Windsurfers, jet bikes, surfing, surf skis, power boating, waterskis and the recent developments in dinghy sailing are all the resultant products of these changes. Each sport, and its different requirements, presents the coastal recreational manager with a different management challenge.

7.3.1 WIND-POWERED SPORTS

Dinghy sailing was really born after the Second World War, with a plethora of designs for plywood construction. Jack Holt, a UK designer was probably at the forefront of this with designs like the Enterprise, which has had approximately 23 000 units built to date. This boat was developed in conjunction with a leading newspaper of the day, which suggests that the influence of marketing is not a modern phenomenon! Prior to the fibreglass revolution (GRP) there were developments in plywood and fibreglass, known as stitch and glue construction. Panels were mass produced in plywood and stitched together with copper wire twists. Once the basic hull was assembled, all the joints were taped with fibreglass tape and polyester resin. In 1963 the Mirror dinghy was designed for the Mirror Group of newspapers by Jack Holt and Barry Bucknel, 70 000 boats were constructed to this method with the vast majority being constructed in kit form by home builders.

The problem with these plywood boats was the high labour costs which prevented their production in any volume by professional builders. These dinghies also required high levels of maintenance. Thus they were fine for low cost entry to a sport by a handyman, but not good for the instant participation society, who wanted to sail rather than maintain and build wooden boats.

Enter the fibreglass revolution, and the arrival of European designers and boats like the 420 and 470. This enabled higher volume professional builders to capture market share. None of these boats was constructed by home builders. It was not long after this period that global communications assisted the marketing of products worldwide and sailing dinghies were no exception. The power of the manufacturers was also protected by the creation of manufacturers one designs, where all the design and supply of the components was supplied by a single manufacturer. Laser was the product and Performance Sailcraft the company who were to set the parameters for small boat production in the 1990s. Lasers are produced using a sandwich construction of the next generation of materials, PVC foam in a sandwich between two layers of fibreglass cloth and polyester resin. These boats have revolutionized the dinghy industry with over 150 000 units sold world wide and the class is about to make its Olympic debut in 1996. Dinghy production had now arrived as an integrated part of the multi billion pound leisure industry and not the cottage industry run by enthusiasts that it once was.

Key manufacturers focus on marketing of product ranges and creation of brand loyalty. Within the UK, the market is controlled by key companies, such as Laser and Topper International. New boats are developed and marketed so that fleets of dinghies can be developed within a year. The small builders cannot compete with this and have resorted to very small niche markets, or have become involved in the production process for the larger companies. Manufacturing techniques have changed again as volume production became necessary to manufacture the numbers required. Materials now being used range from injection moulded polypropylene, in use in the Topper dinghy (tough, cheap and durable), to vacuum bagged, carbon/epoxy, similar to aerospace manufacturing techniques (very light, strong, expensive).

The modern dinghies of today are easy to sail, due to the use of asymmetric spinnakers, with easier handling and far higher performance. The need to race against other boats has been reduced as just sailing them is **fun**! They are more like an offshoot of the windsurfing boom, with high-pressure marketing and less reliance on the club structure. In this respect the sport is following the lead set by catamarans and windsurfers – fast, flamboyant and fun! It is no coincidence that both Topper and Laser have bought or joined existing catamaran suppliers so that the range of products on offer includes all forms of sailing craft.

In parallel to the technology-led boom in small dinghies the development of yachts followed a similar pattern with the introduction of GRP production techniques and the resultant opening up of the sport to the masses.

The Royal Yachting Association have developed a comprehensive training scheme for sailors and yachtsmen. The dinghy sailing scheme is laid out in five levels of proficiency with a ladder of coaching schemes, these are explained in RYA publications G4 Dinghy Logbook (1993) and S7 Dinghy Coaching Logbook (1993). The yachting scheme is based around the yachtmaster qualification which is approved by the Department of Transport. Details can be found in RYA publication *G15 Cruising Logbook* (1993) and *G27 Cruising Instructors Handbook*.

7.3.2 WINDSURFING

Windsurfing, boardsailing and sailboarding are all the same sport. This led to a confused beginning for this watersport as a result of Windsurfer being both a generic term and a brand name. Nevertheless, the name 'windsurfer' has now been adopted as the sports title. In America the courts ruled that the sport was invented by Hoyle Schweitzer, while in the UK the courts ruled that Peter Chilvers was the inventor.

What is clear is that the Windsurfer range of boards, designed by Hoyle and Jim Drake brought windsurfing to the masses. Ten Cate, a Dutch textile company, diversifying into leisure, were licensed to build the boards for the European market, where the large number of lakes provided the perfect location for this new sport. However, the first boards were heavy and cumbersome.

Initially Laser tried to market a windsurfer, but realized that at that stage it did not suit its product range. Perhaps the windsurfer would sit more easily among that range in today's marketplace.

Rapid development in sailing techniques has fuelled the demand for high-tech manufacturing and materials, used in building today's boards. Robot construction and the use of carbon fibre and epoxy resin in sandwich construction are now the norm, together with clear plastic extruded film in the sails (monofilm) and carbon fibre in the mast, battens and booms. Since the 1970s Asia and Hong Kong have become manufacturing centres with China now established as the largest manufacturer of windsurfing sails. Component manufacture and hull construction however, has returned from the Far East to Europe allowing closer quality control on the high-tech construction and more flexible lead times on production runs.

The development of this sport and indeed many of these so called 'new' watersports has been driven by the thrill or excitement of the recreational experience they offer. Windsurfing originally developed when the boards were large and high in volume (200 litres). This easily supported a participant's weight and made learning relatively easy.

Once this stage had been mastered, speed and manoeuvrability were demanded. The boards became shorter and lower in volume, until the stage was reached where they no longer supported the weight of the participant unless they were moving. A technique called 'water starting' was developed and the sport entered its high wind phase. A requirement for constant winds of over force 4 (11–16 knots) restricted the best venues to specific locations. Windsurfers are now looking to spend increasing amounts of time in the air, to achieve this specialist ramps are being constructed at some venues to give the sailor the added impetus of a permanent wave to take off from, enabling participants to experiment and perfect manoeuvres in the air.

As this side of the sport has increased in popularity, manufacturers have concentrated on trying to capture market share with rapid development of equipment. The outcome is a sport where expensive specialist equipment is the norm, with participants mainly sailing when specific wind conditions exist. This has resulted in a reduction in the opportunities to participate in this sport, but opened up new holiday locations where specific conditions exist. For the long-term future of windsurfing a greater emphasis will need to be placed on the participation/beginners element of the market, rather than the performance sector. Nevertheless, high performance produces the excitement that these individuals will want to experience.

The Royal Yachting Association administer a comprehensive training scheme for windsurfing, the reader is guided to the RYA W3 Logbook (1993) for details of the scheme and RYA *W33 Windsurfing Instructor Manual* for details of instructional techniques.

7.3.3 ENGINE-POWERED SPORTS

Jet-ski/personal water craft (PWC)

One of the problems with considering this rapidly growing specialist small craft market is the lack of research and published information.

Japanese technology has developed this type of craft, originally comprising skis and bikes produced by the likes of Yamaha, Kawasaki and Seedo. The sport is now headed in the opposite direction to windsurfing. It started as low-buoyancy, hard-to-use personal water craft. Technological improvements have now produced more stable craft, capable of carrying more people and able to tow water skiers. New jet skis still possess the same attributes of speed and manoeuvrability, while appealing to a wider market.

In 1989 there were an estimated 7400 machines in the UK. Recent research (Anderson, 1994), based at Lee on Solent in Hampshire found that more than half of those sampled had been in the sport for less than two years. Exhilaration and fun are identified as the main attractions for participants. Young and affluent is also a hallmark of these new wave sports, 70% of those sampled in the Lee on Solent Jet-Ski survey were between 25 and 35 years old and almost 50% were within the C1/C2 category.

7.3.4 WATER SKIING

Recent innovations in waterskiing have included people being towed in a variety of inflatable devices other than the conventional skis. Some of these have included lorry tyre inner tubes, circular rafts and the very popular long yellow tube. Many of these devices have already gained commercial acceptability and are frequently practised at the more popular holiday resorts.

While the 'cowboy' element of waterskiing has given the sport in its early days a bad name, the sport is now extremely well administered by the British Water Ski Federation who have a comprehensive network of clubs and training schemes. Training has been revolutionized by the introduction of a bar that can be placed across the ski boat for training purposes bringing the student level with the instructor.

The sport is at its best on flat water and as such suitable areas in the UK are limited. Many harbours limit waterskiing perhaps unfairly as there is a great deal of difference between the safety standards of waterskiing in clubs and the casual users. Trends show that this sport is still developing in terms of participants.

7.3.5 POWER BOATS

The growth in power boating in the last ten years has been phenomenal both in terms of large and small vessels. At the top end of the market the growth has mainly been in power cruisers capable of 'marina hopping' around the country. Smaller boats are dominated by the Ridged Inflatable Boat or RIB. These boats are a development of the early Zodiac type of inflatable but with a ridged GRP hull for speed and stability of which the Avon Sea Rider is probably the best known class. These vessels are extremely dangerous in untrained hands and so the RYA has developed two training schemes. The Motor Cruising scheme is for larger vessels and is explained in RYA *G18 Motor Cruising Logbook* (1993).

The Power Boat scheme is explained in detail in RYA *G20 Powerboat Logbook* (1990).

7.3.6 WAVE-POWERED SPORTS

The early 1990s has also seen the development of sports that are not so expensive in terms of equipment, but still fall into the category of requiring specialist conditions and sites. They can also be classed as exhilarating and participants do not belong to a recognized club structure. Examples of these sports discussed below are body boards and surfing. Admittedly some of these sports such as canoeing have been in existence for quite some time, but marketing by major companies has opened them up to a wider audience.

7.3.7 BODY BOARDS

This is another sport where one of the leading manufacturers has sometimes become confused with the generic term. The sport uses a body board and the leading manufacturer of these is Boogie. Construction of these products has been made possible again as a result of technology developments, with the standard construction now being closed cell, cross-linked polyethylene. This provides enough stiffness and memory retention with a soft finish, which has important attributes when these boards share the water with swimmers.

Surf conditions are the key to enjoyment and exhilaration within this sport, with the advantage that surf can be anything from clean waves to wind-generated and even shore break waves. This gives the sport a tremendous advantage over surfing, where due to the use of skegs, the water does need to be 'clean', i.e. waves formed by swells which are held up by light offshore winds.

The equipment for body boarding is very affordable, with a board/bag/leash and fins costing approximately £125 at 1995 prices. In addition to this the participant requires a wet suit. Size of the board will vary depending on the size of the rider; however, ease of transport is the key, with juniors being able to transport the boards on foot, by bike or using public transport. Ability level to participate is low, so all participants are likely to achieve a base standard. The sport can be seasonal within northern Europe, with waves generally not being suitable in the months of June/July/August. Due to the ease of transport and price the sport is very popular with the youth market. European and world surfing destinations are easily and cheaply reached, with a minimal amount of equipment required to facilitate body boarding. The sport is now firmly established, with its own UK magazine, *360*, and a governing body was established in late 1994.

7.3.8 SURFING

Compared to body boards, surfing has a long history in which the major breakthrough came about with the introduction of polyester resin. This allowed construction around shapable foam blanks with polyester resin and glassfibre cloth surfaces. A whole art form was built around the role of the shaper and air brush. Clear resins and foam blanks allowed individually shaped boards not only to reflect the technical needs of the rider, but also to serve as an expression of himself/herself in art form sprayed on the blank. This technology allowed rapid growth and links have generated a whole sub-culture, which has been well documented in other text books. Around 99% of modern boards now weigh less than 6 lbs. New materials have resulted in radical designs and a range of different shapes, which influence water pressures and water flow.

Conditions have to be very specific for most enjoyment, with plunging breakers generated by ocean swells providing ideal conditions. Travel is again an important aspect, although personal transport is required due to the size of the equipment. The volume of equipment is not large, allowing a group of friends to share the same mode of transport easily. Synonymous with surfing is the VW camper van, stacked high with surf boards and the occupants definitely fulfilling the culture of surfing.

7.4 ACTIVITY MANAGEMENT

With this diverse range of sports and activities all requiring slightly varying conditions in weather, waves and support facilities it is almost impossible to organize a situation where the conditions are ideal for everyone. However, a number of local management arrangements can be used to help control a multiple-use site where a number of activities can be carried out, side by side, on the same piece of water.

Indeed there are probably as many locations for this type of activity to happen in as there are participants. However, the role of the coastal recreational manager (as explained in Chapter 2) is to maximize the recreational opportunities for as many activities as possible while ensuring the best possible recreational experience for each individual. To achieve this goal on behalf of small craft users the following management issues need to be considered.

7.4.1 LOCAL LIAISON GROUPS

Communication between users is essential as a prerequisite for agreeing the use of popular water areas. In many areas local liaison groups have been formed to help promulgate information to all parties. For small craft users this is perhaps the best way to ensure their activity does not conflict with any other. For example Associated British Ports in Southampton have brought together many potentially disjointed groups, to meet three times a year as the Southampton Water Users Recreational Group. The group comprises the organizers and representatives of:

- local harbourmasters,
- local yacht clubs,
- Waterski Federation,
- Personalised Watercraft Association,
- local rowing clubs,
- local sailing associations,
- local universities,
- district and county councils,
- Royal Yachting Association,
- local windsurfers etc.

The role of this organization is primarily to ensure that new legislation or potential bye-laws which the Port authority may wish to introduce are appropriate to the needs of recreational users, to ensure that major events (Cowes Week, start of Whitbread Round the World Race etc.) are coordinated and that the recreational users are aware of the need of the Port and the Professional Shipping companies (and vice versa).

7.4.2 ZONING

Activities using a venue have generally chosen that location for specific reasons such as: access, ease of use, prevailing winds, proximity of launch points, particularly shallow water, expectation of waves or surf. In many locations however, conditions will be suitable for several different watersports. In these circumstances a method of physical zoning may be the only practical solution to the problem, with the introduction of physical markers to indicate to individuals when they have crossed out of one area and into another. There are numerous examples in the UK of locally agreed zones which enable clear demarcation for access and egress of motorized craft to the slipways on busy and crowded holiday beaches. Zoning schemes can be defined in terms of both time and/or area.

Time Controlling activity management by time zoning is perhaps the most effective way of reducing conflict between watersports but in terms of making use of water space the least effective. This technique is often used in small areas of water such as inland lakes. In coastal areas the Ministry of Defence gunnery ranges are the best example where recreational activity is prohibited during certain times, Lulworth range is the most well-known example.

Area Activities can be managed by setting activity zones such as in the recent management plan for Poole Harbour. This allows many watersports to take place at the same time. Its major drawback is that it does not take into account changing seasons and day-to-day weather conditions. This technique may actually be dangerous in terms of compromising safety as recreational activity may be pushed into an area which is unsuitable for the weather conditions of the day. A windsurfing activity may be ideally suited to a certain beach with an onshore wind but extremely unsuitable in an offshore wind where the windsurfers may be blown into deep water with commercial traffic.

7.4.3 PHYSICAL SEPARATION

The International Collision regulations, combined with the International Association of Lighthouse Authorities, provide another example of physical management. Buoys are laid and very strict regulations are set, backed by international law. For safety reasons this is obviously necessary but in some areas such as the Calshot Spit in Southampton Water the regulations and buoyage have had to be supplemented to take into account the conflict between recreation and commercial ships.

7.4.4 POLICY

At a local level activity can be managed by the establishment of 'minor rules and regulations', the maritime equivalent of keep off the grass signs in public places! Some local authority bye-laws are an example of this kind of technique where water ski boats and power craft might be restricted in their access to beaches. Rather like keep off the grass signs they are often ignored and may have to be policed to be effective.

7.4.5 EDUCATION

The Royal Yachting Association have always been advocates of education rather than legislation. Conflict between water users is reduced by understanding other users' needs and points of view. At its most formal this may lead to the formation of voluntary management agreements. However, if training schemes are effective there may be no need to produce formal documents to manage water activity. Training is perhaps the most effective form of activity management.

7.5 WATERSPORTS ORGANIZATIONS

The water-based leisure industry is unusual in that it is led by a number of sporting national governing bodies which represents the interest of their members. Six of these organizations including two of the newer ones are reviewed below. The reader is advised to contact them direct for a full picture. 'Thumb nail' sketches are provided here only in order to give an idea of their influence on coastal development in watersports.

7.5.1 THE PERSONAL WATERCRAFT ASSOCIATION

As we go to press the organization of jet skiing in the UK is being restructured. Originally the federation was supported by Kawasaki, one of the importers. As the sport has grown, the needs of the jet skier are being handled by two organizations.

- Jet Sport Racing Association of Great Britain (JSRAGB),
- Personal Watercraft Federation (PWF).

JSRAGB control the racing programme while PWF are interested in the recreational aspects. In particular the PWF are fighting similar issues as other governing bodies in trying to protect access and developing safety codes. The BMIF (British Marine Industry Federation), comprising manufacturers from all sections of the marine industry as well as specialist jet ski products are currently co-ordinating this general interest role. As the jet ski market becomes more established, then we may see further developments in the running of the UK administration for jet skis.

7.5.2 THE ROYAL YACHTING ASSOCIATION

The Royal Yachting Association (RYA) was formed in 1875, by a small group of gentlemen interested in Yacht Racing. The RYA is the National Governing body for all forms of sailing, windsurfing, motor cruising, sports boats and power boat racing. Today, it has over 70 000 members, and over 1500 affiliated clubs and class associations, representing at least half a million people.

The role of the RYA as seen by its directors (The Council) is to develop the boating interests of its members. While this encompasses a wide variety of activity, the main aims are to ensure that individuals are not prevented from participating in their activity and to ensure that by offering an educational process that government will not see fit to try to legislate against its members. This is achieved by protecting the rights and freedoms of both members and non-members, through legal processes and by applying pressure on legislative bodies. There are also about 1500 recognized teaching establishments and each year over 90 000 people complete their RYA training in sail cruising, dinghy sailing, motor cruising, sportsboats or windsurfing.

7.5.3 THE BRITISH CANOE UNION

The British Canoe Union (BCU) was formed in 1936 and is now the governing body for the sport and recreation of canoeing in the United Kingdom. The Union is a private members' club with limited liability status it is recognized by the British Sports Council and is a member of the Central Council of Physical Recreation. Its headquarters is located at Holme Pierrepont, Nottingham and an information office is located at the John Dudderidge House, Adbolton Lane, West Bridgford, Nottingham. John Dudderidge is one of the Officers of the Union and is president of Honour.

The Union has over 15 500 members and 450 affiliated clubs. Its purpose is to unite everyone interested in canoeing and encourage others to join in. The BCU has divided the United Kingdom into nine regions which each have their own regional committee and regional officers. It is affiliated to the International Canoe Federation and the British Olympic Association, it is responsible for national and international competition and administering of grants. Its aim is to provide a complete, specialist service – educational, informational, training expertise, improved access to the coinable waters – thereby increasing the enjoyment, safety and skills of all paddlers at every level.

The Union is managed by the British Canoe Union Council which has a large management structure with four main committees and several sub-committees. It is composed of directly elected members, and representatives of specialist and regional committees. The Union Council is also responsible for the continuing development of objectives and policies. It gets it finance through membership fees, councils and from sponsorship. Course fees and test fees are also sources of finance. Publicity of the Union is done through the issuing of leaflets and also through the media with television coverage for recreational as well as competitive sectors.

7.5.3 THE BRITISH WATER SKI FEDERATION

The British Water Ski Federation (BWSF) is a body that was set up to fulfil the requirement of the then rapidly growing sport of water skiing. It was realized that the sport of motor boating was becoming ever more popular and more and more people were buying speed boats. With this came the obvious transgression to water skiing. Therefore a body was established to organize the sport of **recreational** water skiing.

The BWSF has many responsibilities today. There are at present about 14 000 members in the UK, a figure which has almost doubled in the last eight years. Membership in 1993 cost about £26 per individual and gives you many privileges: free personal insurance when skiing; free publications; free information leaflets; advice on training and careers in the industry; favourable boat insurance; a host of money-saving discounts; technical support and advice.

Apart from membership the BWSF offers a great deal. In association with the National Powerboat scheme, the federation has established a series of awards which can be undertaken to gain a recognized certificate of competence in pulling a recreational water skier. There are also certificates available for advanced ski boat drivers who wish to tow skiers at tournament level. These particular qualifications are at present only recognized on a relatively small scale and are striving to gain the status of the National Powerboat certificates. In the next three years BSWF hope to develop these certificates to become approved 'National Vocational Qualification' (NVQs). With these certificates the BWSF will command a much larger presence in the watersports field as a recognized employer.

One of the most important responsibilities of the federation is that of the environment. Water skiing has had a lot of bad press in the past due to pollution; damage to the local ecosystem; physical damage to the sites in terms of accelerated bank erosion; noise pollution etc. The BWSF insists that at every site there be a conservation and access officer to liaise as necessary with the local authorities and the regional NRA. A group of BWSF inspectors was established four years ago to try every year to visit every BWSF approved site and inspect the general condition of the site and facilities.

The federation also acts as an advisory service to anyone who wants to start up their own club. It is important that people wishing to start a club should gain the BWSF certificate of approval as company insurance; personal accident liability can have the worst repercussions if unattached to a formative body.

7.5.4 THE BRITISH SURFING ASSOCIATION

The British Surfing Association (BSA) was founded in 1966 to look after the needs of its membership and the sport of surfing. The BSA is made up of five 'federations': Jersey, Guernsey, England, Scotland and Wales. The Association is subsidized by the Sports Council. This funding is gradually being reduced due to current government policy. Other funding comes from sponsorship and membership subscriptions.

There is only one paid full-time employee of the BSA, the Administrator. This person's job is to conduct the affairs of the Association and to keep financial records of all transactions to do with the Association. All other jobs are voluntary and involve being a member of a committee, which usually only follows after a few years' membership of the BSA. Other paid jobs may arise, but these are usually part-time contractual work such as catering for competitions and championships.

The BSA is the surfing governing body and sets down the rules for competitions and selects the national team. It is also involved with coaching schemes and endorsing surfing schools. The BSA offers very limited employment opportunity, but offers many services and benefits to its members.

7.5.5 BRITISH SUB AQUA CLUB

British Sub Aqua Club is the UK-based governing body for diving. The association is a voluntary organization run for its members and funded mostly by their memberships. The association promotes amateur diving and interest in underwater activities.

7.5.6 THE ORGANIZATION OF SMALL CRAFT RECREATION

Traditional sailing school organizations (Chapter 8) are not appropriate for many of the watersports considered in this section. This is mainly because:

1. The new generation of small craft are much more fun to sail and so the temptation is just to sail for fun, without the need to race.
2. Social demands are forcing people away from the voluntary club structure. Time is now more precious, so less time is available on a voluntary basis. With this change in emphasis has come the fact that individuals are far more willing to pay for leisure facilities.

7.5.7 PUBLIC RELATIONS

Coastal recreation managers need actively to promote these sports in order to foster support for new activities. Often activities and events that individuals do not themselves participate in can be perceived as unacceptable by them. It is imperative that managers fund solutions to prevent an activity being perceived as intrusive by the local populous. The very nature of some of the activities such as windsurfing, canoeing and PWC users means that they will move to the best venue for the prevailing conditions, often without consideration for others.

To achieve acceptability from many locals, i.e. the people that permanently live in an area, an activity has to have been practised there for a considerable time, with perhaps the second generation being the current participants. All activities started somewhere, somehow. Modern watersports have not yet matured enough to have an acceptable following within the older, more vocal and wealthier generation. Consequently there are few supporters of these sports and activities in council chambers predisposed to fight battles on behalf of the younger generation of enthusiasts. Once a sport is established and there are people interested in the activity, but perhaps too old to actively participate, they are more likely to help develop and administer it. As yet the new age watersports have not reached a level of maturity for this to have happened. This same problem can be seen on a smaller scale within established sailing clubs where the new sport of windsurfing is simply seen as an activity that will go away if ignored.

Windsurfing in the UK would never have grown as a sport and been accepted as quickly as it was if a few far-sighted individuals in the Royal Yachting Association had not seen the possibilities for the sport, and set up and developed teaching and learning strategies. However, in the 1990s the sport began to move backwards as it reached a stage in its evolution that meant it needed support and assistance from people with more time to serve on committees to administer the sport.

On a local basis if activities are seen to be controlled and coordinated then acceptability will soon come. Bude in Cornwall has now accepted surfing as an acceptable activity and now the tourist trade and the leisure industry is geared up to the requirements of the sport rather than to provide opposition. The opposition is now focused on the windsurfers and their activities which can often conflict with the surfer.

As sporting organizations begin to appreciate the need to ensure a high profile for their sport so more and more activities will be moved to venues where the public can spectate. Watersporting activities must be taken to the crowds to achieve a high coverage, unlike the more easily covered televised sports where the crowds will travel to watch the activity. The consequence of this is that the manager must be aware of how different activities will be viewed by the public and steps need to be taken to control adverse effects such as car parking pressure and litter.

7.5.8 ACTIVITY PLANNING

The coastal recreational manager needs to be able to plan activities temporarily as well as spatially. A simple summary of different sports and their requirements is given in Table 7.1.

7.6 CONCLUSION

The providers of facilities for these 'new wave' sports have a problem, due to the speed of change and also the very specialist conditions that participants now require. Often a venue will become popular due to the physical conditions, rather than because facilities have been provided. The most recent example of this development has been the Greek resort of Vassiliki. A natural phenomenon creates a pressure gradient which adds to the thermal effect and produces winds of approximately force 4+ on a regular basis throughout the summer. This sleepy fishing resort has now been turned into the most popular catamaran and windsurfing high wind site in Europe, with often in excess of 1000 boards on the water at any one time! Other examples of this are Lake Garda in Italy, The Gorge in USA, and Tarifa in Spain. Even Britain has accelerated winds through the Solent which, when combined with wind against tide conditions, provides superb reaching conditions. All these venues have specific wind and sea states and have grown in importance as the windsurfing market has become more high wind orientated. On the other hand beginners may be attracted to shallow water, as in Poole Harbour, and surfers may be attracted to a certain surf break which may be the result of a sand bar.

Table 7.1 Activity weather requirements and water conditions

Activity	Competence	Equipment	Water type	Wind	Land facilities
Bodyboarding	All levels	Specialist board	Surf	Any	Beach
Canoe	Beginner		Sheltered	<F3	Slipway or beach
Canoe	Advanced			<F6	Slipway or beach
Canoe	Surfing	Specialist ski	Surf	<F9	Exposed beach
Dinghy sail	Beginner	12–16 ft boat	Flat	<F4	Slipway
Dinghy sail	Advanced			>F2	Slipway
Dinghy sail	Competition		Any	Any	Slipway
PWC	Beginner		Flat	<F3	Slipway
PWC	Advanced		Rough/waves	>F3	Slipway
Surfing	Beginner	Hire board	Small surf	>F4	Beach with waves
Surfing	Competition	Surf board	Surf	Any	Exposed beach
Surfing	Recreational	Surf board	Surf	<F9	Exposed beach
Waterski	Beginner		Flat	<F3	Slipway and beach
Waterski	Advanced		Flat	<F3	Slipway and beach
Waterski	Competition		Flat	<F3	Slipway and beach
Windsurf	Beginner	Board>340 m	Flat	<F3	Beach
Windsurf	Intermediate			F2–3	Beach
Windsurf	Advanced	Board>240–390	Rough	>F3	Beach
Windsurf	Competition	Board>240–390		>F2	Beach
Windsurf	Recreational/comp.	Board>240–390	Waves	>F3	Beach

The providers of facilities have very little say about where the venue will be if natural features are the key. Local managers will frequently have to manage the problem of participants, while only controlling parking, toilets and café. The other feature of the participants in this 'new wave' is that they generally do not belong to voluntary sector clubs. On the whole the equipment is personal, expensive, specialized and easily transported. The fact that participants are on the whole affluent allows for easy transportation and storage of the equipment.

Modern-day sailing clubs now resemble small businesses in terms of attitude, services and staff employment. We have also seen the launch in 1994 of the first commercial sailing club, where the dinghies and keel boats are owned by the club. You simply ring up and book a boat in exactly the same way that you book a squash court. This operation has been launched by Sunsail at Port Solent, near Portsmouth.

These factors present a problem for the coastal recreational manager who is likely to be a shore based supplier of facilities. Managers need to know what specific facilities these sports need, as well as having an insight into the optimum water conditions. Requirements change with the expertise of the participants and also in some cases with the wind conditions. The excitement factor experienced by these participants and the mobility of the participants may make one venue popular in the morning and another site popular by the afternoon. Inevitably continuing experimentation and development of the variety of 'fun watersports' and 'small craft' will provide coastal recreational managers with an ongoing challenge.

REFERENCE

Anderson, J. (1994) *Perceptions of Jet Skiers: A Case Study*. Unpublished report for Southampton Institute.

Sea School Management

8

8.1 INTRODUCTION

Over the last 30 years there has been a tremendous boom in establishing sea schools in the UK. Many of the training schemes associated with them are administered by the Royal Yachting Association who in many ways have become the world leaders in pioneering water-based training schemes. This chapter provides a guide to the key issues that should be considered when developing or managing sea schools, these issues are provided in bullet points in a series of tables.

8.2 THE OBJECTIVES OF MANAGING SEA SCHOOLS

The majority of sail training in the UK is undertaken by the voluntary sector, with commercial and public sector schools making up the remainder. Many instructors working for the public and commercial sectors do so for 'pin money'. The bulk of UK sailing instructors in the UK provide their services for fun and/or a desire to put something back into the sport. This voluntary ethos is reflected in the Royal Yachting Association's policy of education rather than legislation.

Within this split of public and private provision there exists a myriad of organizations providing sail training for a wide variety of reasons. To a certain extent no two sailing schools are alike in their management objectives. However, the objectives at course level are very similar from sailing school to sailing school. Many courses adopt the quality control and assurance systems laid down by national governing bodies. An outline of the key factors influencing the specific objectives of sailing schools is laid out in Table 8.1. Government intervention in sailing schools varies from country to country. In the UK intervention takes place mainly through health and safety legislation but with the development of the European Union this is likely to change very rapidly.

Coastal Recreation Management Edited by Tim Goodhead and David Johnson. Published in 1996 by E & FN Spon, London. ISBN 0 419 20360 5

A successful sailing school must have clear objectives; for the organization as a whole, the course and the individual teaching session. Balanced against this must be the objectives of the student which may be sporting or social. The student's motivation for taking training may be extremely complex. These reasons must be identified from the outset. Often students arriving in groups or pairs should be split to avoid one person becoming dominant and possible personality conflict. For example husband and wives/brothers and sisters are extremely difficult to teach in the same boat as one tends to 'take charge' of the other. Having identified the key objectives potential health problems should be identified preferably at the booking stage as this will be a critical factor in terms of how the student should be treated.

Table 8.1 Objectives of sea schools

Organizational objectives
Possible commercial profit but in most cases training objectives will apply.
Specific objectives
Courses must be enjoyable and consider: repeat custom; structured learning and progression; building student confidence and raise self-esteem.
Objectives of activity time
Maximum time on the water, scheduled time slots, e.g. summer evening sessions, shore-based courses in the winter. The maximum number of people on the water is a function of safety ratios.
Student objectives
Students must be extended as much as possible: students should be divided into ability, e.g. split husband and wives, pick sympathetic instructors (this may conflict with social objectives).

8.3 SHORE FACILITIES

Shore facilities vary considerably from sea school to sea school varying from operating from the back of a minibus to multi-million pound centres. One type of facility should not be regarded as a 'better' training establishment than another as they are likely to be operating to very different objectives. Sailing schools should be judged against their objectives and perhaps against the safety policy of the organization and in relation to policy laid down by national governing bodies such as the Royal Yachting Association and the British Canoe Union. The key facilities that might be found at a sea school are outlined in Table 8.2. Safety provision is critical in a shore facility. A first-aid kit, telephone and some method of warming students who are suffering from extreme cold are critically important. Teaching aids might be considered to be a luxury as inevitably the best teaching aid is often the boat on the water, but, if more sophisticated facilities are acquired it does extend the potential for teaching during the day and may in some cases extend the season where night school classes are operated.

A potential sea school proprietor should plot the movement of an imaginary student from home to the point when he/she steps into a boat in order to consider welfare and safety when determining provision. This will start with joining instructions, detailing what the student should bring and a map explaining the location of the site. Car parking should be provided. Sailing involves transporting a fair amount of equipment and a facility for dropping off this equipment as near to the changing facility as possible should be provided. The facilities for changing in the base may vary from a wooden hut to 'four star' facilities. The common denominator should be warm showers, a toilet and a hand basin with hot running water. The shower can be used for warming very cold students and the basin provides hygiene for cuts on hands which might provide an entry for leptospirosis or Weils disease. Having provided these basic facilities any enhancement may be a function of marketing.

Having changed the customer the next provision must be access to the water. This will vary according to location but as a general rule it should take the student no more than 15 minutes to go from the changing room to being afloat – however large the group. Slipway congestion often slows this process down and so sailing schools may have to schedule launch times for differing student groups or provide more launching facilities. It is not possible to define exact standards for launching boats as different boats need different facilities and this varies according to weather conditions, and the students' ability. The 15-minute rule should be used as a guide and facilities for individual locations organized accordingly.

Repair facilities at a sea school are extremely important. Broken boats equate with a loss in teaching time and possible loss of income. This can be overcome by acquiring spare boats and equipment but this results in capital being tied up that is under utilized. Successful sailing schools use boats such as Topper Dinghies which are extremely difficult to damage, require low maintenance and have a readily accessible network of retailers supplying spares. Where possible, boats should be standardized to reduce the cost of holding spares and to make the interchange of equipment more feasible.

Table 8.2 Minimum shore facilities

Basic facilities Adequate changing facilities, showers, toilets, dual purpose rooms, visual aids, drinks machines, power points, RCBs, blackout facilities, telephone, medical aids. *Provision for conflicting groups* Slipway congestion, timing zones, outside water for cleaning boats. *Facilities for both sexes* Male/female and disabled *Car parking* Encourages repeat custom Safety and security *Bosun's department* Adequate repair facilities Spares System

8.4 WATER FACILITIES

Water space must be regarded as a resource. This resource will be suitable for some activities and unsuitable for others. In different wind and tide conditions this suitability may change dramatically. For example an onshore light wind on a beach may be ideal for training novice windsurfers. If they get into difficulty they will simply be blown onto the beach. However, an offshore wind on the same beach may be extremely dangerous as the windsurfers may be blown offshore if they get into difficulties. The practice of zoning waterspace permanently for specific activities should be regarded with extreme scepticism. In this situation, activities should be zoned according to local weather and tidal conditions and reviewed and monitored on at least an hourly basis with constant watch on the natural elements being made. In the same way launching facilities need to be different for different craft and weather conditions. A successful sailing school needs a variety of water facilities so that students can practice and develop a wide variety of skills and techniques. This obviously entails a financial cost and some schools may have a natural advantage to the variety of facilities in their home location. The variety of harbours, tidal effects, estuaries, rivers and ports in the Solent perhaps partly explains the success of some of the sailing schools in this region. For novice sailors an area of light constant wind is required. This can be manipulated in strong winds by towing the fleet of sailing boats into the lee of a headland or physical feature. Flexibility as to the choice of sailing area is extremely important to the successful operation of a sailing school, but the choice of area must be made by suitably qualified staff with appropriate training and safety equipment for that area. A list of key points to be considered when choosing an appropriate sailing area is contained in Table 8.3.

8.4.1 LOCATION

In terms of location the two key factors that should be considered are firstly the prevailing wind direction and strength, and secondly the local tidal conditions. These two factors will determine the type of operation which is feasible.

8.4.2 RATE OF TIDAL STREAMS – TOWING THE FLEET

Where sites are limited by perhaps light wind strengths and strong tides, perhaps behind a headland, motor boats or road trailers can be used to make the operation mobile in order to overcome the problems. Extensive tidal and meteorological research must be undertaken before considering the provision of a sea school at a specific site.

8.4.3 LOCAL EFFECTS OF WIND AND TIDE

The local environment can severely effect regional weather conditions. This may be an advantage or a disadvantage. As explained in Chapter 3, coastal areas often experience a sea breeze effect in the early afternoon. If this supplements the gradient wind then the total wind strength increases normally for a period of two or three hours. For training purposes this can produce ideal light winds in the morning building up as the student's confidence builds. If the sea breeze kills the gradient wind it can result in serious training problems. In a similar way wind with tide produces a smooth wave pattern but wind against tide produces a short sharp chop. These local effects must be built into training programmes and also the business plan.

Local hazards A chart will identify many local hazards but local knowledge of the kind built up by fishermen over many centuries must not be overlooked. Local hazards can be used to advantage in some training situations. An area with a wide variety of hazards ironically can make for a very good training area. However, it is critical that instructors are aware of these hazards and thorough briefing and updates must be provided by the management.

Local information centres Local information is, as has been seen, very important. Students and staff at sea schools should be trained to consult local organizations on a regular basis for safety reasons.

Table 8.3 Water facilities tidal

Points to consider: location, launching and recovery, time on the water, ownership of HW-LW, depth of water, shelter from the elements, prevailing winds, capacity of launch site, pontoons, cost of slipways, stowage of boats, storage of rescue craft

Rate of tidal streams-towing fleet
Capability of rescue craft
Distance to safe sailing area
Springs and neaps
Time taken to tow to sailing area
Time on water

Local effects of wind and tide
Average wind speed light and strong
Can beginners cope
Funnel winds/deflected winds
Gust patterns
Local sea breeze/land breeze
Wave patterns
Wind against tides/wind with tide

Local hazards
Buoyage
Depth
Formation of sea bed
Isolated hazard
Local currents
Obstructions
Sand banks–mudflats
Sea bed
Sea bed, sand gravel rock
Sea bed adjacent to area

8.5 GENERAL SAFETY

Participation in watersports always entails a degree of risk to personal safety as the elements can never be completely predicted. However, the safety risks to individuals can be minimized with the development of an effective health and safety policy together with adherence to the guidelines laid down by sporting national governing bodies and appropriate legislation. Central to any safety strategy will be the knowledge, skill and understanding of individual instructors. Safety awareness must be an attitude that runs from top to bottom in a sea school. It is critical that all staff and students operate the same system. The development of a safety scheme in a sailing school is similar to developing a Total Quality Management system in the workplace. Safety and quality of provision of service go hand in hand. Recent actions by the Health and Safety Executive in the UK show that failure to adopt a corporate heath and safety policy may result in the closure of the facility. Table 8.4 illustrates some of the key factors contributing to safety but this only provides a thumbnail sketch. The reader is guided to the policy of the national governing bodies for watersports for further detail.

Table 8.4 General safety

Thorough briefing of instructors
• rules and regulations • hazards • tides • ability of students • safety procedures • flares • safety drills • clothing
Qualified safety boat drivers Buoyancy Chain of command – senior instructors/management bear the ultimate responsibility Clothing Declaration of ability to swim 50 m First aid Footwear–non slip Group control Instructor to set examples Knife and torch Oilskins/waterproofs Set exercise according to ability Warm clothing Weather forecast

8.6 SAFETY BOATS AND EQUIPMENT

Safety boats are vital to the operation of a sailing school. Ironically they are probably the most dangerous items of equipment that can be found in the sailing environment. Sadly there have been a number of deaths in recent years involving these craft. The problem appears to be highly skilled sailors operating very high-powered motor boats in which they have little experience. The Royal Yachting Association have instigated a comprehensive training programme in the UK which, judging by the number of people attaining qualifications, appears spectacularly successful. However, the sailing school manager should always view a powerboat in untrained hands as a potentially lethal weapon and act accordingly. These boats can be divided into two categories, namely displacement and non-displacement. The former, operating at much higher speeds than the latter is perhaps the cause for most concern in two areas; firstly safety of operators and students with regard to their proximity to high-speed propellers and secondly the fuel costs of operating such craft. Successful sailing schools tend to operate a variety of safety boats so that some act as teaching platforms, with a safety role as last resort (an example might be the use of a canoe to teach young children in Optimist sailing dinghies), with other more powerful boats such as ridged inflatables providing a 'sheepdog' safety role in trained hands. An outline of key points regarding safety boats can be found in Table 8.5. The Royal Yachting Association Powerboat scheme provides an example of good practice in the management of power boats and safety boats (RYA *G20 Power Boat Logbook*, 1996).

8.7 OPTIMUM COURSE DURATION

The length of training programmes will be a function of the objectives set for that programme. A considerable financial cost may be incurred by offering customers too much as part of their programme. Conversely, offering too little will perhaps turn out students whose belief in their own ability is higher than their skill. One of the main arguments against compulsory training is that there will be tremendous pressure to push people through courses too quickly as customers will only be interested in 'chasing tickets' and not in the inherent value of the training programme. Sailing courses are complex because students require different instructional techniques depending on their age. Children tend to learn by doing, so they are suited to training in single-handed boats, while adults tend to learn from explanation and are more suited to instruction in boats with the instructor on board. In the same way that a sailing school manager might be advised to segment the market for marketing purposes there is a training need for market segmentation. This has commercial implications.

Table 8.5 Safety boats and equipment

Types
Planing

Advantages
- high speed
- high manoeuverability
- good in rough water
- open cockpit
- good righting capabilities
- unsinkable

Disadvantages
- easily damaged
- low initial stability

Displacement

Advantages
- easily driven at low speeds
- low fuel consumption
- good directional stability
- performance not greatly affected by load
- good in bad weather

Disadvantages
- max. hull speed governed by length
- difficult to handle at close quarters
- cannot usually be beached
- freeboard makes MOB recovery difficult
- can be very costly to repair

Inland/coastal
Inland Dory is best as it is stable at rest and at speed on relatively flat water, (not coastal). RIBs can also be used

8.8 HIGH-TECH EQUIPMENT

A move away from basic instruction into high-level instruction brings with it a need for more sophisticated equipment and a higher capital base. If this capital cost cannot be offset on to the customer the sailing school manager may be courting financial disaster. There are, however, ways round this problem. The manager could, for example, use the customer's own boat or charter. A modern lightweight high-performance boat a very expensive item of equipment. Uffa Fox is reputed to have said that 'the only place for weight is in a steam roller' and that 'offshore sailing is rather like standing in a cold shower tearing up five pound notes'. His comments seem very apt when considering high performance sailing. Customers are attracted to up-to-date equipment which is an incentive to provide it. The dilemma is that it may be damaged easily. Race training is a specific market niche, as is offshore sailing, and the entrepreneur who wishes to break into these markets is advised to tread very cautiously.

Table 8.6 High-tech equipment

Maintenance problems
Ratios of staff to students are very expensive
Speed of boats creates safety problems
Electronics and sea water tend not to mix
Cost of instruction can be very high
Variety of boats may be required
Pre- and post-sailing checks are required
Safety policy needs to be adapted
Spares need to be held leading to high inventory costs
Simulation may be a safer financial option
High-tech equipment normally leads to racing
This may have training benefits
Gives an aim to training
Builds up general awareness
Speeds up reactions
Team work is developed
Knowledge is tested
Tactics can be practical
Confidence should be built up
Achievement can be measured

8.9 FOUL WEATHER

The demand for sail training will be influenced by weather and season. This demand can be manipulated by taking deposits so that customers cannot withdraw if they spot 'bad weather on the horizon' and by price differentiation against time of booking (perhaps the smarter commercial operators opt out of the system altogether by relocating to better climates!). The operator of sailing services is always faced with a problem when the weather turns inclement. Contingency plans have to be considered. These may have shore-based facility implications and can be extremely costly. For this reason a contingency plan is essential. Also the individual yacht should also have a contingency plan or bolt hole to go to when the weather closes in. These contingency plans should be built into the sailing school's standing orders.

As an added incentive to plan for foul weather the decision to abandon
sailing incurs a possible refund to the client unless an alternative
programme can be found. The two most common solutions are:

1. **Safety cover** By increasing the number of safety boats in operation
    or restricting the sailing area it may be possible to continue. This
    assumes that instructors have high wind ability.
2. **Simulation** As a second-best alternative videos and presentations
    can be offered. There are now many computer simulation packages
    available that can provide realistic alternatives to being on the
    water. The cost of these must be balanced against refunds or
    postponements.

8.10 STAFFING

Recruitment of staff of an appropriate calibre is critical to the success of a
sailing school. Qualifications must be checked before staff meet students
and the personality of the instructor must relate to the students. Young
children relate to young instructors, mature students relate in the main
to mature instructors. The credibility of the instructor in the eyes of the
student, rather than just in the eyes of the employer, is very important
(the financial implications of hiring staff are reviewed later in this
chapter). Key staffing issues are detailed below.

1. **Continuity of staff** It is important for safety reasons that there is
    some continuity of staffing from one season to the next. Staff can
    then pass on good practice from one season to the next whether it
    be in administration or instruction. Continuity can be financially
    expensive as there may be little to do during the winter months
    other than basic maintenance and evening classes. As a very rough
    rule of thumb one permanent member of staff to every five
    visiting/seasonal instructors should be employed.
2. **Cash flow** Because of the costs of holding non-productive staff
    through the winter particular attention should be paid to the
    monitoring of cash flow. The sailing school manager may have to be
    ruthless in laying off labour during this period to ensure financial
    viability. The use of student labour is particularly suitable for sailing
    schools as students leave of their own accord during the winter
    months. Many sailing schools have developed leisure management
    courses, so that these students both instruct and pay for training, in
    imaginative attempts to alleviate cash flow problems and provide a
    service.
3. **Wage rates** These vary tremendously in sailing schools varying from
    £20 per week to £30 pounds per hour. The determination of these
    rates will be a function of what competitors are offering or the

national pay bargaining power of local authority unions. Some sailing schools retain some pay and award at the end of the season as a loyalty bonus. Catering/accommodation can be used to supplement low wages and this has the advantage that live in instructors contribute to the social life of the centre and are on call during an emergency.

4. **Qualifications** It is absolutely critical that staff have appropriate instructional qualifications. These must be checked before the instructor commences work, there have been cases of non-qualified instructors misrepresenting their qualification with disastrous results.

5. **Progression** The national governing bodies all have a progression of instructor qualifications. A staff development policy together with training must be implemented to retain enthusiasm and develop safety skills.

6. **Enthusiasm** The enthusiasm of the individual instructor can make or break a sailing school. Skill in staff selection is required. Planning of staff deployment should be considered six months in advance of the course to be offered, references as well as qualifications need to be checked.

7. **Safety boats** The modern sailing instructor must have safety boat qualifications as well as a current first aid certificate.

8.11 FINANCE

The main financial problem in operating sailing schools, particularly in the UK, is the length of the season. For many months of the year very expensive equipment will probably be lying idle. The success of some sailing schools in the UK, out of necessity, has been a function of offering discount or adapting equipment to other use during quiet periods and the off season. The most obvious example of that is that many sailing schools during early spring and late summer offer discounts for large school groups. The season can be extended by using property for conferences or simply renting out property during the darkness of winter months. The successful management of a sailing school often seems to be as much a function of cash-flow management as training. The maritime leisure industry has major problems with cash-flow management due to the seasonal nature of demand. In devising a cash-flow schedule for the successful operation of a sailing school there are two main aspects of sailing school management that must be considered.

Firstly the operation and safety of the sailing school. Given that sailing is a risk sport it is hoped that in most people's eyes safety and operational matters should always come first. Safety comes at a cost and so this cost must be built into the business plan of the sailing school right from the outset. If these costs cannot be met the sailing school should cease its operation.

Table 8.7 Financial considerations

Expenditure
Administration
Depreciation of equipment
Expenses
Hire of equipment
Insurance
Yacht insurance
Third-party cover
Instructors' insurance
Building Insurance
Marketing
Overheads
Spares and damage
Students
Wages
Income
Council/government grants
Course fees
Hire of equipment
Hire of facilities
Merchandise
Selling of equipment
Sponsorship
Vending machines and bars

Secondly at a strategic level business plans for sailing schools need to consider some kind of long-term projection which considers the competition from other providers both nationally and internationally.

Many sailing schools operate on a year-to-year basis. The more successful ones can be differentiated from the rest in that they have very clear corporate objectives that are projected forward for many years. Sea school management is unusual in that particular attention needs to be taken in terms of managing staffing costs as instructor/student ratios are often as low as one instructor to three students. Student labour may be prime staff for the average UK sailing school, not only because they may be young fit and enthusiastic with sailing skills, but also because they are relatively cheap to employ. Even students who do not have sailing skills can be used in roles such as attending to children, looking after accommodation or simply cooking lunches. Together with this the young person's most useful attribute is perhaps that they can be laid off at the end of the summer! This makes student labour extremely suitable for staffing sailing schools providing that there is a bedrock of experienced sailing school staff to support them. Student instructors are used particularly in the UK where the vacation closely corresponds with the summer season for dinghy and windsurfing instruction. Yachting instructors tend to come at a higher price as they are required to work a longer season and so require an annual salary. It is critical that staff hold the appropriate qualifications.

Table 8.8 Publicity – safety information

Publicity for sailing courses is unusual in that it may also have to portray safety information. Typically it will include:

Application forms
Book list
Changing and shower facilities available
Clothing requirements
Contact name
Food and hot drink facilities
Instructor ratios
Insurance cover
Time of start and finish
Travel instruction
Types of dinghy used

8.12 MARKETING AND PRICING

In terms of managing sailing schools both marketing and pricing have very clearly defined roles. Firstly marketing: finding out what the customer wants, would seem to be extremely important in an industry that is experiencing constant change. Twenty years ago the windsurfer was only the figment of one person's imagination, ten years ago the UK had not seen the jet bike, five years ago at an average international boat show most sales would have been in sailing yachts, now the growth market would seem to be in power cruisers. Analysing what the customer wants and delivering it is critical together with the price that the product is sold at. In terms of setting a price for the services provided by sea schools there is one major problem: sailing schools operate in a market that is very similar to the market of perfect competition (i.e. there is relative freedom for new suppliers to enter the sailing school markets and there is relative freedom for consumers to investigate prices). If the consumer looks through the back of current yachting magazines he or she will very quickly identify a fair price and perhaps an unfair price. As a result pricing as a whole tends to be a function of the industry rather than of an individual sailing school. Due to this market structure the manager will have to monitor costs very keenly as margins may be very slim.

Studies of various sailing schools in the UK will show that successful ones have adapted the use of property very adeptly. One of the best examples to illustrate this is perhaps the early years of the world renowned PGL children's activity holidays organization. PGL initially developed around providing canoe holidays near Ross on Wye. This gave young people a taste of adventure by letting them canoe down the river Wye and accommodating them in tents. During the winter months the business was carrying very little capital, tents could be sold off and are relatively cheap to buy. Successful ventures followed promoted by other operators using caravans as accommodation. These were only rented in the summer months. Where property is a feature of the equity of the sailing school, as in most local authority sailing bases, an environment is created where it is extremely difficult to obtain a reasonable return/break even, simply because the property and the capital tied up in it lies empty for so much of the year. In any event the returns from sailing schools on capital employed are very low, possibly as low as 5% or even negative. With very low returns it is at first sight very difficult to see why anyone invests in the sailing industry at all. They possibly invest because many are romantics at heart, attracted by the sport rather than the investment. As a result opportunity costs may be very high when investing in sailing schools. The companies that seem to have done well have done so because they have both analysed the market for sailing tuition/holidays and they have organized their property management in such a way that they are carrying as few costs as possible through the winter.

8.13 FACILITIES

The site In terms of running sailing schools there are three golden rules (these have been borrowed from estate agency), location, location and location. Since sailing uses a natural resource, at its most obvious the wind the sea and a beach, the more attractive the resource is to the customer the more likely you are to succeed. There are some enterprises which get round this by having a movable facility, e.g. small windsurfing schools operating from the back of car trailers, water ski operations which can move from bay to bay and indeed yachting operations which can move from harbour to harbour. The problem with dinghy sailing is that often you cannot move your base, but you can sell it! The cash flow of a dinghy sailing school must be carefully manipulated. To illustrate this, one financial technique might be something like this:

Setting up a dinghy school

The following example is included to demonstrate the importance of monitoring cash flow.

1. Investigate the London Boat show and negotiate trade status.
2. Buy preferably single-handed dinghies so that you can operate on ratios of one instructor to six pupils.
3. Boats are ordered in January and paid for by cash on delivery in April.
4. When the boats arrive they are immediately put up for sale to be delivered at the end of the season.
5. Advertisements perhaps should read 'Brand new boats slightly used, one-third of retail price'. This will not be far off the bulk trade price.
6. As soon as you take customers your instructors should try to sell the boats. This will immediately help to alleviate cash flow problems. In an ideal world all of the equipment should be sold off at the end of the season if it is not going to be used through the winter.
7. The aim is to 'winter' carrying as little capital as possible. The customer in return has the advantage that they are always using relatively new equipment, the boat builder gets bulk orders.

This example is, perhaps, a little simplistic because it is unlikely that all of the equipment could be sold and then repurchased at the correct time – deadlines and pressure may be obtained from suppliers who might see this activity as reducing their potential margins to new customers. However, the basic concept outlined here is practised by many sailing schools to help alleviate the problems created by short seasons.

There are some costs that cannot be economized, they are the costs of providing safety for staff, customers and third parties. However, safety costs can be managed. Different boats for different applications need different safety equipment. If, for example, a Ridged Inflatable Boat is taken for illustration the safety equipment that it needs to operate 100 yards from the beach may be totally different from when it is operating ten miles off shore from the same beach. Customer needs in terms of training should be carefully evaluated against operational safety requirements that have been drawn up with different safety equipment in mind. Moving customers away from the home base may have a cost in terms of fuel and safety devices. If there is a training need for this then provision must be made, however, it may be more financially viable to operate close to the home base or even use shore-based simulation. Fuel bills in small sailing schools can be very large, particularly if petrol-driven outboard boats are being used.

8.14 CONCLUSION

To summarize and conclude this chapter the following section reviews the main facilities and services that the Royal Yachting Association inspects before awarding recognition of firstly a powerboat/dinghy establishment and secondly a yachting establishment. These requirements represent a guide of good practice and it is critical that anyone considering establishing a water sport operation should consult the national governing body for the sport before commencing activity.

Principal
- Name and qualifications of chief instructor

Supervision and administration
- Accuracy of brochures
- Course programmes adhering to syllabi
- Correct balance between theory and practice
- Standard of supervision

Operating area/facilities
- Nature of venue
- Grade of water
- Suitability of sailing water
- Are instructors aware of local hazards?
- Designation of operating areas
- Launching facilities
- Do beginners have to be towed to the sailing area/towing arrangements?
- Running time to the nearest telephone
- Walking time from the slipway to the nearest WC

Shore-based facilities
- Is suitable main first-aid kit provided and location indicated?
- Is dry teaching area suitable?
- Are visual aids available?
- Are female/male changing areas suitable?

- Are showers available?
- Is hot water/soap available?

Instructional staff

- Details and qualifications of all instructional staff
- Standard of teaching observed

Dinghies and keelboats

- Normal teaching ratios for RYA beginners' courses
- Junior boats available
- Are boats seaworthy?
- Can sails be reefed?
- Are boats suitably equipped for area?
- Number of dinghies tested for buoyancy during inspection
- List of all boats used

Safety boats and equipment

- Is personal buoyancy provided in good condition for all students?
- Make and model
- Are safety boats suitable for the area of operation?
- Are engines adequately fixed to boats?
- Does each boat have an alternative means of propulsion, anchor and warp, towing warps, basic first-aid kit, kill cord?
- Is VHF used?
- Do staff have VHF licences?
- List of safety boats used
- Comments on boats seen driven

Powerboat recognition

- Name of powerboat instructor
- Are boats suitable for instruction?
- Are boats fitted with kill cords?
- List of boats used

Conclusion and recommendation

- Inspector's Report
- Statement by School Principal

REFERENCES

Royal Yachting Association publications
(These publications are reviewed every four to five years. The number after the booklet code represents the last date of revision, i.e. 93 equates to the year 1993.)
G4/93 Dinghy Logbook

G14/93 Dinghy Instructor Handbook
G16/90 Safety Boat Handbook
G19/90 Powerboat Instructor Handbook
G20/90 Powerboat Logbook
W3/93 Windsurfing Logbook
W33/90 Windsurfing Instructor Manual
G15/93 Cruising Logbook
G18/93 Motor Cruising Logbook

Marinas and Yachting 9

9.1 INTRODUCTION

The origins of yachting have been well documented in an earlier chapter but what has yet to be discussed is the infrastructure that is required to service those yachts. While it is recognized that there are many different organizations that service yachts, for the sake of clarity, this chapter will analyse only marinas and yacht harbours. The basic criteria for managing yachts in marinas however, is transferable to rivers, estuaries and boatyards.

Marina development in the UK took off in the mid 1970s culminating in a frenzy of activity in the late 1980s. However, the origins of this form of leisure development go back to the turn of the century when some very large yacht yards such as Camper and Nicholson at Southampton were established to service the very large racing yachts in fashion from the late Victorian era. Since then, as the nature of yachting and watersports has changed, so the requirements for boat yards and moorings has changed. This change has been very rapid with the advent of the plastic boat and transformation of keel shapes.

9.2 HISTORICAL DEVELOPMENT

The history of marina development has passed through seven distinct phases:

1. the development of tidal estuaries;
2. the development of existing boat yards;
3. the introduction of civil engineering;
4. the renaissance;
5. the boom;
6. the collapse;
7. stabilization.

Coastal Recreation Management Edited by Tim Goodhead and David Johnson. Published in 1996 by E & FN Spon, London. ISBN 0 419 20360 5

This historical development is reviewed briefly below.

9.2.1 THE DEVELOPMENT OF TIDAL ESTUARIES

Yachts constructed up until approximately 1960 were predominantly made of wood. Estuaries and creeks were ideal for mooring and maintaining these vessels, as wooden boats deteriorate badly if they dry out. The mud berths used in these estuaries kept these wooden hulls moist through the winter months but protected them from the worst of the British winters. Yacht maintenance during this period went hand in hand with the maintenance of fishing boats and other small craft with a multitude of small craft being maintained at yards throughout the country. During this period, racing and cruising yachts were usually left on swinging moorings during the summer months and either brought ashore in the winter or moth-balled in the mud. After the Second World War rapid advances in technology using laminated wood baked in an autoclave or the more modest plywood opened up the sport of yachting to the masses in the form of dinghy sailing. These boats required dry storage and had a requirement for areas of dry land. With the advent of this form of low-cost sailing a multitude of sailing clubs were established linked normally to the friendly services of local boatbuilders or repair yards.

9.2.2 THE DEVELOPMENT OF EXISTING BOATYARDS

As the sport of sailing grew then the demands on the local boat yards grew as well. Swinging moorings were often replaced by pile moorings in the proximity of a boat yard and long wooden piers constructed to give access. Fairly rapidly during the 1960s the pile moorings were linked with pontoons and the birth of the modern marina was witnessed. Rapidly the natural sites in the south of England were developed, particularly in the Solent area. The River Hamble perhaps witnessed the most rapid development with marinas being established from the mouth of the river to Moody's yard on the upper tidal reaches. All of these marinas were relatively easy to construct as they simply required piling into soft mud.

9.2.3 THE INTRODUCTION OF CIVIL ENGINEERING

During the 1970s with many of the prime sites already having been developed and the leisure boating and sailing industry growing rapidly, marina development became more ambitious. Major civil engineering work created retaining walls and in some cases locked harbours were built. The most ambitious of these projects was the marina development at Brighton. Built directly into the English Channel it cost approximately £65 million to construct. Supported by the Town Council on tourism grounds and financed by a pension fund and banks, it was the most ambitious project in the country at that time. Two years after construction it ran into serious financial difficulty and was sold on to Brent Walker for a repudiated £17 million. An area within the marina was again sold on to the Gateway Supermarket chain resulting in the new marina operators being able to service a much lower capital debt. This financial disaster left many investors and financiers feeling very reluctant to support marina development. There were some notable exceptions such as the development of St Katherine's Dock in London, one of the first comprehensive projects to regenerate an area of redundant dockland.

9.2.4 THE RENAISSANCE

Following a relatively slow period of development in the 1970s, the beginning of the 1980s saw tremendous activity. This was initiated by the activities of a south coast company known as Dean and Dyball. This company had observed integrated residential housing developments and marinas on the South Coast of France such as Grande Motte/Port Grimaud and attempted to emulate them on the south coast of England. Their development at Hythe on Southampton Water was spectacularly successful. They carefully phased the development building and released houses as they found customers, much of their promotional activity relating to models and brochures. During the construction phase there was a very high rate of inflation in the values of residential property. Purchasers of waterside property saw their values rise very rapidly, giving very satisfying capital gains on their investment. At the same time historic docks at Liverpool, the Albert Docks of Jessie Hartley design, were being refurbished as part of urban regeneration programmes adding to the image of waterside property as being an up market place to live, particularly if one's boat could be 'moored at the bottom of the garden' as well.

9.2.5 THE BOOM

The mid 1980s saw a tremendous boom in mixed waterside development. It also saw the opening up of many areas of redundant dockland as privatized port authorities began to realize the potential development value of their land, e.g. Southampton, Swansea Marina Village and Penarth. The construction of residential houses effectively paid for the civil engineering of the marina, considerably reducing the payback period for capital employed. Marinas such as Port Solent in Portsmouth Harbour took this mixed development to the extreme with yachting, residential housing, shops, offices, light engineering, pubs and restaurants all rubbing shoulders with one another; all enhancing each other's business and property values. At Southampton a different approach was taken at Ocean Village where the marina development was the focus for a major tourist speciality shopping arcade. Shamrock Quay, Southampton saw the transformation of the old Camper and Nicholson Yard, it retained a working boatyard and developed a mixed use scheme with a marina, sail loft, speciality shops, pub, restaurant and small office units.

During this period the traditional boat park form of marina saw a transformation of boats and yachts virtually all being constructed of glass reinforced plastic. These boats need to be hoisted out of marinas by mobile gantries for the winter months. In some cases racing boats are even hoisted ashore between races. Around these marinas developed a small boat industrial hinterland of manufacturers and servicing agents. In some areas the provision of marinas replaced traditional port functions such as Portmadoc (old slate port N Wales) and Amble (old coal port NE England).

9.2.6 THE COLLAPSE

The late 1980s saw another collapse in confidence in the potential for developing marinas together with the collapse of some of the key players such as the Brent Walker group. The general collapse of the property boom in the UK was mainly to blame. To cure the cash flow problems involved in providing the civil engineering works needed to create modern marinas, residential development had been used to great effect. With the collapse in UK housing values at the end of the 1980s many schemes ran into serious financial difficulties. In an attempt to ease cash flow problems some very inventive financial packages were offered. Perhaps the most common was the offer of a long-term lease on berths of up to 25 years for a one-off cash payment.

Rents for berths dramatically increased at this time, leaving many marina customers feeling that they were the victims of the collapse in property values. During this period a marina company Marina Developments Plc (MD) consolidated its holdings, taking over many marinas in the Solent and elsewhere. It received severe criticism in the yachting press over alleged monopoly powers although this was never effectively proven. The Office of Fair Trading found little scope for proceeding under the monopoly provisions of the Fair Trading Act of 1973. The argument in reply was that in certain regions this company owned 80% of the berths. MD claimed that increases in fees were necessary to invest in upgrading the quality and facilities of the marinas. Following this intense criticism which overlapped on to the Royal Yachting Association a number of working groups were established. This debate was further complicated when the Crown Estate Commissioners, managing agents of approximately 75% of the intertidal land in England, started to increase its rents. As a result some owners moved their boats to the north coast of France. Despite the ferry crossing this was still cheaper than mooring on the south coast of England.

9.2.7 STABILIZATION

The early 1990s has seen yachtsmen and boat-owners applying pressure on marina operators for better services and more realistic fees. Much of this pressure has been focused through the editorial pages of a well-known yachting magazine. The Royal Yachting Association has responded by creating a forum to consider the needs of the boat-owner and marina berth availability. There is evidence that boat owners are continuing to vote with their feet and move their boats abroad or to cheaper locations. Certainly at the time of writing marina fees seem to be static or falling. Chichester Harbour Conservancy has recently reduced its mooring charges for small craft. The quality of service being offered in marinas appears to be improving as a result of operators having to compete for custom. In the marinas themselves there is evidence of boat-owners leaving their boats in the water all season to avoid laying up charges (made possible in part by the development of epoxy coatings). Further details of the development of marinas can be obtained from the National Yacht Harbour Association which is the trade association for marina operators.

9.3 REGIONAL IMPACT

9.3.1 DEVELOPMENT

Permitted development in the UK has followed a chequered history. In many cases marinas have not complied with development plans and a great deal of justification has had to be provided by developers and operators so that other material considerations could be taken into account in order to obtain planning permission. This has included:

1. the aesthetics;
2. the operation in practice;
3. density and height of buildings;
4. scale of development;
5. impact on service infrastructure;
6. traffic generation;
7. car parking provision;
8. impact on the environment.

The modern marina may be a compromise between recreational demand and local policy. However, detailed policy guidelines give the operator substantial guidance in terms of site development. Significant site design features to be considered are:

1. elevations;
2. scale;
3. massing;
4. proportion;
5. layout;
6. materials and colours;
7. landscaping and seascaping;
8. access, roads and footpaths.

Local highway authorities will also impose specific design standards such as:

1. design widths of roads;
2. sight lines;
3. traffic levels;
4. junction design;
5. turning circles;
6. parking spaces;
7. provision of footpaths;
8. service areas;
9. access for emergency vehicles.

As well as the regional and local impact, the local infrastructure must be able to support the marina in terms of services. These might include:

1. water;
2. foul and surface drainage;
3. sewage and waste disposal;

4. refuse disposal;
5. gas;
6. electricity;
7. telecommunications;
8. community facilities;
9. public transport;
10. roads and footpaths.

Planning matters have been dealt with in earlier chapters but it must be recognized that the marina that is finally constructed may have been designed by a committee and may not be exactly what the operator had in mind as a product to meet a demand.

9.3.2 ENVIRONMENTAL IMPACT ANALYSIS (EIA)

Marinas are listed as Schedule 2 developments in the Town and County Planning Environmental Impact Assessment Regulations 1988. The EIA process is detailed in other texts (Glasson, J. *et al.*, 1994) but the following are recognized as key impacts of marinas, which would need to be 'scoped' for any new development and their significance assessed.

1. noise;
2. pollution;
3. traffic;
4. danger;
5. nuisance;
6. hours of operation;
7. loss of privacy;
8. overlooking;
9. overshadowing;
10. visual intrusion;
11. loss of visual quality;
12. loss of amenities;
13. loss of habitats;
14. reclamation;
15. dredging of estuaries;
16. erosion/sedimentation of estuary/coastline.

9.3.3 ECONOMIC IMPACT

The Keynesian Multiplier effect was designed for use on a national level looking at the results of changes in injections or withdrawals into the economy. Since these theories were developed by Keynes in the 1930s economists have applied this technique to compare the interaction of regional economies. These studies are commonly known as impact studies because they attempt to measure the economic impact of changes in investment and expenditure on one particular region's income and employment. They have been used in tourism research but this application of the technique has been hindered by different assumptions and definitions making comparison of research difficult (Archer, 1977).

Multiplier analysis has been adapted over the years for a number of research applications. In terms of the context of marinas the research that has been conducted into tourism together with sport and recreation is the most relevant. However, many of these studies do not calculate the multipliers but 'borrow' them from other studies, making the analysis of this research complex.

Multiplier analysis explains how over time an increase or decrease in expenditure in an economy eventually affects the level of expenditure, income and employment. Methods of assessing changes in expenditure and the resultant changes in the level of a regional economy's expenditure, income and employment vary considerably.

Using a marina as a model, the multiplier can be seen to operate in the following way when assessing the impact of tourist expenditure within the boundaries of a local authority. An increase or decrease in expenditure by marina customers will create the following effects on a regional economy.

1. Direct income – organizations directly serving the marina will be affected by the change in expenditure.
2. Indirect income – firms supplying the organizations directly supplying the marina customers will be affected by the change in expenditure.
3. Induced income – the changes in income caused by the direct and indirect effect will cause further changes in expenditure and hence employment.

These changes can be expressed as a tourist income multiplier which is a coefficient expressing the amount of income generated in an area by an additional unit of tourist spending. Expenditure outside of the economy will decrease these effects. Any expenditure outside of the economy is known as a leakage, such as savings, imports or taxes, because of these leakages, the multiplier will eventually become zero.

Using the basic principles of National Income calculations, multipliers can be expressed in relation to sales, output, income or employment. Thus a grid of possible multiplier types and multiplier value indicators can be constructed, from a marina manager's viewpoint. Modern marina development is often supported on the basis of these multipliers but it is critical that these are also viewed in the context of environmental impact.

9.4 DESIGN

The installation of finger pontoons in marinas has become almost universal. Companies such as Walcon can supply and erect modular systems extremely rapidly. An example of this is the pontoon system at Southampton International Boat Show which is erected and dismantled on an annual basis. What is not so straightforward is the retaining or bund walling around the marina. This will be a function of wave height and extensive hydraulics research must be undertaken before construction. Every marina location is different and has different strengths and weaknesses. As has been stated, many of the sites with natural advantages in terms of construction have already been developed. Marinas can be categorized by their physical characteristics as follows:

1.   natural rivers;
2.   dredged areas of rivers or harbours;
3.   converted docks;
4.   bund walled marinas;
5.   bund walled marinas with a sill;
6.   bund walled marinas with a lock.

9.4.1 HYDRAULICS RESEARCH

Critical to the design of a marina is an analysis of tidal conditions and the impact of waves. Using modern technology problems created by tidal conditions can be overcome with the installation of locks and sills together with the appropriate dredging. What is far harder to overcome is the destructive nature of waves on man-made structures and extensive research needs to be conducted before development into offshore and inshore waves. This should include beach dynamics and offshore transport of sediment and shingle. The development of a marina may well change the physical environment many miles from its site by severely modifying the natural sediment pattern. Also the implications of predictions of global warming and sea level rises must be taken into account.

9.4.2 DETAILED DESIGN

The design of a marina will be very much a function of the objectives set by the developers. A large-scale commercial multi-use development will obviously have very different objectives to those set for a private members sailing club marina. Having said that, the old estate agent's saying 'that there are only three import factors when developing property; location, location and location' seems very appropriate. Access from the land and sea is critical. Before undertaking any development a detailed marketing strategy needs to be considered. During the 1980s there appeared to be an almost insatiable demand for marina berths. In reality this was only in certain locations of the UK and primarily on the River Hamble and at Lymington. Areas such as Chichester Harbour, while having long waiting lists for deep water mooring, had a number of half tide moorings to let throughout this period.

The key features that might be considered in the design of a marina can be seen in Figure 9.1. This list of features will obviously not apply to all marinas but all should be considered at the design stage. It is critical that marina operators should consider the customer's total leisure experience when operating a marina from departure from home, while on the site, the return journey and even the customer's possible recollection of the trip. Quality of service is critical when operating marinas including the safety of clients and protection of the marine environment.

9.4.3 LOCATION

The location of the marina should be considered both from the land access and with regard to the accessibility by sea of other marina venues. Accessibility to other harbours and safe havens is critical. The bulk of marina customers travel very short distances in their boats and so marinas in areas such as the Solent with many harbours within easy reach together with a large number of racing circuits are extremely attractive.

9.4.4 ESSENTIAL SERVICES

Boat-parking and car-parking facilities are obviously the most essential service that a marina can provide with, preferably, 24-hour access to the sea. The Solent has natural advantages due to its unique tidal conditions. These can be created artificially, for example the barrage scheme for Swansea Maritime Village, but may prove extremely expensive. The design of the marina must make for a safe approach to the facility at all states of the tide and in all weather conditions. The more that this is compromised the lower the rent that can be charged for marina services. A modern boat needs to be fed and watered rather like a horse and so the marina must be able to provide water, electricity, and access to fuel as a bare minimum. These services can all be provided on the pontoons. As a guide the depth of a marina should be at least 2.2 metres with access and certain berths being at a depth of 3 metres. Boats need to be maintained during the off season and so hardstanding and lift-out facilities must be provided. Toilets are perhaps the last essential service! Very few UK yachts have holding tanks and to use the yachts heads while in a marina is both extremely anti-social and environmentally damaging.

9.4.5 OTHER MARINE AND HOSPITALITY SERVICES

Further services provided by the marina will be a function of client demand and the nature of the surrounding region. The larger marinas act as honeypots for sailing activity creating a sizeable economic impact. It is important to try to develop a mixed economy within a marina so that one enterprise adds value to another. Services such as brokerage can be linked through chains of marinas to provide a substantially enhanced service. The exact mix of facilities will vary from area to area, but central to it will be the provision of hospitality facilities. As a nation, our three largest leisure pursuits by expenditure are drinking alcohol, eating out and gambling. Other leisure pursuits pale into relative insignificance in terms of expenditure. With this in mind the provision of a bar, catering facilities and a restaurant may be fairly central to an operator's provision of facilities. In themselves they may generate a financial surplus but they also generate a secondary effect of creating a social nucleus to the marina, encouraging people to spend more time on the site and hopefully consuming more services. There is however a business risk to be evaluated. Empty units and lack of custom during the winter will have a knock-on effect on the marina as a whole.

9.4.6 RESIDENTIAL DEVELOPMENT

In the 1980s developers considered housing development was essential for any marina scheme to be viable. The success of developing residential housing within a marina now will be very much a function of the current property markets. A cynic might view the modern-day marina as a vehicle to enable residential properties to be constructed on waterside sites under the guise of sport and recreation. For some developments in the 1980s this may have been true but a modern-day developer will have a hard battle justifying this form of development to the planners. Current strategic policy for the Solent, for example, is to resist strongly any further marina development (Hampshire County Council, 1991). In developing housing schemes in marinas the location in terms of air, road and rail links is critical but so also is the general ambience of the development. Research must be undertaken into, regional economic growth, regional household size, local housing supply, population growth, development planning policies, non-statutory briefs and management plans before even considering this form of development. Each marina typically has a different balance of second homes and housing for local people.

Location	Hot water
Accessibility from land	Landscaping
Accessibility from the sea	Lifting bridge
Safety	Office parks
	Post box
Essential services	Racing facilities
Car parking	Rigging service
First aid	Rubbish disposal
Fuel	Sail repairs
Hardstanding	Sailing school
Liftout facilities	Sailing area
Security	Scrubbing grid
Telephones	Sewage pump out
Toilets	Showers/laundry
Walkways	Slipway
Water and electricity	Travel hoist 30 ton
Water depth 2.2 m	Trolleys
	VHF watch
Other marine services	Visitors and waiting pontoon
Boat repairs	Waste oil disposal
Boat park	Workshop
Electronic repair	
Engine repairs	*Hospitality services*
Entry control	Club house
Brokerage	Groceries
Calor gas	Hotels
Chandlery	Hire
Charter	Restaurants
Cradles	Self drive
Customs	

Figure 9.1 Key points for consideration in the design of marinas

9.4.7 GENERAL LEISURE

Recent developments at marinas such as Port Solent and Ocean Village, which have both introduced cinema facilities, would have been unheard of 20 years ago. Marina development must consider the local provision for leisure facilities as well as being part of the regional recreational provision. This will be to the benefit of the marina operator and the regional community. Marinas are becoming more adventurous in terms of their provision of general facilities. Recent developments have incorporated one or more of the following: an arts centre, cinema, health suite, heritage museum, ice skating, sports centre, tennis/squash, theatre or water park.

9.4.8 FEE INCOME

The income from a traditional marina can be obtained from a wide variety of sources. The major sources are outlined below:

Berths	Hoist
permanent short term visitors	haulage high pressure wash down storage
Boat park	Retail
storage racking slipway	brokerage chandlery restaurants bars groceries fuel
Service	Commercial docking
maintenance construction electronics service engineering survey hire	

9.5 OPERATIONAL REQUIREMENTS

9.5.1 LIFT OUT

Once the layout of the marina has been planned in terms of access and pontoon structure the next major consideration is how should yachts be lifted in and out of the water. The simplest method is to haul boats out of the water on a slipway using a tractor and trailer or boat sledge and then chocking the boat on dry land using wooden props with the use of a crane. This method is both time-consuming and in some cases extremely dangerous. Sadly there have been a number of fatalities when boats have fallen on operators or clients, either when transported or when in storage. More sophisticated operations use travel hoists and galvanized steel cradles, which is the most efficient method both in terms of time and safety. However, this comes at a cost of up to £500 000 for a sophisticated system and tends to be used only at large marina developments. The more sophisticated the lifting technique, the greater the cost to the client. There are however some hidden benefits in using travel hoists. Boats can be quickly moved away from the prime waterside sites and stored at the rear of the development enabling the water frontage to be used for hospitality services or residential purposes. The cost of a travel hoist should be viewed against the enhanced land values and business operations.

9.5.2 SERVICES

The modern yacht requires electricity, sewage disposal and fresh water when in harbour. Whether these services are plumbed in to the yacht when on the quayside or simply services provided on the hardstanding will vary according to the customer's ability to pay and the type of yacht. Water and electricity are extremely dangerous when mixed and this can be overcome in a number of ways. Firstly by providing low-voltage electricity. Secondly by installing residual circuit breakers and finally by providing independent generators. Whatever the solution it is the responsibility of the operator to provide reasonable care when dealing with these services. Sewage disposal from yachts is relatively straightforward at present in the UK. Offshore yachts discharge directly into the sea and in marinas and estuaries yachtsmen and women should use the shore facilities. If it was possible to predict EC legislation it is likely that in the future yachts will have to use holding tanks.

9.5.3 TOILETS

The operation of toilet and shower blocks can present a nightmare for any recreational manager, marina operators are no exception. The main problems are those of hygiene and vandalism. The cost of servicing these blocks must be thought through together with a charging and access policy. The control of a toilet block gives great control over the customer and many marinas only issue keys to customers who have paid or booked in to the marina. Since most yachtsmen need to use these facilities this is a very effective weapon for extracting marina dues.

9.5.4 CARS

Cars need to be strictly controlled in a marina complex. They can destroy the ambience and create security/safety problems. A car catching a boat prop can cause a catastrophe – potentially toppling any number of boats rather like dominoes. Most customers will also require a facility to move equipment from the car to the boat. The use of cars should be zoned and trolleys provided for transportation. The trolley itself can create a safety hazard and customers should not on any account allow children to ride in them.

9.5.5 COLLECTING REVENUE

Accounts are normally invoiced in advance in a marina based on the customer's anticipated needs at the start of every season, together with a contract for berthing. A mechanism must be provided for monitoring actual expenditure together with an invoicing system. There are a number of computer programs that have been devised for the management of marina administration which can now be bought 'off the peg'. A computer database is perhaps the minimum that should be provided. Bad debts to a marina can be overcome by retaining possession of the yachts until bills have been paid. This can create problems with some owners simply abandoning craft – a phenomenon that any one who has managed a dinghy pen will understand. This leads to the complex problem of disposing of a craft that is not owned by the operator.

9.6 YACHT TECHNOLOGY

9.6.1 VHF

Communication between yachts is normally undertaken through VHF radio but cellphone also has its uses. Most marinas keep a VHF watch on a specific channel while also maintaining a listening watch on Channel 16 which is used for communication distress calls as well as other important radio traffic. For the marina operator this may be costly to install but it does give the capability of knowing in advance who is about to enter the marina. Both the operator and the yacht must have a licence.

9.6.2 ENGINES, MASTS, SAILS, CHANDLERY

The Royal Yachting Association organize short courses for the maintenance of diesel engines. Since the engine on a yacht might be regarded as a safety device it is critical that yacht owners understand them. However, there are so many varieties and makes of marine engines that most yachtsmen rely on qualified engineers to service their equipment. In the same way with masts, sails and yacht fittings there is some self-help among yachtsmen ranging from books to courses but the majority of breakage and damage is repaired by professionals both in and out of marinas. Yachtsmen mainly concern themselves with winter maintenance and routine servicing. The marina operator must develop a charging scheme for professional tradesmen, whether it is by sole franchise or by a fee for operating on the site.

9.6.3 GRP/EPOXY ANTIFOULING

At first sight modern yachts may look as if they have all been constructed in the same fashion, but the reality is very different. The modern plastic yacht may have been constructed from glass-reinforced plastic or high-tech epoxy composites or a variety of other materials. These materials need very different conditions for repair but the two most important are temperature and humidity control. When first developed the modern yacht was thought to require little maintenance, but this has not proved the case. Plastic yachts require epoxy or paint coatings to protect them from marine life and osmosis. Whether these are applied at the construction stage or ten years into the life of a yacht is very much the owner's decision. To protect against marine life a yacht is normally antifouled once a year although dry sailing or copper coating are alternatives. The construction of a modern yacht introduces many hazardous chemicals into the marina environment not to mention repair sheds and great care must be taken to conform to the relevant health and safety legislation.

ELECTRONICS AND SAFETY DEVICES

In the last ten years the pace of electronic development has been bewildering. The modern yacht uses electronic navigation systems that only a few years previously would only have been found on US nuclear submarines. As the cost of this electronic technology has fallen a whole new service industry has been created around the modern marina in terms of selling and servicing safety and navigational devices. Should he/she wish the modern yacht owner could spend as much on electronics as they did purchasing the yacht in the first place. For the marina operator this is a new and lucrative service market.

9.7 MARINA ACCESS

The marina operator can contribute a great deal to the security of clients and their yachts by considering access to the facility. The following design criteria should be considered in the design of all marinas. Implementation will be a function of location, the value of the yachts in the marina and the geography of the site. High-value yachts may have owners who are prepared to pay for high-technology security systems negating perhaps some of the operators responsibility but it is unlikely that they will be adopted by owners of low value yachts and equipment. Listed below is a series of bullet points that should be considered by the developer or manager of any marina both at the design and operational stages in order to ease security problems and provide as much access for the marina visitors and boat owners alike.

9.7.1 DESIGN

Marinas should be designed with specific security and access zones incorporated from the outset. The type of restriction to access will be a function of the mix of facilities within the marina.

The marina operator should consider the following.

- Bridgehead security points fixed on to the pontoons designed in sympathy with the aesthetics of the marina.
- Sightlines from the central harbour office so that vigilance can be maintained by harbour officers, together with a design that minimizes blind spots.
- Where blind spots exist CCTV should monitor them.
- In a conventional marina a control point at the entrance to the marina should be manned by security personnel or swipe card machines. In the case of a marina with tourism implications a more discreet form of monitoring should be introduced. There is a very difficult balance to be struck between assuring security and putting off visitors and customers.
- Tourists/visitors should be managed in terms of footpaths and signposts so they have a view of the yachts but no access to the pontoons and areas where high-value equipment is kept. An effective visitor flow can also increase visitor spending.
- Illumination and lighting is critical for safety access and security reasons.

- Lock-up facilities for movable electronics/equipment should be provided.
- A bottleneck to control the exit should be constructed, thus enabling the monitoring of visiting workmen/vehicles perhaps with random checks. Vehicle movement should be restricted and it is perhaps the control of vehicles that is the key to visitor management in a marina.

9.7.2 INTELLIGENCE

- Links should be developed with local business groups to promote crime awareness.
- The development of good relations with police marine units and crime prevention officers who will offer local knowledge is essential. Police and marina operators need to operate as partners.
- All criminal events should be logged to define the weak spots and build up a portfolio of evidence for the factor.

9.7.3 OBSERVATION

- Self-help groups should be encouraged within the marina, boat-owners should be encouraged to take collective responsibility. The marina manager needs to establish a neighbourhood watch type of scheme, in partnership with the boat-owners.
- Collaboration with neighbouring sites to give a collective fight against crime and to define the standards of access to marinas may pay long-term dividends. Over reaction in terms of providing security and restricting access may put off existing customers.

9.7.4 ALARMS

- Marina operators need to establish a VHF base station for alarms and provide a monitoring service for the system chosen. This should include a response to alarms going off.
- Mobile patrols over a site add a surprise element and as such timing should be erratic, these patrols could simply be the marina manager making daily inspections of the site at different times.

9.7.5 PROSECUTION

- Thieves and vandals must be prosecuted no matter how small an offence to send a message to the criminal that it is unwise to visit the marina.

9.7.6 SECURITY COMPOUNDS

- Winter compounds need to be fenced and patrolled. This is perhaps the biggest problem for the marina manager. Fences are extremely unsightly.
- Strong points must be provided on the hardstanding for padlocking equipment these have the advantage that they aid security but are not unsightly.

9.7.7 INSURANCE

- A package of cheap premiums could be negotiated with a specific broker for both the boat-owners and the operator as an all encompassing package for mutual benefit.

Deciding on how much access to allow to a marina is an extremely difficult problem. On the one hand perimeter fences and dog patrols keep boats safe from criminal activity, but on the other hand it totally destroys the ambience of the marina. If this ambience is destroyed it is then extremely difficult to use the marina as a tourist feature generating many small businesses. Zoning of the marina has to be considered from the design stage. Physical barriers are not the solution to crime a much more subtle approach to visitor management must be considered (for more detail see Goodhead and Kasic, 1995).

9.8 CONCLUSION

Marina development has developed rapidly since the Second World War. From early beginnings of small rivers marinas can now represent very large tourist facilities involving hundreds of millions of pounds of investment. The future success of these developments will be a function of mooring demand and how they have been linked into the economy of the local community. It is likely that developments will continue but at a somewhat slower pace than of recent years. Robin Knox-Johnson in his opening address to Marina 95 summed up by emphasizing that 'it is not the moorings we should be selling but the whole rich ambience of yachting and matters maritime' (Knox-Johnson, 1995). For the future attending to customer care will be critical if a marina is to be successful.

REFERENCES

Archer, B. (1977) *Tourism Multipliers the State of the Art*, Bangor Occasional Papers in Economics No. 11, Cardiff University of Wales Press.

Blain, W. R. and Webber, N. B. (1989) *Marinas: Planning and feasibility. Design and Operation*, Computational Mechanics Publications, Southampton.

Glasson, J., Therivel, R. and Chadwick, A. (1994) *Introduction to Environmental Impact Assessment*, UCL Press, London.

Goodhead, T. and Kasic, N. (1995) The considerations of maritime crime in the planning, design and operations of a marina. In W. Blain (ed.), *Marina III Planning, Design and Operation*, Computational Mechanics Publications, Southampton, 73–9.

Hampshire County Council (1991) *A Strategy for Hampshire's Coast*, County Planning Department.

Knox-Johnson, R.(1995) *Marina 95: Opening Address*, St Raphael, France, Wessex Institute of Technology.

RYA (1994) *Marina Guide*, Royal Yachting Association.

RYA (1993) *Buying a Secondhand Yacht – the Legal Aspects*, Royal Yachting Association.

RYA (1994) *Cruising Yacht Safety*, Royal Yachting Association.

Commercial Harbour Operations and Recreation

10

10.1 INTRODUCTION

There are in excess of 400 ports and harbours along the coastline of the United Kingdom which range in size from complex dock areas to small fishing harbours. These ports often have a very long commercial history, but some have been developed relatively recently due to changing and developing trades. Being an island-trading nation, the UK is highly dependent on its commercial ports, but in many of these ports and harbours, the commercial operations have to carry on alongside recreational activities. Many of the most popular areas for marine recreation are in some of the busiest commercial waters in the vicinity of the country's most important ports. Examples of these are the Solent with the ports of Southampton and Portsmouth together with other locations such as the Thames, the Medway, Harwich and Plymouth along with their many surrounding creeks and rivers. Yachtsmen, power craft users and other water enthusiasts are free to use these waters, but it is important that they have an understanding, and give due consideration, to the problems faced by the commercial operations that are taking place in the quite often congested waters around them. The desire to live in harmony is advantageous for both parties. The aim of this chapter is to give an overview of commercial shipping and port operations along with details of the problems which exist and the precautions or management solutions that are taken to ensure safety and minimize the potential conflict that can occur between the various commercial and leisure users. The responsible authorities in harbour areas are investigated and the role of the International Regulations for Preventing Collisions at Sea, Port Bye-laws and Vessel Traffic Services are described.

Coastal Recreation Management Edited by Tim Goodhead and David Johnson. Published in 1996 by E & FN Spon, London. ISBN 0 419 20360 5

10.2 COMMERCIAL OPERATIONS

Virtually all international trade is carried by sea (some 90% in volume and 80% in value), and a considerable amount of this cargo (estimated at over 50% by the International Maritime Organisation) is classified as dangerous goods. Even though the transportation of goods by sea is the most environmentally friendly method of transport, the cost of a small error in judgement for the 'super' vessels of today is enormous. Whether it be risk from collision, fire, spills of toxic substances, grounding etc., the threat of major disasters has grown substantially as ever-increasing volumes and ranges of dangerous and noxious substances are transported by sea.

Thirty years ago commercial vessels went to sea with crews of typically 40 or more persons, whereas today, much larger vessels sail the seas with crew that number as low as 10. This reduction in manning level reflects more than a century of technical change, and these changes are far from having run their course. Ship technology is continuing to move forward (at an accelerating rate in some fields) around the world. All this has been brought about by owners and operators seeking economies of scale and to make the most efficient use of labour and new technologies in their aim to achieve cost competitiveness and maximum profits.

Modern vessels have highly automated engine rooms that no longer require watchkeepers and bridges where propulsion, navigation, cargo operations, safety and emergency systems and communication functions have been centralized. The bridge of a modern vessel has become a 'ship operation centre', with the integration of all functions necessary for running the vessel a fundamental necessity to achieve the concept of reduced manning. It could be argued that these large commercial vessels, with such low manning, are cutting the safety margins in terms of operation and safe navigation to the absolute minimum.

10.3 THE PORTS OF TODAY

The commercial operations that take place in ports and harbours are key to the economy of their country. Ports are an important interface in the transport chain as they are the principal point of arrival and departure of goods and commodities. Around 500 million tonnes of cargo is handled yearly in UK ports. The transportation of goods by sea is the most cost-effective way of transporting raw materials and the everyday items we require. In addition, people use the ports to board ferries and cruise liners for both business trips and for pleasure purposes. These commercial ports operate in a highly competitive environment, with economic pressures demanding vessels spend as short a time as possible in port, time which is measured in hours, even for the largest vessels. Commercial ports need to remain competitive to survive.

But the ports of today do not have it all their own way. The explosion in marine recreational activities has produced a conflict of interest. The continuing boom in the number of people taking to the water for recreational purposes has resulted in increasing pressure on both the water itself and accessible water frontage, especially those areas located near to large population centres which are home to the majority of marine recreational participants. These are the same areas that have been traditionally attractive to commercial operations due to their close proximity to the consumer. Indeed, the change of use of redundant dock facilities into marinas, described in Chapter 9, has brought the recreational user into the heart of the commercial scene.

The conflict of interest between recreational craft and commercial vessels leads to a requirement for a fair and safe 'share' for all such mixed-use areas. The problem for the authorities in charge of ensuring commercial vessels safely navigate the approaches to their ports or through their waterways is that the vast commercial ships of today are regularly restricted by their size to relatively narrow channels, with the manoeuvrability of these vessels, along with visibility from the bridge, being severely restricted. This has led the authorities in charge of busy waterways to operate positive management over their area of responsibility, leading to the introduction of strict rules for vessels to observe, and the creation of Traffic Separation Schemes (TSS) – literally one-way traffic lanes, and Vessel Traffic Services (VTS) which monitor vessel movements using techniques such as shore based radar to obtain a traffic image.

10.4 THE PORT/HARBOUR AUTHORITY

The definition of a harbour or port is a place for ships to shelter and where they can load and discharge their cargo. Ports in the UK are not under the administration of a single authority, but are owned and operated by a variety of bodies. Almost every port and harbour, whether in commercial or recreational use is managed under statutory powers, giving the Harbour Authority, or Competent Authority, the power to regulate the activities of users, particularly the movement and mooring of all vessels and to make local bye-laws for their area of responsibility. The statutory powers may be either embodied in a local Act of Parliament, which normally also incorporates parts of the Harbours,

Docks and Piers Clauses Act 1847, or in subordinate legislation made under the Harbours Act 1964.

The Harbour Authority, or the Competent Authority, is defined in the Harbours Act as:

> any person in whom are vested under this Act, ... powers or duties of improving, maintaining or managing a harbour. (Douglas and Geen, 1993)

The structure of the UK ports industry is complex. It is argued that it is the most diverse in the world, but generally the functions which any port authority performs are quite similar. These functions can be specified as:

- regulation of activities in the area of jurisdiction, e.g. movement and berthing of vessels, etc.;
- provision of port facilities, e.g. quays;
- conservancy functions, e.g. buoyage and lighting of the channels, dredging, etc.
- provision of a pilotage service.

10.4.1 TYPES OF HARBOUR AUTHORITY

In the last 15 years there has been a considerable change in the ownership of ports due to the privatization policy instigated by the Conservative Government. This has resulted in a complex mix of different owners and operators in the UK ports industry. During the process of privatization, the role of the Competent Authority has been included in the activities undertaken by the new port owners. This is largely against the beliefs of other European countries and international states who maintain the Harbour Authority as a function of the State, although in the UK, the Competent Authority is subject to statutory obligations. A particular port can generally be categorized as being either a part of Associated British Ports, a Company Act Company Port, a Dockyard Port, a Fishing Harbour, a Municipal Port, an Own Account Harbour, a Statutory Company Port or a Trust Port. In some areas, such as the Solent, there can be a complex mix of different types of port ownership, each with its own interests.

10.4.2 ASSOCIATED BRITISH PORTS (ABP)

ABP came into being as a result of the Transport Act of 1981, and took control of the 19 ports that remained of the 31 ports originally vested in the British Transport Docks Board under the Transport Act of 1962 (the other 12 ports had been sold or transferred to other port authorities). These in turn had been transferred from the Railway Companies to the British Transport Commission under the Transport Act of 1947. ABP is a statutory corporation, controlled by a company, Associated British Ports Holdings Plc, set up by the state under the Companies Act. This means that ABP is a wholly owned subsidiary of ABP Holdings Plc.

ABP is the country's largest single port operator, now owning 22 ports of varying sizes. The ABP ports are Southampton, Hull, Grimsby, Plymouth, Goole, Immingham, Newport, Cardiff, Barry, Port Talbot, Barrow, Swansea, Ayr, Troon, Silloth, Whitby, Fleetwood, Garston, Lowestoft, Kings Lynn, Teignmouth and Colchester. It is important to be clear that ABP are not a company, although they are a subsidiary of a company formed under the Companies Act.

10.4.3 COMPANIES ACT COMPANY PORT

As stated earlier, most of the Railway Company Ports were vested in the British Transport Docks Board in 1962 with the restructuring of the British Transport Commission, but some, mainly those with direct rail services and concerned with shortsea passenger transport, were vested in the British Railways Board, others came under the control of the British Waterways Board, for example the Canal Ports of Sharpness and Gloucester. The British Railways Board ports were managed by a subsidiary, Sealink, along with the British Rail ferries. These ports included Folkestone, Holyhead and Newhaven. Under the Transport Act of 1981, a subsidiary of Sealink, Sealink Harbours Ltd, was created under the Companies Act, to manage the ports, which was eventually sold to companies which are subsidiaries of Sea Containers Ltd. Hence, these are Companies Act 1985 Company Ports.

As a result of the Ports Act of 1991, four major Trust Ports were transferred to companies formed under the Companies Act. Those ports were the Medway Ports Authority, the Tees and Hartlepool Port Authority, Forth Port Authority and the Clyde Port Authority. In addition, Port of Tilbury London Ltd was created by transfer out of the Port of London Authorities control. Other Trust Ports which fall within the criteria set down in the 1991 Ports Act may be transferred in the future (Trust Ports are discussed later).

10.4.4 DOCKYARD PORT

These are the Naval Ports such as Plymouth and Portsmouth. Each has a Queens Harbour Master who has precedence over any commercial harbours in their area of responsibility, an example of this is Dockyard Port of Portsmouth and Portsmouth's Municipal Continental Ferry Port.

10.4.5 FISHING HARBOUR

This is a small harbour, or landing place, which is principally used by the fishing industry. This is defined in the Sea Fishery Industry Act of 1951 (in Scotland this is a Marine Works harbour).

10.4.6 MUNICIPAL PORT

A Municipal Port, or Local Authority Port, is one that is managed by the local or district council through a committee. Examples of these are the Continental Ferry Port in Portsmouth, the Port of Ramsgate and Sullom Voe in the Shetlands. If a Municipal Port makes a profit, the local authority are able to set aside money for future requirements, but if a loss is incurred the deficit has to be raised from local taxes. Examples of municipal recreation harbours are the River Hamble (managed by Hampshire County Council), Langstone Harbour and Chichester.

10.4.7 OWN ACCOUNT HARBOUR OR PORT

These are usually quays or jetties which are operated by a company under statutory powers and are utilized for the loading and discharge of goods by that company in connection with their own business. An example of an Own Account Harbour is the Port of Par in Cornwall, owned by the English China Clay Company and used for the export of china clay.

10.4.8 STATUTORY COMPANY PORT

These are ports that are owned by a statutory company, an example of a Statutory Company Port is Felixstowe (called the Felixstowe Dock and Railway Company), which was constituted by a local Act of Parliament and not under the Companies Act of 1948 or the 1985 replacement. These privately owned ports are required to operate within their relevant Acts of Parliament.

10.4.9 TRUST PORT

A Trust Port, or Port Trust, is a body created for the purpose of managing a harbour. The Trust does not have share capital, is non-profit making, is able to issue port stock and to borrow money at preferential rates. In many cases, Port Trusts were set-up to take over the administration of private ports which, due to financial problems, were unable to continue in operation. Trust Ports were created by individual Acts of Parliament which established self-governing statutory bodies to administer each port. These bodies, the Harbour Commissioners or Trustees, are entrusted with the care of the area of jurisdiction, with the responsibility to conserve, regulate and improve their area of authority. Examples of major Trust Ports are Dover, Tyne and Poole, along with Harwich Haven Authority and the Port of London Authority whose functions do not include the provision of port facilities. Trust Ports more concerned with recreation include Cowes and Great Yarmouth.

There were 114 Trust Ports in existence in 1991, but this number has decreased due to the current governments privatization philosophy. The larger Trust Ports are currently required to be privatized under the Ports Act 1991, with the threshold for privatization being set at ports with an annual turnover of £5 million or more (in 1991 prices) in any of the years 1986–91. The 15 ports that fulfil the requirements were obligated to produce privatization proposals by 1993, and although some did and were duly privatized, the Government does not appear in a hurry to enforce further sales after the 'scandal' of the privatization of the Trust Port of Medway. Medway was sold in March 1992 in a management and employee buyout for £29.7 million, at £1 a share, with the Government receiving only £13.2 million (under the terms of the enabling legislation) and most of the remainder, as laid down in the Ports Act 1991, being returned to the new owners. Twelve months later, the port was valued at £2.50 a share by KPMG Peat Marwick (an international management consultancy firm), only to be purchased six months later, in September 1993, by the Mersey Docks and Harbour Board for £104 million – £38 a share! It is expected that the government will require two more Trust Ports (Tyne and Ipswich) to privatize themselves in 1996.

10.4.10 PORTS WORLDWIDE

There is no general model for port ownership worldwide, although it is far more likely that ports will be under the control of either local or national government. In an attempt by states to attract private capital into ports, in excess of 40 countries are currently involved in port privatization in one form or another, but in almost all cases the responsibility of marine safety is being retained as a function of the state.

10.4.11 THE HARBOUR MASTER

The Harbour Authority, or Competent Authority, employs a Harbour Master to carry out their requirements derived from either the local act or national legislation. It is the responsibility of this Harbour Master, along with his authorized assistants, to ensure the safety of navigation in his area of responsibility and to carry out the earlier mentioned functions of the Port Authority. This can place the Harbour Master in a difficult position due to his employers being a commercial enterprise concerned with making money, while his responsibility is largely ensuring safety. This can result in a clash of interests, especially if there is a direct commercial conflict or benefit.

Whether or not the functions carried out by the Competent Authority should be a responsibility of the port owner is open to debate. As previously mentioned, many other countries reserve the role carried out by the Competent Authority and the Harbour Master as a responsibility of the state. In the UK it is argued that the safety/commercial conflict is not a problem because the Harbour Master is acting on behalf of the Harbour Authority and it is this authority, and hence the port owners, who are responsible for any incidents due to negligence. In addition, the role and powers of the Competent Authority are clearly defined in the port's enabling legislation. But, when you consider the commercial interests at stake and some of the cases of overzealous application of the considerable powers vested in the Harbour Master, this must be questioned.

10.5 THE MANAGEMENT OF SAFETY OF NAVIGATION IN PORTS AND HARBOURS

10.5.1 THE INTERNATIONAL REGULATIONS FOR PREVENTING COLLISIONS AT SEA

The International Regulations for Preventing Collisions at Sea, which were produced by the International Maritime Organisation (IMO), include rules concerning steering and sailing conduct, conduct of vessels in sight of one another, conduct of vessels in restricted visibility, lights and shapes to be exhibited along with sound and light signals. Rule 1a of these regulations states that:

> These rules shall apply to all vessels upon the high seas and in all waters connected therewith navigable by seagoing vessels. (IMO, 1972, amended 1983 and 1989)

All vessels and small craft (even windsurfers!) in ports and harbours fall under these collision regulations, but Rule 1b states that:

Nothing in these rules shall interfere with the operation of special rules made by an appropriate authority for roadsteads, harbours, rivers, lakes or inland waterways connected with the high seas and navigable by seagoing ships. Such rules shall conform as closely as possible to these Rules. (*ibid.*)

From this, it is evident that the collision regulations apply to vessels within the confines of a harbour and its approaches, but are also subject to additional local bye-laws made by the competent authority.

For recreational craft in harbour areas, rule 9 of the regulations is of primary importance as it concerns the behaviour of vessels in narrow channels (rules of particular importance appear in bold). The old saying that 'steam gives way to sail' is dispelled by this rule. Rule 9 states:

a) **A vessel proceeding along the course of a narrow channel or fairway shall keep as near to the outer limit of the channel or fairway which lies on her starboard side as is safe and practicable.**
b) **A vessel of less than 20 metres in length or a sailing vessel shall not impede the passage of a vessel which can safely navigate only within a narrow channel or fairway.**
c) A vessel engaged in fishing shall not impede the passage of any other vessel navigating within a channel or fairway.
d) **A vessel shall not cross a narrow channel or fairway if such crossing impedes the passage of a vessel which can safely navigate only within such channel or fairway.** The latter vessel may use the sound signal prescribed in Rule 34(d) if in doubt as to the intention of the crossing vessel.
e) (i) In a narrow channel or fairway when overtaking can take place only if the vessel to be overtaken has to take action to permit safe passing, the vessel intending to overtake shall indicate her intention by sounding the appropriate signal prescribed in Rule 34(c)(i). The vessel to be overtaken shall, if an agreement, sound the appropriate signal prescribed in Rule(c)(ii) and take steps to permit safe passing. If in doubt she may sound the signals prescribed in Rule 34(d).
(ii) This Rule does not relieve the overtaking vessel of her obligation under Rule 13.
f) A vessel nearing a bend or an area of a narrow channel or fairway where other vessels may be obscured by an intervening obstruction shall navigate with particular alertness and caution and shall sound the appropriate signal prescribed in Rule 34(e).
g) Any vessel shall, if the circumstances of the case admit, avoid anchoring in a narrow channel. (*ibid.*)

The important part of this rule is that a small vessel shall not impede the passage of a vessel confined to a narrow channel.

It is probably wise to consider rule 10 in conjunction with rule 9 as this deals with behaviour of vessels in Traffic Separation Schemes (TSS). TSS are lanes that are marked on charts and are designed to split opposing traffic flows so as to prevent head on situations arising. Although generally found in busy through traffic situations, for example the Dover Strait, they are also utilized in the approaches to busy ports, and the rule directly mentions small craft. In this case, a small vessel is obliged to try and avoid crossing the traffic lane but, if it is necessary, to do so at as near right angles as possible. Rule 10 states:

a) This Rule applies to traffic separation schemes adopted by the [International Maritime] Organisation and does not relieve any vessel of her obligation under any other rule:

b) A vessel using a traffic separation scheme shall:

 (i) proceed in the appropriate traffic lane in the general direction of traffic flow for that lane;

(ii) so far as practicable keep clear of a traffic separation line or separation zone;

(iii) normally join or leave a traffic lane at the termination of the lane, but when joining or leaving from either side shall do so at as small an angle to the general direction of traffic flow as practicable.

c) **A vessel shall so far as practicable avoid crossing traffic lanes, but if obliged to do so shall cross as nearly as practicable at right angles to the general direction of traffic flow**.

d)(i) A vessel shall not use an inshore traffic zone when she can safely use the appropriate traffic lane within the adjacent traffic separation scheme. **However, vessels of less than 20m in length, sailing vessels and vessels engaged in fishing may use the inshore traffic zone.**

(ii) Notwithstanding subparagraph (d)(i), a vessel may use an inshore traffic zone when en route to or from a port, offshore installation or structure, pilot station or any other place situated within the inshore traffic zone or to avoid immediate danger.

e) A vessel other than a crossing vessel or a vessel joining or leaving a lane shall not normally enter the separation zone or cross the separation line except:

(i) in cases of emergency to avoid immediate danger;

(ii) to engage in fishing within the separation zone.

f) A vessel navigating in areas near the terminations of traffic separation schemes shall do so with particular caution.

g) A vessel shall so far as practicable avoid anchoring in a traffic separation scheme or in areas near its terminations.

h) A vessel not using a traffic separation scheme shall avoid it by as wide a margin as is practical.

i) A vessel engaged in fishing shall not impede the passage of any vessel following a traffic lane.

j) A vessel of less than 20 metres in length or a sailing vessel shall not impede the safe passage of a power-driven vessel following a traffic lane.

k) A vessel restricted in her ability to manoeuvre when engaged in an operation for the maintenance of safety of navigation in a traffic separation scheme is exempted from complying with this Rule to the extent necessary to carry out the operation.

l) A vessel restricted in her ability to manoeuvre when engaged in an operation for the laying, servicing or picking up a submarine cable, within a traffic separation scheme, is exempted from complying with this Rule to the extent necessary to carry out the operation. (*ibid.*)

These two rules, rules 9 and 10 deal with factors directly affecting the navigation of recreational craft in harbour waters, but should not be taken in isolation from the rest of the International Regulations for Preventing Collisions at Sea. This is especially the case if a risk of collision develops. In this situation the normal steering and sailing rules apply. Particular navigational considerations for recreational users are highlighted later.

10.5.2 HARBOUR BYE-LAWS

As mentioned earlier, the international collision regulations apply to all vessels within the confines of a harbour and its approaches, but these are subject to additional local bye-laws made by the Competent Authority.

Using the powers bestowed upon the Competent Authority in the various Harbour Acts and Orders, the authority is able to form bye-laws to regulate the occurrence of any water activity, from the passage of the largest vessels down to sailing dinghies and even swimming. These bye-laws are the Harbour Authority's main instrument in the management of their port area and will of course vary depending upon local circumstances. Generally, bye-laws will include rules concerning the navigation, berthing and mooring of vessels, movement of goods and road and rail traffic, along with other general rules. These general rules will normally include sections relating to the regulation of recreational activities, for example exclusion of particular activities from areas such as channels and anchorages; areas where particular activities can take place, for example water skiing; and the governing of public events such as regattas. It is only in Dockyard Ports that the Queen's Harbour Master has the authority to refuse entry to a harbour by any vessel, commercial or recreational, with other Harbour Authorities only able to prevent vessels from entering the port area if they are in a dangerous condition or carrying dangerous cargo.

In many commercial harbours, bye-laws exist for the Harbour Authority to ultimately control the use of waters by recreational users to prevent conflict occurring between the commercial interests of a port and the recreational events happening around them. This is to ensure minimal adverse impact on the port operations and to facilitate the general smooth running of the port. Commercial operators want to avoid the situation where recreational users are unable to come and go as they please, except in very special situations. Therefore it is in the interest of both sectors to cooperate and avoid discord.

Copies of bye-laws for a particular port or harbour can be obtained from the relevant Harbour Master.

10.5.3 VESSEL TRAFFIC SERVICES

Most ports, along with busy seaways, operate a Vessel Traffic Services (VTS) system in one form or another. Basically a VTS system is utilized by a Competent Authority to monitor shipping in a certain area and operate some form of management or regulation over the vessels, although direct control does not occur. The Competent Authority is able to obtain an image of the traffic situation in their area of responsibility by using various devices such as shore-based radar stations, closed-circuit television cameras and VHF radio.

The installation of VTS systems have largely occurred since the early 1970s, with the principal expedient for their deployment being the fear of a major pollution spillage, or ship collision. VTS was, and is, seen as a major solution to the need for increased safety. Port authorities also discovered that VTS had a major role to play in the efficiency of the transport logistics chain, by operating as the centre of information exchange in the port community and linking up the different bodies involved, such as customs, pilots, berth operators and tugs.

The basics of VTS are now a mature technology and are acknowledged as having much to contribute to the safety of navigation, efficiency of traffic flow and in reducing the risk of marine pollution. This contribution to safety of navigation can be accomplished by the anticipation of avoidable situations of high risk, positively assisting those vessels involved and as the centre of information exchange between the different parties that interact with the traffic. A wide variety of VTS sophistication exists, ranging from the very simple, for example a system that just broadcasts general traffic information from a pilot office, to highly complex traffic management systems, such as that installed in the Port of Rotterdam which includes 26 radars, 8 closed-circuit television cameras and 12 VHF channels in its system.

The VTS centre will act as the coordinator of response to an incident and as such may well be equipped with an incident room from where the ports emergency plan will be brought into action. These plans have to cover a multitude of possible incidents or disasters and will generally include consideration of recreational activities.

10.5.4 THE VTS TASK

The latest generation of VTS are becoming increasingly complex systems, utilizing the ever-growing computer processing power that is becoming available and allowing expert systems to aid the VTS operators in their task of monitoring the safety of traffic and improving efficiency.

The VTS task can be summarized into three basic (external) functions. These are:

- information service,
- traffic monitoring, and
- traffic organization.

The information service may include the broadcasting of relevant information regarding the movement of traffic, visibility and tidal conditions or the intentions of vessels, as well as the exchange of information with vessels on all relevant safety matters, traffic conditions and traffic situations.

Traffic monitoring is aimed at ensuring the compliance of vessels with international, national and local requirements and regulations as well as the interpretation of the traffic situation. These rules are primarily the International Regulations for Preventing Collisions at Sea, but are supplemented by local rules, for example Traffic Separation Schemes and port bye-laws. Depending on the situation, different sensors for the acquisition of the traffic image are utilized, together with environment sensors and the necessary communications equipment.

The final function, traffic organization or 'traffic management' is concerned with the forward planning of vessel movements in order to avoid dangerous situations or congestion, and therefore provides a safe and efficient flow of traffic within the VTS area. To assist in this task, the VTS Centre will be connected to many different parties, allowing it to act as the centre of information exchange between the vessel and others involved in the immediate transport chain. VTS can be considered as an information processing system concerned with maritime traffic.

It is important to note that a VTS does not physically control the traffic by giving manoeuvring orders, it purely provides information and advice to shipping. This is where the service offered by VTS is different to that of Air Traffic Services and to the level of control in Air Traffic Control regions.

10.5.5 VESSEL TRAFFIC SERVICES AND RECREATIONAL CRAFT

Recreational craft are usually exempt from reporting to VTS Centres in the same way as commercial vessels. But, for safety purposes, it is recommended that recreational users monitor the relevant VHF channel to obtain an appreciation of commercial vessels' movements that might affect them. A VTS situated in busy waters will, in most cases, regularly transmit relevant navigational information, for example details of manoeuvres vessels are going to make and other applicable information including weather reports and tidal information. In some locations special small craft broadcasts are transmitted in which the information is specially tailored to their requirements. In the case of Southampton VTS, hourly 'Traffic Information Broadcasts' addressed to recreational craft are transmitted on VHF Channel 12 on the hour from 0600 to 2200 Fridays to Sundays inclusive and Bank Holiday Mondays from Easter to the last weekend in October. In addition, in the busy summer months from 1 June to 30 September the broadcasts are made every day of the week. The broadcast includes details of large vessel movements, approximate times for when a vessel will be transiting a designated 'Area of Concern' and any other relevant information for the safety of small vessels.

In virtually all circumstances it should be sufficient for recreational users to just monitor the relevant VHF channel, without the need for reporting to a shorebased VTS Centre. But this is where problems arise as, presently, there is no requirement for recreational craft to carry a VHF radio, and some would find it very difficult, if not impossible, to fit one. In addition, the available VHF channels already suffer from misuse and overcrowding without more users being added. This exposes the real problem of competence and legislation of recreational vessels, a contentious issue that will not be debated here.

10.6 NAVIGATIONAL CONSIDERATIONS IN THE VICINITY OF LARGE COMMERCIAL VESSELS

In the UK there is no requirement for the completion of formal training courses before recreational users take to the water, so it is up to the individual to obtain education relating to navigation skills and their responsibilities to other users. Many recreational users are aware of the various regulations in existence and the navigational problems encountered by commercial vessels when they are in the confines of a harbour or its approach, and take care in ensuring that they act safely. Unfortunately it is the few who conduct themselves in an unreasonable manner, who do not realize the danger they put themselves in, along with their crew and the commercial vessel they are hindering the passage of, who can cause problems. Current training schemes are possibly lacking in their coverage of the potential conflict between recreational and commercial users. After all, ignorance is no defence in the eyes of the law and the greater the understanding of a situation, the better safety benefit for all.

Some of the problems associated with large vessels operating in harbour areas are described below.

10.6.1 RESTRICTED ROOM TO MANOEUVRE

It is usually the case that large vessels are restricted to using a narrow channel due to their draught. In some cases these vessels may have a draught of 15 m or greater, which in confined waters severely limits their ability to manoeuvre. Small craft have far greater space in which to manoeuvre and, as stated by rule 9b of the Collision Regulations, they should not impede the passage of a vessel restricted to a narrow channel (see Figure 10.1). Vessels that are restricted in their ability to manoeuvre will display the correct visual signal, a black ball over a diamond over a ball by day and a red light over a white light over a red light by night. If a large vessel is forced to alter her course the manoeuvre will take time to occur and it is unlikely the vessel will be able to regain her original track. If a small vessel finds itself in close proximity to a large vessel, it should get clear as early and quickly as possible – a strong sense of self-preservation is a good help! It is also important to question what is considered close proximity? What is considered safe speed? The various parties involved may have very different perceptions.

Some ports, for example Portsmouth and Harwich, have a designated small craft channel which is outside the main shipping channel and is intended for recreational users. In Portsmouth's case, all craft under 20 m in length are obliged to use this channel. This was initially subject to protest as it was viewed as the removal of the right to freedom of navigation, but is now accepted and makes a valuable contribution to safety in the very narrow entrance. All craft should keep as near to the starboard side of any channel as is safe and practicable. In addition there may be recommended small vessel tracks and main channel crossing areas. It is prudent that small craft should cross a channel as near to right angles as practicable and as quickly as possible.

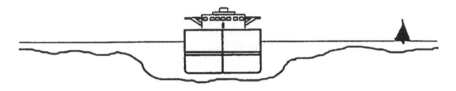

Figure 10.1 Deep draught vessels may have limited room to manoeuvre

In most of the Solent large vessels, some in excess of 100 000 tonnes DWT with draughts up to 13 m, are restricted to narrow channels and have little room to take avoiding action. The problem of their restricted manoeuvrability is exacerbated when vessels are entering or leaving Southampton Water. Here, as they approach the Guarnard buoy, off Cowes, the vessels have to execute a very exact 110° turn and once they are committed to this manoeuvre they have no room to take avoiding action without seriously jeopardizing their own safety. All vessels of over 150 m length overall undertaking this manoeuvre and transiting the narrow channel into Southampton Water, elected an 'Area of Concern', have what is called a 'Moving Prohibited Zone' designated around them. This is a zone of 1000 metres ahead and 100 metres either side of the vessel in which small craft of under 20 m length overall are prohibited from entering. This zone is designed to keep the path of a large commercial vessel clear of recreational craft which may impede its progress in a narrow channel where there is very limited room to take avoiding action.

10.6.2 RESTRICTED VISIBILITY FROM COMMERCIAL VESSELS

Some larger vessels, especially laden container vessels and empty VLCCs (very large crude carriers), have very restricted visibility ahead of them. Visibility from a large fully laden container vessel could be obscured for as far as 1000 m ahead (Figure 10.2). This should be borne in mind by recreational craft, who should avoid crossing the bows of on-coming commercial traffic.

Figure 10.2 Restricted visability

10.6.3 SPEED OF LARGE VESSELS

Large vessels often have to travel at relatively high speeds, even in confined areas, so as to maintain manoeuvrability. If the vessel has to slow down it may well lose its ability to manoeuvre and if its engines are put astern, steerage may be lost altogether. Minimum speed to maintain manoeuvrability for a modern container vessel may be in the order of 6 or 7 knots in good conditions and 10 to 12 knots in strong winds.

The speed of a large vessel can often be very deceptive. A large vessel may have a very small bow wave even at 15 knots, whereas a speed boat at this speed would be bouncing across the waves and sending spray everywhere. At 15 knots it only takes 4 minutes to cover 1 nautical mile, and at 10 knots it only takes 6 minutes, so a vessel can very quickly change from being a speck on the horizon to being on top of you.

The latest generation of fast ferries often travel at speeds in excess of 30 to 40 knots, making it very important that a careful lookout is kept astern as well as ahead, even if you are in a speed boat!

10.6.4 STOPPING DISTANCE

If the engines of a large vessel are put astern, it may take 5 minutes or longer to come to a complete stop. In this time the vessel may well have travelled in excess of half of one nautical mile. If a single screwed vessel goes astern, its bow will usually swing to starboard during this kind of manoeuvre and may cause the vessel to leave the channel.

10.6.5 VISIBILITY OF SMALL CRAFT

The recreational user may be able to see a large commercial vessel, but can the crew on her bridge see them? The sailor or motorboat user should ensure that they do everything possible to make themselves visible to others. A good quality radar reflector, correctly positioned, will enable others to see you on their radar screen, but it is important that it is an effective reflector and at a reasonable height to ensure that it is visible at sufficient range. It is no use having a poor reflector that is only visible at short range, as clutter (interference) and a large vessel's blind sectors may obliterate their image for one nautical mile, or further, from the vessel depending on conditions.

In addition, at night, navigation lights should be bright and unobstructed. Modern yachts and power craft often have these mounted high on their masts which makes them visible at a greater range, but background lights from the shore can sometimes make it difficult to identify navigation lights.

10.7 ACTION TAKEN BY THE PORT AUTHORITY TO IMPROVE SAFETY

The Competent Authority has the responsibility to regulate activities of all users within its area of jurisdiction, and this is carried out in a number of ways in relation to recreational activities.

10.7.1 HARBOUR LAUNCH

Most Harbour Authorities operate some form of launch which, among other uses, may be used to enforce the collision regulations and local bye-laws, for example speeding. The launch may also be used to escort large commercial vessels ensuring their route is kept clear of recreational craft to allow for safe transit. Southampton Port Authority operates one such launch which accompanies most large vessels that are moving in the busy recreational areas and will 'usher' recreational craft out of the path of commercial vessels.

10.7.2 PUBLICATIONS

Some commercial ports that are also popular recreational areas publish guides for recreational users, examples of these are the *Pleasure User's Guide to the Tidal Thames* published by the Port of London Authority and *The Yachtsman's Guide to Southampton Water and its Approaches* published by the Associated British Ports. These are designed to provide recreational users with enough information to enable them to operate safely and with consideration to other users, while at the same time enjoying themselves. These are sometimes reinforced by newsletters which are sent to user groups, such as berth/mooring holders. In addition a useful contribution can be local information and events diaries, published annually, which may include port information, contacts, tide tables and a programme of events for the forthcoming year with details of the organizers.

10.7.3 NOTICES TO MARINERS

These are issued by the Competent Authority to promulgate information concerning such matters as changes to navigation marks, depths or port entry regulations. To ensure that these are accessible to recreational users they are often displayed in yacht clubs, marinas and published in the press. Due to the time it takes to have new bye-laws approved by the state, the Competent Authority may use a Notice to Mariners to implement proposed bye-laws.

Before a major event in the harbour area, a Notice to Mariners will probably be published laying down the 'rules for engagement' which would have been jointly agreed between the Harbour Master and the organizers of the event. For a regatta, or an event such as the start of the Whitbread Round the World Race or powerboat racing which may attract hundreds or even thousands of competitor and spectator craft, the Notice to Mariners may include start times, restricted areas, spectator areas, speed limits, press areas and arrangements for press launches, manoeuvring areas and lanes for the competing craft along with information relating to commercial operations during the event.

10.7.4 TRANSMISSIONS ON VHF RADIO

If recreational craft are equipped with a VHF radio they should monitor the VTS working frequency, on which regular information broadcasts concerning vessels navigating in the port, weather forecasts and safety messages will be transmitted (described in sections 10.5.3–10.5.5 above on VTS).

10.7.5 ZONING OF RECREATIONAL ACTIVITIES

Some recreational activities are not particularly compatible with commercial vessels or other recreational activities. Examples of these include waterskiing, jet skis, parascending, rowing and windsurfing (particularly if the equipment is being hired out to occasional users). To cope with this problem, the Port Authority may limit certain types of activity to particular areas or zones, or totally prohibit activities from set zones. These zones can be temporarily established for a particular activity such as a regatta.

10.7.6 PRESENTATIONS BY THE HARBOUR AUTHORITY

The education of water users, in the problems of conflict and the rules, is an ongoing process. This can be achieved by a variety of means, for example the publications mentioned earlier, or lectures given to clubs and schools, articles in specialist magazines and the local press, and posters displayed near to launch sites explaining relevant points.

10.7.7 HARBOUR DUES

All the above activities, and others such as buoyage, have to be paid for and this results in harbour dues being levied, predominantly on the commercial user. This is a highly contentious issue for recreational users, but it can be argued that it is unfair for commercial activities to be forced to subsidize the recreational user and a fair and true cost of the services provided should be levied on the recreational user. This charge can be difficult to collect, so it is generally limited to vessels over a certain size and visiting craft. Car style licence discs or stickers are often used to identify those who have paid the levy.

10.8 AUTHORITIES RESPONSIBLE FOR SAFETY

The Competent Authority has the role of ensuring safety in the port environment, but other international and national organizations have the responsibility for safety at higher levels and for formulating legislation.

10.8.1 INTERNATIONAL MARITIME ORGANISATION (IMO)

The IMO is a specialized agency of the United Nations dealing with maritime affairs. It has been in existence since 1958 and is the body responsible for improving safety in maritime organizations at an international level. The subjects which the organization addresses include safety of navigation, radio-communications, search and rescue, life-saving, training and watchkeeping, carriage of dangerous goods and the prevention and control of pollution from ships. Although these subject areas predominantly effect commercial vessels, due regard has to be given to recreational craft.

10.8.2 MARINE SAFETY AGENCY (MSA)

The MSA is responsible for the implementation of the UK Government's marine safety strategy. This includes the development, promotion and enforcement of high standards of marine safety for shipping and safe navigation in UK coastal, estuarine and inland waters. Formerly the Surveyor General's Organisation, the MSA was established as an Executive Agency within the Department of Transport on 1 April 1994. The MSA manages the provision of statutory surveys and certification services for all types and classes of vessels down to small commercial motor and sailing vessels. It is also responsible for advising the government on the need for new legislation, provides the input required for the drafting of this legislation and publishes advice and instructions to the maritime community. The MSA carries out an advisory role for recreational craft safety and, with the Coastguard Agency, represents Department of Transport interests in this area at meetings of safety organizations, such as the Royal Society for the Prevention of Accidents. The MSA has also played an active part in inter-Departmental initiatives touching upon the safety of recreational craft and their users.

10.8.3 COASTGUARD

On 1 April 1994, the Marine Emergencies Organisation of the Department of Transport, which included HM Coastguard, became an Executive Agency called the Coastguard Agency, known as 'Coastguard' for short. Coastguard is responsible for marine search and rescue and counter-pollution operations in our waters. Within Coastguard, HM Coastguard has the responsibility for coordinating all civil maritime search and rescue, in the process of which it is able to call on, and coordinate, all available resources such as its own helicopters, boats and cliff rescue teams, together with the Royal National Lifeboat Institution lifeboats, the Royal Air Force and Royal Navy helicopters and other emergency services. Coastguard operates the English Channel VTS system, called the Channel Navigation Information Service (CNIS), which is mainly concerned with monitoring the traffic and broadcasting relevant safety information.

Coastguard also has the responsibility in providing safety advice for recreational users, transmitting weather forecasts on VHF radio, giving general advice and producing free literature. In addition, the agency mounts a specific safety campaign every year. In 1994, the campaign aimed at reducing incidents involving sea canoeists.

10.9 CONCLUSIONS

It may well seem that commercial and recreational activities are mutually exclusive. However, although problems do occur, in the main it can be said that with education, cooperation and careful planning, the two activities can safely take place side by side. Nevertheless, with increasing participation in maritime recreation, conflicts are inevitable. This emphasizes the need to educate recreational users in the difficulties inherent in the navigation of large vessels in confined waters and in the complexities of commercial port operations. Without this education, the management solutions implemented at international, national and local levels will only be of limited benefit in ensuring a safe and harmonious environment for the enjoyment of everyone wishing to use harbour areas.

REFERENCES

Douglas, R. P. A. and Geen, G. K. (1993) *The Law of Harbours and Pilotage*, 4th edn, Lloyd's of London Press Ltd, p. 2.
IMO (1972 amended 1983 and 1989) *The International Regulations for Preventing Collisions at Sea*, International Maritime Organisation.

BIBLIOGRAPHY

Branch, A. E. (1986) *Elements of Port Operation and Management*, Chapman & Hall.
Douglas, R. P. A. and Geen, G. K. (1993) *The Law of Harbours and Pilotage*, 4th edn, Lloyd's of London Press Ltd.
Hayman, B. (1986) *Harbour Seamanship*, Pergamon Press.
IMO (1972 amended 1983 and 1989) *The International Regulations for Preventing Collisions at Sea*, International Maritime Organisation.
IMO (1992) *IMO – What it is, What it does, How it works*, International Maritime Organisation.
Nettle, S. (1988) *Port Operations and Shipping*, Lloyd's of London Press.
NI (1988) *The Work of the Harbour Master and Related Port Management Functions*, Nautical Institute.
Phelan, A. (1970) *The Law for Small Boats*, 2nd edn, Charles Knight.
Southampton Institute (1992) *Proceedings of the Symposium on The Future Prospects for Vessel Traffic Services*, Southampton Institute, September.
Southampton Institute (1993) *Proceedings of the Conference on The Impact of New Technology on the Marine Industries*, Southampton Institute, September.

PART FOUR
Management

Looking Ashore: A Comparison with Inland Waters and Waterways

11

11.1 INTRODUCTION

The increasing pressure on the coastal environment and the dramatic rise of many water-based recreational pursuits in recent years, necessitate an holistic review of the use and management of all available water resources including inland waters and waterways, so that a strategic approach to the management of water-based recreation can be adopted at a national and regional level. Inland waters, particularly lakes and rivers, have traditionally been used for a number of recreational pursuits, notably angling and sailing, but with the growth of water-based recreation, even man-made water areas, reservoirs and reclaimed mineral workings, have been utilized. Together these provide a significant part of the resource available for water-based recreation in England and Wales. However, the dynamic interrelationship between water recreation resources, both coastal and inland, in the satisfaction of recreational opportunities is complex and not always well understood. This chapter attempts to explain this relationship, reviewing the opportunities and limitations of the inland water resource compared with those of the coastal zone, so facilitating an assessment of the extent to which the demand for coastal sites could be diverted to inland sites and vice versa.

The different pattern of ownership and accessibility to inland sites as well as their more confined nature have often resulted in more easily controllable management solutions to recreational problems on inland waters compared with those possible in coastal locations. The presumed generation of wealth associated with the recreational development of many inland sites has been a catalyst for the formulation of effective and sometimes quite sophisticated management regimes. In the latter sections of the chapter, the management of inland sites is compared with coastal sites and those techniques transferable between the two are considered.

Coastal Recreation Management Edited by Tim Goodhead and David Johnson. Published in 1996 by E & FN Spon, London. ISBN 0 419 20360 5

Particular attention is focused on Wales, where there are 30 700 acres of lakes and reservoirs and 3600 miles of river as well as 800 miles of coastal waters available for water-based recreation (WWA, 1980). This Welsh focus provides a context for the two case studies, the Lower River Wye and Llandegfedd Reservoir, which are used throughout the chapter. Both these sites are of national importance for water-based recreation, accommodate a wide range of recreational users, are of high conservation value and have well developed recreation management regimes.

11.2 OPPORTUNITIES OFFERED BY INLAND SITES

The wide variety of inland sites, including both linear waters (rivers and canals) and open water spaces (lakes, reservoirs and flooded mineral workings), provides for a range of recreational users. Figure 11.1 shows the range of inland waters and waterways available for recreational use in Wales.

British rivers are mainly used for canoeing, rowing and angling, with limited dinghy sailing on wide rivers; sailing, water-skiing and motor cruising being only possible on navigable sections. Within Wales angling is the traditional and major recreational use of rivers, as most rivers within the Principality, apart from those along the Welsh Borders, do not contain lengthy navigable sections. However, this sport is generally in decline, particularly coarse fishing, whose participation rates have dropped by about 2 to 3% each year in some regions (Sidaway, 1991). Conditions for canoeing, particularly white-water canoeing, are excellent on many of the fast flowing rivers draining the Snowdonia and Plynlimon ranges and have resulted in many sites being used for training and major competitions. The Afon Treweryn near Bala is the National White Water Centre for Wales and one of the few permanent white water canoeing sites in Europe (Aitchison and Jones, 1994). On the Wye however, angling and canoeing are the main activities although a wide range of other activities do take place along certain sections of the river. This river is arguably the best salmon fishery in the British Isles outside Scotland with 1300 salmon licences issued in 1990. Canoeing is a more recent development, having attracted over 30 000 participants in recent years, including both trainees and white water canoeists (Crease and Penning-Rowsell, 1985). Other activities include a limited amount of rowing, rafting and swimming, as well as some sailing and water-skiing on the tidal reaches (Figure 11.2).

Restored canals provide for a similar range of water-based recreational activities, although cruising tends to dominate many

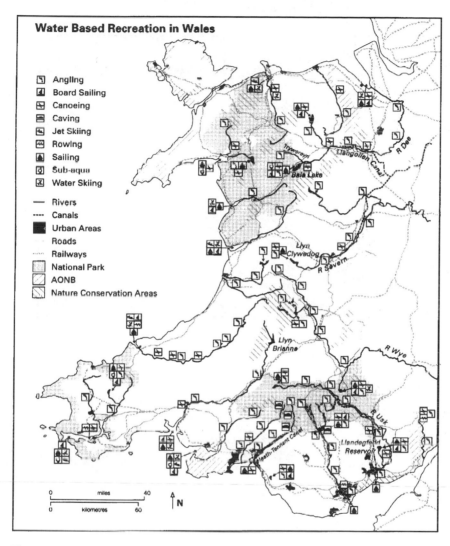

Figure 11.1 The distribution of inland sites for water-based recreation in Wales. (Source: adapted from Sport Council for Wales, 1991.)

sections. The potential of these former arteries of industrial Britain in providing green corridors and recreational and development opportunities within some of the most populated landlocked regions of England and Wales has now been realized. As Figure 11.1 shows, the network of canals within Wales is limited although some, such as the

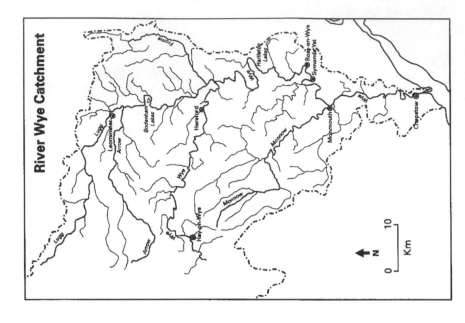

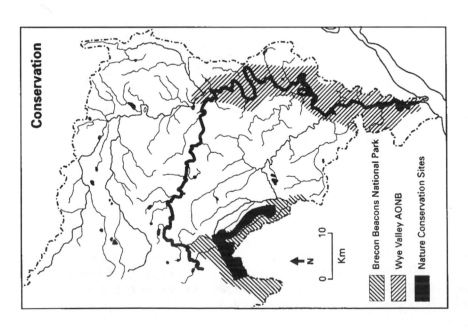

Figure 11.2 Recreational use of the River Wye. (Source: adapted from National Rivers Authority Lower Wye Catchment Management Plan, 1994.)

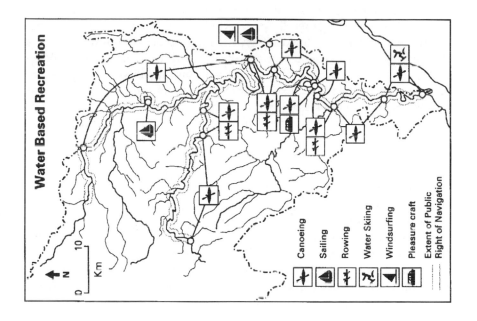

Water Based Recreation

Canoeing
Sailing
Rowing
Water Skiing
Windsurfing
Pleasure craft

Extent of Public
Right of Navigation

N

0   10
Km

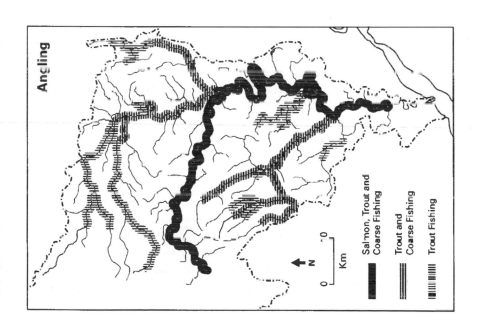

Angling

Salmon, Trout and
Coarse Fishing

Trout and
Coarse Fishing

Trout Fishing

N

0   10
Km

Llangollen Canal in north-west Wales provide miles of high quality recreational resource. Restoration of the scenic sections of canal in mid and north Wales has generally proceeded more slowly than in England. Within South Wales, unfortunately, the enormous recreational potential of many of the canals previously serving the industrial South Wales Valleys has been lost with a few exceptions, notably the Neath and Tennant Canal near Swansea, which has been restored by a local preservation society. With limited available land for development in Wales, many have been infilled and many, such as the former canal along the Taff valley, have provided the routeway for major road developments (A470). Within the Cardiff area, some canals have been lost to road development: today, these would probably have been seen as a major asset to the city, linking the centre with the Cardiff Bay Development.

Natural lakes are an important additional resource for a wide variety of sports, notably angling and wildfowling, with some sailing, canoeing, rowing and water-skiing taking place on a few waters. Most lakes occur in scenically attractive locations in Britain, notably in the Lake District and Snowdonia National Parks. Within Wales only Lake Bala in the north is of major recreational potential, but overall within the Prinicipality there are 1790 lakes, 50 of which are over 50 acres in size (WWA; Figure 11.1). Some of these, such as Lynn Llangorse are close to urban centres of population, although most lie in fairly remote mountainous locations.

Reservoirs, even though they have been constructed for other purposes, are an important recreational resource in the upland areas of Britain, particularly the mountainous and scenic areas of northern England and Mid-Wales (Figure 11.1). With improvements in water treatment, an increasing number have become available for recreational use: within Wales 118 out of 137 reservoirs are now used (WWA, 1980), four of which are of national importance (Brenig; Llandegfedd; Clywedog and Trawsfynedd: SC). Provision for recreation in the more recent reservoirs is usually good, having been considered from the outset of the planning stage, for example at Llyn Briane and Llyn Clywedog. A similar range of recreational pursuits can be found on the larger reservoirs to those practised on natural lakes, but their geographical remoteness generally limits their development and makes them less of a competitor with coastal sites. At Llandegfedd Reservoir, which is within easy travelling distance of the major population centres of south-east Wales, dinghy sailing and fly fishing are the main activities, with windsurfing, subaqua, canoeing occurring to a lesser extent (Aitchison and Jones, 1994).

Flooded mineral workings are an additional, and increasingly popular and vital resource in Britain, particularly in the Thames and Trent valleys as well as in the East of lowland Britain (ECSR, 1987). These tend to be the most commercialized sites. Most types of recreation which do not require vast acreages of water area can be catered for, although sites are often dedicated to a particular activity as frequently a number of workings occur in close proximity, so offering a range of pursuits. Despite the rapid development of sites, this has not been able to keep up with the rapid growth of water-based recreation, so there is still a shortfall in Hertfordshire, South Hampshire and along the M4 corridor (Elson et al., 1989).

Figure 11.3 provides a general comparison of the relative use of coastal and inland sites for a selected range of water-based recreational activities. It also gives an indication of recent trends in the participation of these sports, and a summary of the general environmental conditions required by each sport.

As Figure 11.3 shows, the use of inland waters for most of these activities is generally lower than for coastal waters, although within each particular watersport, there may be considerable variety in the preference and use of each resource. For example, the requirements for water ski racing contrast with the needs of tournament skiing. The former takes place mainly (75%: Elson et al., 1989) at coastal locations where a rough sea provides a challenge to competitors; conversely, calmer inland waters tend to be more suitable for tournament skiing. The conditions required by each activity are so specific that the availability of one resource does not automatically provide a substitute for another. For canoeing this is particularly the case: surf canoeing only is possible in coastal waters and white water canoeing on fast-flowing rivers. Surface water conditions, water depth, area and quality are the main determinants governing the use of each resource. Inland waters, with generally smoother, more sheltered water surfaces tend to favour motorized sports, such as rowing and sailing. Sports requiring surf conditions such as windsurfing are located in coastal waters, although the release of overflow waters from regulating reservoirs can provide an invaluable resource for white watersports. The main restriction for inland waters compared to coastal waters, however, is the small size of many water bodies, particularly flooded mineral sites and linear waters, only comparable with the most confined upper stretches of rias or lochs. However, inland sites do not suffer from the main disadvantages of coastal sites, namely large tidal variations, restricting use for a few hours either side of high tide, and very severe sea states which preclude the use of the sea for most watersports during the winter months.

The huge growth in some watersports in recent years has put a lot of pressure on all sites and has necessitated the review of inland, alternatives for many activities although exact participation rates are difficult to establish for such activities. The rapid growth of water-skiing in particular has resulted in a national shortage of sites with over 25% of clubs having waiting lists: the British Water-ski Federation are particularly concerned over the lack of inland sites, notably in some of the counties of the East Midlands (EMRCSR, 1987). Similarly, a study by Leisure Consultants (1989) has shown a major deficit of marinas and moorings, particularly in inland areas, compared with the potential demand for recreational boating use. Even the known plans for expansion of such facilities would only raise the number of inland sites from 190 to 209, and the number of coastal sites from 306 to 355 (*ibid.*). On the National Facilities Database for Wales 88 sailing locations are recorded, but most of these are along the coast.

Resource	Water-clubs	Skiing casual	Jet skiing	Power boating	Sailing	Canoeing	Angling	Sub-aqua
General trends	High growth	High growth	High growth	Medium growth	Low growth	Medium growth	Decline	Medium growth
Major sport requirements	Large water area; boat access points; non-sensitive environment Relatively calm waters				Large water area; calm waters	Variable water state; canoe access points	Clean, uncongested waters	Clean safe waters; low turbidity
Coastal waters	33%	High	High	High	High	High (Surf; touring; sailing)	Sea angling	Limited sites
Linear waters	13%	High	Medium	Low	Low	High (white water; slalom racing; touring)	High	N/A
Enclosed waters	24%	Medium	Low	Low	High	Medium	High	Low
Mineral sites	30%	Low	Few sites	Few sites	Medium	Low	Medium	Low

Figure 11.3 A comparison of the use of coastal and inland sites for water-based recreation. (Source: adapted from Elson, 1992.)

11.3 ENVIRONMENTAL ISSUES AT INLAND SITES

Water-based recreation is probably a greater threat to the environmental quality of inland waters than it is for coastal waters (Chapter 5), although the restoration of canals and defunct mineral workings, frequently driven by recreational needs, has resulted in the formation of new and sometimes valuable conservation habitats. The movement of low levels of boat traffic along canals has been shown to encourage diversity of flora through maintaining open water and preventing invasive marginal species from swamping the whole channel. The following section evaluates the erosional and ecological effects of watersports, before finally investigating water quality issues at inland sites.

Erosion of the shoreline, banks and bed of inland waters can be induced and accelerated by recreational boating, and is often a major reason for banning water-skiing at inland sites. Propeller damage, hull impact, particularly from launching and land operations, and boat-induced wash can result in physical damage. The latter is particularly severe in the acceleration and deceleration zones of power boats, often close to busy access points, where boats below planing speeds can create disturbed and potentially damaging water surfaces. In general, the lack of a wide beach 'buffer' and a tidal variation in water level, results in such erosion being much more concentrated and severe than in the coastal environment, even though limited seasonal changes in water level may occur. Reference should be made to some of the numerous reports describing the factors influencing the severity of this impact (Liddle and Scorgie, 1980; Klein, 1991; Bhowmik, 1975; Zabawa and Ostrom, 1980) and the consequences of this increased erosion (Youssef, 1974; Gucinski, 1982).

The most significant effect of this erosion is an increase in turbidity caused by sediment resuspension. This can cause further abrasion, scouring and reduce light penetration of the water with further consequences for the biota of the water column. Submerged aquatic vegetation (SAV) and fish productivity may be threatened by changes in turbidity (Klein, 1992) and emergent vegetation alongshore may be damaged: bare patches of shoreline, 2–3 m wide, are common features alongside launching/beaching points on shores which otherwise have well developed marginal vegetation. Figure 11.4 summarizes these effects on a canal ecosystem.

On the Wye there is little evidence that physical damage from boats is a serious problem, although there is some erosion of the banks and islands at Symonds Yat, one of the honey pot sites for canoeing on the river. Of more concern is the physical modification of the river through the construction of croys, the creation of underwater obstacles and excavation of the river bed: between Rhayader and Chepstow the NRA have recorded 500 such croys (NRA, 1994). Apart from their visual impact, they are thought to affect underwater habitats and water circulation in the river.

Enclosed inland waters make a significant contribution (40%: Sidaway, 1988) to sustaining migratory wildfowl and waders over the

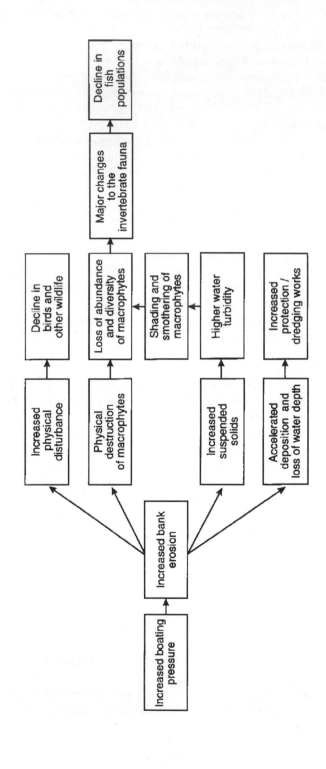

Figure 11.4 Physical and ecological effects of boat traffic on a canal ecosystem. (Source: Piggott, 1992.)

winter season. Man-made sites alone provide for 19% of all the estimated over-wintering populations (*ibid.*) and constitute a new conservation resource. The construction of single schemes, notably Rutland Water with a water surface area of 1254 ha including 60 ha of lagoons, has resulted in attracting significant bird numbers, in this case a resident population of 10 000 and an additional over-wintering population of 21 500 have become established since 1976. Llandegfedd Reservoir, being the largest inland open water habitat in Gwent, is an important refuge and ornithological site for a number of species, including large numbers of widgeon, pochard and mallard. Ironically, such wildfowl can be adversely effected by water-based recreational pursuits: recreation on Llangorse Lake, the largest natural lake in south Wales, has reduced the wildfowl carrying capacity of this SSSI, particularly during the daytime and in midwinter when substantial movements of birds off the lake have been noted (Tuite *et al.*, 1983). Conversely, on Llandegfedd Reservoir, Welsh Water in their report 'Winter Sailing and Wildfowl' did not identify any major deleterious impacts from winter sailing trials on the over-wintering bird populations (Welsh Water, 1991).

The scale and type of disturbance is thought to be related to the bird species and its activity, the type of recreational use, the size and nature of the waterbody and the distance from alternative sites (Ward, 1990). Some species, notably the Goldeneye and Gadwall are much more susceptible to disturbance than others, for example the tufted duck, pochard and coot (*ibid.*). Studies by Tuite *et al.* (1984) have shown coarse fishing, sailing and rowing pose the greatest overall negative impact on British wildfowl populations, because of the large recreational involvement with these sports. On a site basis though, the impact of noisy watersports is far more significant: Watmough (1983) has suggested a tolerance distance of 250 m for fishing boats and 450 m for motor boats. However, most disturbance to wildfowl, as well as being of local impact, is only temporary (Watmough, 1983). Where there are a number of waterbodies within a region most birds are quite able to redistribute themselves and use alternative, refuge sites.

Unlike coastal waters, the water quality of inland recreational waters rarely hits the headlines. However, this is no reason to be complacent, because water-based recreational users can contract similar illnesses from inland sites as they can from coastal waters. In fact, the National Rivers Authority (NRA) specifically advises not to swim in inland sites and British Waterways surveys have recently revealed that some of their urban sites do not comply with the EU Bathing Waters Directive (76/160/EC). This directive, however, has not officially been applied to inland locations: no bathing beaches have been designated at inland sites, unlike in some continental EU countries. However, statutory Water Quality Objectives produced by the NRA (1991) do specify aesthetic criteria for inland sites.

Inland waters lack the capability to 'dilute and disperse' compared with most coastal waters apart from the most confined bays. The survival of pathogens tends to be more prolonged in fresh than coastal waters and some species, such as Leptospirosis, is only present in freshwater. In particular, the spread of Weil's Disease is a major threat to freshwaters: figures vary, but some estimates indicate that the risk of a canoeist contracting the disease is about 1:200 000 (Philipp and Hughes, 1992). Even so, various national watersport associations, notably the British Canoe Union, provide advice for their members on codes of practice to reduce the risk of contracting the disease.

The other danger which is much more of a threat in inland than coastal waters is the growth and spread of toxic blue-green algae. This afflicts mainly shallow waters, particularly lakes and reservoirs in hot, dry summers and can produce neurotoxins, which attack the central nervous system, hepatoxins, which cause liver damage, and endotoxins which cause skin rashes. The monitoring of sites at risk by the National Rivers Authority has resulted in the closure of a number of reservoirs for recreational use over the last few years, although in some seasons the RYA Code of Practice has allowed clubs to remain open for dinghy sailing on lakes where windsurfing has been banned (Whelan, 1990/91).

11.4 OTHER LIMITATIONS AND ISSUES RELATING TO INLAND SITES

The relatively confined nature of inland waters can result in conflict and collision between different water-based recreational users similar to that witnessed in enclosed coastal waters, such as Poole Harbour. Figure 11.5 provides a summary of the extent to which a range of water-based activities are compatible on enclosed waters.

Conflicts between traditional users of inland sites and the newer activities can be a major problem: this is particularly true on rivers where boat-based sports conflict with the traditional angling use. This is the only significant inter-recreational conflict on the River Wye with 66% of anglers reporting problems with other recreational users in a recent survey (Crease and Penning-Rowell, 1985). This survey also showed that many of the anglers believed that the presence of canoes and to a lesser extent rafts was a major disturbance and was affecting the behaviour of the fish as well as their own enjoyment of the peace and tranquillity of the river (*ibid.*). The different age and attitudes of the boating fraternity compared with the generally older and more conservative anglers was also cited as a possible reason for the conflict between the two groups (*ibid.*). As with coastal areas, noisy and fast-powered watersports tend to be in competition with other river users, often with their needs being relegated to a subsidiary position. However, unlike coastal sites, there is considerable scope for 'no conflict situations' to occur, with individual watersports commanding exclusive use of enclosed sites, particularly at privately owned locations.

	Fishing	Wildfowling	Canoeing	Rowing	Sailing	Water skiing	Power boating	Cruising
Swimming	X	Z	Z	Z	Z	Z		Z
Fishing			PZ	PZ	PZ	X	X	PZ
Wildfowling						X	X	
Canoeing	PZ			PZ	PZ	PZ	PZ	
Rowing	PZ		PZ		PZ	P	P	PZ
Water skiing	X	X	PZ	P	PZ		PZ	n/a
Power boating	X	X	PZ	P	PZ	PZ		n/a
Cruising	PZ			PZ	Z	n/a	n/a	

X	Incompatible	P	Programming
Z	Zoning	n/a	Not applicable

Figure 11.5 The compatability of watersports on enclosed inland waters. (Source: *A Strategy for Water Recreation*, Sports Council for Wales.)

Conflicts with non-recreational use occur as much at inland sites as in coastal waters. As indicated in the previous section (section 11.3), a large number of enclosed recreational waters are of ornithological interest and difficulties may arise from the disturbance caused by recreational activities, particularly noisy watersports. Consequently, achieving the balance between recreation and conservation is as much an issue on inland waters as it is at the coast, although it is recognized that without recreational use some inland sites, particularly canals, would not have much conservation interest. The renotification of Sites of Special

Scientific Interest (SSSI) under the Wildlife and Countryside Act, 1981 in particular, brought the issue of wildlife conservation of canals to the fore. Potentially damaging operations have had to be defined and maximum movements of recreational craft calculated for such sites. At Llandegfedd Reservoir, an SSSI, because of its overwintering bird populations (NCC, 1981), there are a large number of notifiable operations, which include watersports as well as land-use practices around the reservoir. Along the River Wye recreation and tourism have also had to be very carefully managed as the river valley is of such great conservation value: as well as the Area of Outstanding Natural Beauty which extends from Mordiford to Chepstow, the whole river is an SSSI and there are a number of other designations along its length, including National and Local Nature Reserves (Figure 11.2).

Potential incompatibilities with nonconservation interests also exist: on wide, navigable rivers commercial users' interests may conflict with recreational usage just like in busy coastal waters such as the Solent. On most man-made enclosed waters, with the exception of some flooded mineral workings, it must be remembered that their whole *raison d'être* is nonrecreational. Hydroelectric power generation, water storage, river regulation and cooling water are the prime functions and recreational use, where allowed, takes a secondary role. Llandegfedd Reservoir is in fact a pump storage reservoir, providing drinking water for South East Wales.

Because many of the enclosed man-made water sites are privately owned, access is much more of an issue than for coastal waters. Traditionally, access to reservoirs was restricted as there were major fears over pollution. In addition, water companies and river authorities bought large expanses of land which were often let to the Forestry Commission for tree planting. Despite a relaxation in attitudes, particularly in the 1960s and 1970s, which was partly fuelled by changes in government legislation, there was a general reluctance by the water companies and the later water authorities to extend recreational use of their water (Ravenscroft, 1992). By 1980, only the Welsh Water Authority had produced a comprehensive strategy for the recreational use of water space; the other authorities were generally spending less than 1% of their budgets on recreation, namely angling and fisheries protection (*ibid.*). The privatization of the water utilities under the Water Act 1989 rekindled fears over access to sites (Morgan, 1989). Negotiating public access to water-filled mineral extraction sites is also difficult, particularly as other more lucrative developments may take precedence. Country club and marina-type developments with extensive housing are increasingly popular; in these watersports are seen to be of little priority or even as a nuisance. Some sites, such as Thorpe Park near Chertsey in Surrey, have even been developed as theme parks, whereas others have formed the focus for out-of-town superstores such as in the Blue Water Park in Dartford: the water area then becomes only available on a pay-and-ride basis (UK CEED, 1993).

The Right of Navigation in inland waters is a major issue. Rights of Navigation for such waters are immeasurably complex and have been the subject of a recent Sports Council study. Where there have been major improvements to waterways, involving Acts of Parliament, public rights of navigation exist, but otherwise *de facto* use is made of the water. A few rivers, such as the River Trent, and lakes, notably Lake Windermere, enjoy an undisputed Right of Navigation, but on many rivers, such as on the upper sections of the River Wye above Hay on Wye, this right is not always clear. Even below this point on the river those wishing to gain access to the water still have to do so at a public access point or with the permission of the riparian owner. With the exception of this river, the Severn below Pool Quay and a few individual agreements between canoeists and fisheries interests, there is no other authorized public use of rivers for canoeing in Wales.

11.5 MANAGEMENT OF INLAND WATER-BASED RECREATION

The responsibility for the provision and regulation of water-based recreation at inland sites falls to a range of different organizations (Figure 11.6). Some of the organizations shown in the diagram, such as the regional Water Companies and the British Waterways Board, are major providers. The latter are responsible for 2000 miles of navigable canals, including much of the canal network of the English Midlands, plus 90 feeder reservoirs which together are used by 22 000 privately owned powered craft and 1500 hire boats (BW, 1994). Many Water Companies now have contracted private consultancies to manage their leisure interest, for example Dŵr Cymru Welsh Water's recreational strategy is overseen by Hamdden its subsidiary company. Under the Water Act 1989, Water Companies have a statutory obligation to provide opportunities for recreation. On Llandegfedd Reservoir this provision includes interpretation, refreshment and recreational facilities.

The range of management techniques available for inland sites is very similar to those used in coastal waters, but, because of the confined nature of the enclosed waterbodies, control of recreational use is, at least theoretically, much easier. Ownership of sites, including water space, can further aid management and allow sites to be customized. Elson *et al.* noted that 33% of waterski clubs were the sole recreational users of former mineral workings and owned about 15% of these sites (Elson *et al.*, 1989). In particular, access may be used as a management tool and owners of inland waters have applied many techniques which have been suggested, but so far rejected for the coastal environment, including registration schemes and insurance standards for boats (British Waterways Boat Safety Standards Scheme and Pleasure Boat licences) as well as seasonal and daily permit systems. Commercial owners also have the finances to pay for educational materials: for example, British Waterways have produced a video version of their Waterways Code. Zoning techniques are particularly effective on enclosed inland waters and often provide the basis of water management schemes, whereas sharing water offshore may be difficult, because of the open access and general Right to Navigation. Spatial zoning may be designed for a single site or for a range of sites.

Providers (examples)	Regulators (examples)
Water Companies	National Rivers Authority
British Waterways Board	Local Planning Authority
Minerals operators	Harbour Commissioners
Local Authorities	English Nature (CCW)
Private landowners	Countryside Commission (CCW)

Figure 11.6 Organizations responsible for the provision and regulation of water-based recreation at inland sites

Broad zoning of water parks consisting of a number of individual waterbodies, is a popular option on flooded mineral workings. This approach has been adopted at the Kingsbury Water Park, where Warwickshire County Council have graded a range of water and other sports across the 21 lakes according to the degree of noise and visual intrusion of the activities. As Figure 11.7 shows, motorized watersports are confined to the southern end of the park, whereas the quieter activities occur to the north, the most northern stretch of water being a nature reserve with access limited to permit holders only (Elson *et al.*, 1989).

Many larger, single sites employ spatial zoning, with examples such as Kielder Water and Rutland Water, demonstrating the range of activities that can be accommodated within an individual waterbody, from water-skiing to angling. In the former case a mere 0.01% of the total water space (2684 acres) has been earmarked for water skiing where the 6 mph speed limit applying to the rest of the water has been lifted. The main constraint for such zoning is the actual size and morphology of the waterbody, but for inland sites the latter can be sometimes modified by the construction of artificial islands. At Llandegfedd Reservoir, the shape of the waterbody lends itself to spatial zoning: feeding grounds for the birds are confined to the three northern arms of the reservoir and so are relatively easily protected (Figure 11.8). Users are channelled to certain areas of the shore and access to the reservoir for recreational use is controlled via a permit system, operated by on-site wardens (Aitchison and Jones, 1994). Certain sports, notably water-skiing are completely banned from the reservoir, because of their potentially disturbing nature.

Temporal zoning is often introduced at inland sites. On some small water areas full-time zoning has been introduced to accommodate different watersports, such as on Bodymoor Heath Water at Kingsbury Water Park, where the local sailing club and hydroplane club each use the water on alternative days throughout the summer. Seasonal zoning, employing close seasons is well established on many inland waters, including rivers. These ensure that the wildlife interests are not damaged by recreational activities and are developed according to local and specific needs. They were traditionally observed in angling and shooting to protect the breeding seasons, but now can include protection for the nesting and breeding seasons of birds and fish as well as the over-wintering period for migratory wildfowl and the growing season for plants (Sidaway, 1991). Figure 11.9 demonstrates the close seasons which has been developed along the River Wye. At Llandegfedd management is based on 'summer recreation and winter conservation', with the peak of recreational activity occurring between May and August. However, limited winter sailing is now allowed within the spatial zoning plan shown above. The effects of this winter sailing are, however, monitored by the Gwent Ornithological Society and the Countryside Council for Wales.

However, zoning is not just restricted to enclosed waters, rivers may have speed limits imposed on certain sections: for example, British Waterways, the navigation authority for the River Trent, has lifted the normal 6 mph speed limit along eight stretches of the river for a number of waterski clubs (R). The National Rivers Authority in their Lower Wye Catchment Plan (NRA, 1994) suggest imposing further bylaws to restrict speed of boats.

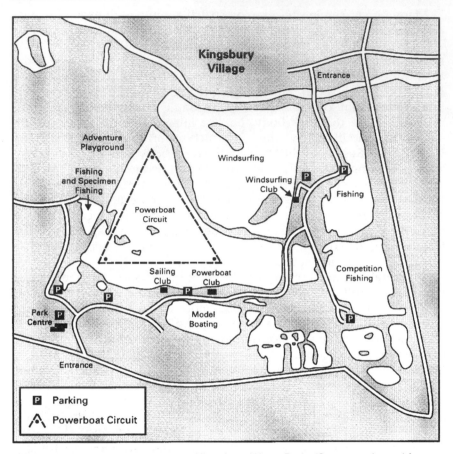

Figure 11.7 Broad zoning across Kingsbury Water Park. (Source: adapted from Elson *et al.*, 1989.)

For both case studies, zoning has to be supplemented by a range of other management techniques. Codes of Conduct, extensive interpretation programmes and user liaison groups (Llandegfedd User Liaison Group; Wye Users' Group) are equally important management tools just as they are at coastal sites.

11.6 CONCLUSION

The notable growth in watersports over the last 25 years has taken place both in inland and coastal locations, particularly in newer sports such as windsurfing and water-skiing. The fragmented organizational structure of the water-based recreation industry, particularly the providers (Figure 11.6) however, has resulted in a very parochial view of the potential of inland waters and waterways for water-based recreation. The growth of new man-made sites, particularly flooded mineral workings and restored canals, has greatly supplemented the supply of suitable natural sites and has necessitated a serious consideration of inland sites within a national water-based recreational strategy. For the manager of recreational activities at coastal locations too, there is much to be learnt from the application of techniques to inland waters and waterways. Some of these, just being considered for the coast, have been tried and tested for some time at inland sites.

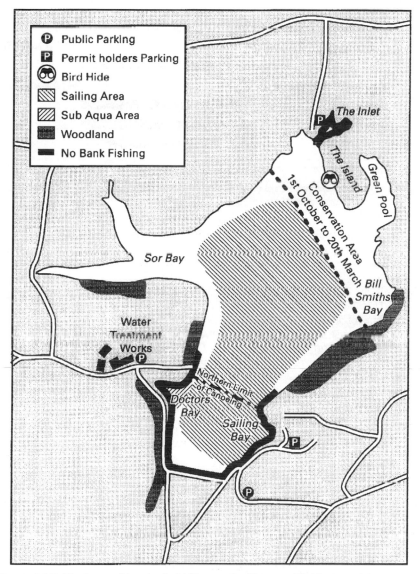

Figure 11.8 Zoning on Llandegfedd Reservoir. (Source: Aitchison and Jones, 1994.)

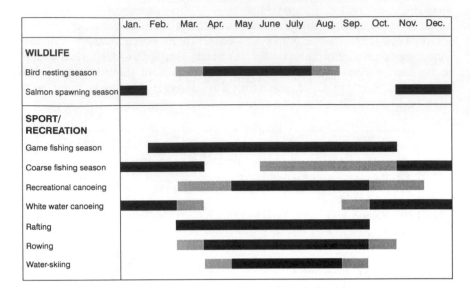

Figure 11.9 Close seasons on the River Wye. (Source: The Wye Challenge.)

REFERENCES

Aitchison, J. and Jones, P. L. (1994) *A Sporting Chance for the Countryside: Sport and Recreation in the Welsh Countryside. Case Studies of Good Practice*, Report prepared for the Sports Council for Wales and the Countryside Council for Wales.

Bhowmik, N. G. (1975) Boat generated waves in lakes (Technical Notes), *Journal of Hydraulics Division*, Proceedings of the American Society of Civil Engineers, **11**, HY11.

British Waterways (1994) *Leisure and Tourism Strategy*, BW.

Crease, D. and Penning-Rowsell, E. C. (1985) *Pressure and 'Conflict' – Managing Recreation and Sharing Water Space on the River Wye*, School of Geography and Planning, Middlesex Polytechnic.

East Council for Sport and Recreation (1987) *Mineral Extraction Areas – Their Importance to Sport and Recreation*, ECSR.

East Midlands Regional Council for Sport and Recreation (1987) *Water Recreation in the '90s: A Review of Strategy in the East Midlands*, Nottingham: EMCSR.

Elson, M. J., Lloyd, J. and Thorpe, I. (1989) *Providing for Motorised Water Sports*, Study 36, Sports Council, London.

Elson, M. J. (1992) *Planning and Provision for Motorised Watersports*, Facilities Factfile 3: Countryside and Water Recreation, Sports Council.

Gucinski, H. (1982) *Sediment Suspension and Resuspension from Small-craft Induced Turbulence*, Environmental Protection Agency, Annapolis, Maryland.

Klein, R. D. (1991) *Comments on a Water-skiing Slalom Course prepared for a site in St Leonard Creek, Maryland, USA*, Community and Environmental Defence Services.

Klein, R. D. (1992) *Middle River: An Assessment of Options for Halting the Decline and Restoring Former Water Quality*, Community and Environmental Defence Services.

Leisure Consultants (1989) *Boating and Water Sports in Britain: Market Profiles and Prospects*, Leisure Consultants.

Liddle, M. J. and Scorgie, H. R. A. (1980) The effects of recreation on freshwater plants and animals: a review, *Biological Conservation*, 17, 183–206.

Morgan, A. (1989) The Water Bill, *Yachts and Yachting*, September, 19–20.

National Rivers Authority (1991) *Proposals for Statutory Water Quality Objectives*, NRA Water Quality Series no. 5.

National Rivers Authority (1994) *Lower Wye River Catchment Management Plan*, NRA Welsh Region.

Nature Conservancy Council (1981) *Llandegfedd Reservoir: A Nature Conservation Appraisal*, NCC, South Wales Region.

Philipp, R. and Hughes, A. (1992) Understanding of Weil's disease among canoeists, *British Journal of Sports Medicine*, 26(4), 223–7.

Ravenscroft, N. (1992) *Recreation, Planning and Development*, Macmillan, 151–9.

Sidaway, R. (1988) *Sport, Recreation and Nature Conservation*, Study 32, London: Sports Council.

Sidaway, R. (1991) *Good Conservation Practice for Sport and Recreation*, London, Sports Council.

Sports Council for Wales, *Database*.

Tuite, C. H., Owen, M. and Paynter, D. (1983) Interaction between wildfowl and recreation at Llangorse lake and Talybont Reservoir, South Wales, *Wildfowl*, 34, 58–63.

Tuite, C. H., Hanson, P. R. and Owen, M. (1984) Some ecological factors affecting winter wildfowl distribution on inland waters in England and Wales and the influence of water-based recreation, *Journal of Applied Ecology*, 21, 41–62.

UK Centre for Economic and Environmental Development (1993) *Water-skiing and the Environment: A Literature Review, UK*, CEED.

Ward, D. (1990) Recreation on inland lowland waterbodies: does it affect birds?, *RSPB Conservation Review*, 62–8.

Watmough, B. (1983) The effects on wildfowl of recreation at reservoirs in the Mid-Trent Valley, paper given at the *Water Space Amenity Commission Workshop on the Impact of Water Recreation upon Wildfowl in Great Britain*, 25 February.

Welsh Water (1991) *Winter Sailing and Wildfowl. A study. Llandegfedd Reservoir*, 1990/9 Welsh Water.

Welsh Water Authority (1980) *A Strategic Plan for Water Space Recreation and Amenity*, Welsh Water Authority.

Whelan, E. (1990/91) Pollution: in the thick of it, *Water Start*, 6, 1.

Wye Project (1992) *Conservation and Recreation: The Wye Challenge*, Vols 1 and 2.

Youssef, A. (1974) *Assessing Effects on Water Quality by Boating Activity*, National Environmental Research Centre, Ohio, US.

Zabawa, C. and Ostrom, C. (1980) *The Role of Boat Wakes in Shore Erosion in Arundel County, Maryland*, Coastal Resources Division, Maryland Coast Report 5.

Regional Strategies for Coastal Recreation

12

12.1 INTRODUCTION

In recent years there have been a range of regional strategy initiatives for recreation on the coast. This chapter evaluates some of the points to emerge from their development. It highlights some of the different approaches which are being taken, and makes observations on good practice.

12.1.1 WHAT ARE REGIONAL STRATEGIES FOR COASTAL RECREATION?

The words 'regional' and 'strategy' are difficult to define and may mean different things to different people. Both are used in a broad sense in this chapter. 'Regional' can be taken as shorthand applying to strategies which cover substantial areas of coast with a geographical integrity (for example the Scottish Firths), or which deal with administrative areas covering more than one county. In strictly geographical terms some of the latter might be termed sub-regional. Sports Council 'regions' have been the basis for a number of strategies and illustrate this distinction. Their extent varies considerably, with the Southern Region, for example, covering the coastline of Hampshire and the Isle of Wight only (a sub-region in geographical terms) while the South West Region covers the 800 miles of coastline in Gloucestershire, Avon, Somerset, Devon, Cornwall and Dorset very definitely a geographical region.

The original meaning of 'strategy' is the art of war; here, however, it should be taken as meaning a process through which policies and action are agreed, implemented, reviewed and developed. Regional strategies for coastal recreation have not always lived up to this definition.

Coastal Recreation Management Edited by Tim Goodhead and David Johnson. Published in 1996 by E & FN Spon, London. ISBN 0 419 20360 5

Regional strategies for coastal recreation have been, and continue to be prepared by a variety of organizations and through a variety of initiatives. However there are at least two factors which all have in common. Firstly they are *non-statutory* – there is no legal requirement to produce regional strategies. Any action they achieve will be with the consent of organizations and individuals rather than by insistence. Secondly, they are *multi-agency* projects. Although frequently led by one body, they seek to influence the actions of a number of different organizations. Widespread ownership of strategies among the organizations they seek to influence is therefore fundamental if they are to succeed.

It is vitally important at the outset to understand that strategies are not simply a set of written documents. One of the major criticisms of past practice is that it has over-emphasized the importance of a written statement, and has undervalued the process of consultation, communication and consensus-building involved.

12.2 WHY HAVE A COASTAL RECREATION STRATEGY?

Five key factors provide the incentive to the development of regional strategies for recreation in the coastal zone. These are as follows, and are not listed in any order of priority. Different strategies will weight the importance of each differently.

12.2.1 THE IMPORTANCE OF THE COAST FOR RECREATION

Perhaps as many as 50 different sport and recreational activities take place in the coastal zone ranging from the formal and organized to the very informal. Each activity has its own ranges in terms of time, intensity and location. Sport and recreation activity is fundamentally a positive use of the coastal zone. As stated in Chapter 4 it has been confirmed as a legitimate land use and activity by recent government planning policy guidance for statutory plans (Department of the Environment/Welsh Office 1991, 1992). Possible objectives which a regional strategy might address include the following:

- **To improve and extend opportunities for recreation.** Recreation and sport are widely accepted as of substantial value to society, and a strategy is a positive means of articulating and promoting that value, and of seeking better and wider opportunities for recreation and sport.
- **To give a voice for recreation.** The level of organization of outdoor sport and recreation is generally limited by staff resources,

particularly within the governing bodies of sport and also the Sports Council (Sports Council, 1994). Most coastal recreation is informal and where events and activities are organized they are often reliant on voluntary effort. Strategies can provide a vehicle to highlight the demands for sport and recreation to the organizations which are in a position to provide for them. They can highlight sports development needs at a range of different levels of skill and ability from foundation, through participation and performance to excellence.

- **To provide a framework for facility development.** Some activities require major facilities, or intensive use of areas of water space. A regional rather than local perspective may be required to identify where such facilities might be best located and to justify their development. Examples might include the designation of water-ski and jet-ski areas, the creation of marinas and decisions on no-go areas for particular activities and developments.

12.2.1 CONSERVATION OBJECTIVES

Much of the coast is of high nature or landscape conservation value, and there are also a number of important archaeological sites both on land and underwater. There is public support and considerable legislation for the protection of these values. As explained in Chapter 5 this can place significant constraints on recreational activity and objectives for the development of recreation need to be tempered with the need for development to be sustainable, or to avoid environmental damage. A further objective of a regional strategy therefore may be.

- **To ensure sport and recreation is compatible with sustaining the value of the natural environment.** Strategies may consider the ability of the coastal resource to provide for recreation, and seek a means to ensure demand and facilities can be managed within this threshold. They might for example highlight preferred and no-go areas for different activities, set out a framework for zonation, and consider the needs for increased regulation, better management, information, research or codes of practice.

12.2.3 OTHER ACTIVITIES

Aside from conservation, the coast is subject to a wide range of other activities which interact with recreation; for example sewage disposal and commercial shipping are two uses considered in Chapters 6 and 13 respectively which can have substantial impacts. Strategies therefore will also need to recognize these as additional constraints on the opportunities for recreation development. Strategy objectives might be:

- **To harmonize recreational activity with other uses of the coast.** Strategies might highlight particular conflicts and identify means of achieving their resolution, through education, regulation and communication.
- **To improve the quality of the environment for recreation.** Strategies might seek to highlight concerns about litter and pollution on recreation, and to find means of reducing them.

12.2.4 ADMINISTRATIVE COMPLEXITY

Strategies can have an important role with regard to communication and coordination between the wide range of different organizations which have an interest in the management and development of coastal recreation. Strategy objectives could be:

- **To improve communication between recreation interests and other users of the coast.** A strategy can provide a vehicle for bringing together the wide range of bodies involved in coastal recreation and evaluating their respective roles and the links and consultation mechanisms between them and with other users of the coast.
- **To improve co-ordination and set standards for coastal recreation management.** Some aspects of coastal recreation may require co-ordinated management. A strategy can be used to identify these factors, and develop the means to achieve the necessary co-ordination. Issues which might be considered include public launch points and the provision of information and interpretation.

12.2.5 GAPS IN INFORMATION AND UNCERTAINTY ABOUT THE FUTURE

Finally there is often uncertainty about existing patterns of recreation and more particularly on future trends. It is quite clear that recreational activity on the coast has grown considerably over the last 150 years, and particularly in the last 25–30. However, this growth has been episodic, at times very rapid but also sensitive to economic trends. It has also been characterized by the appearance and rapid booms in new markets. The growth in marina developments (Chapter 10) and the appearance of windsurfing and personal watercraft (Chapter 7) are good examples. Strategies can provide a framework for discussing possible growth and contraction in different activities, and the implications this may have for management arrangements. A possible objective might be:

- **To assess the future demand for coastal recreation and its implications for the planning and management of the coast.** This might be achieved through specially commissioned research, improved information sharing or the establishment of monitoring systems.

To illustrate the objectives which may motivate regional strategies, some examples from two Sports Council strategies are given in Table 12.1.

Table 12.1 Examples of objectives from Sports Council coastal recreation strategies

---

Southern Council for Sport and Recreation (1991) Coastal Recreation Strategy (6 stated objectives):

- To build a picture of the type and scale of participation in and provision for sport and active recreation on the coast and the location and intensity of different activities.
- To investigate the present and future demands for recreation on the coast, locally and nationally.
- To look at the physical attributes of the coast and at the ability of the coast to supply the current and future demand, taking into account its environmental sensitivities.
- To identify and examine any issues and concerns relating to the recreational use of the coast, and constraints on its use from the perspectives of participants, managers and planners.
- To identify any opportunities for the development of additional facilities or opportunities for different activities, and the constraints on such development.
- To produce a strategy which will include planning goals and mangement options, policies and recommendations, and suggested methods of implementation for enhanced coastal management.

South Western Council for Sport and Recreation (1990): A Strategy for Coastal Recreation

- To provide a strategic overview of the present and future demands for and constraints on, provision for sport and active recreation on the coast, and to develop appropriate policies which can be followed through into regional strategies, statutory plans and local planning and management frameworks of other relevant agencies.

12.3 THE STRATEGY PROCESS

The importance of clearly understanding the process of production for a non-statutory strategy cannot be over-stressed. Strategy development should be thought of as a process which is continuous and progressive – it is not about producing a comprehensive blueprint for recreation and does not have an end product.

In general terms there is no difference between the process of producing strategies for coastal recreation and producing other non-statutory initiatives. A simple model of the process of strategy production is shown in Figure 12.1. It can be thought of as consisting of four related phases of equal importance.

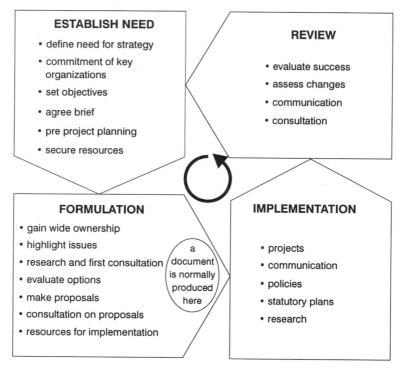

Figure 12.1 The strategy process

12.3.1 ESTABLISH THE NEED FOR A STRATEGY

The first requirement is to determine whether a strategy is needed, identify what it should achieve and the issues which it should address, and begin to bring together the organizations which need to be involved. There is a need for good pre-project planning which will culminate in the creation of a clear brief. From the outset it is important to begin to make contacts with the organizations who it is hoped will be part of the strategy process. As noted above most strategies are led by a single organization, and they may take the role of bringing together the key interests to discuss the project and work up a brief. Since most coastal strategies, whether recreation-led or not, are likely to address recreational issues it is ideal that a recreational interest should be included at the pre-project planning stage. This role might be performed by the Sports Council, a local authority leisure department or an appropriate governing body of sport.

The key questions to be resolved at this first stage of the process are to decide whether a strategy is needed, and agree on what it should achieve. This implies careful consideration of the possible issues which a strategy could address (which for recreation might be based on those in 12.2 above), and the formulation of a clear set of objectives. The production of a strategy has resource implications in both staff time and money. Part of pre-project planning will be to identify these costs and how, and by whom, they will be met.

12.3.2 FORMULATION

The formulation of a strategy embodies the process of developing and gaining agreement on the issues and actions which it should address. This involves much more than simply writing a document. The process involves working with and bringing together the range of organizations who can contribute to the achievement of the strategy. As a non-statutory initiative there is a key need for the strategy to achieve ownership by all these organizations. Research will be required to highlight a range of possible concerns and opportunities, to identify those which are real issues for the strategy and to produce measures or policies for how each might be addressed. A further key element will be to determine the resources which are required to develop these proposals.

There are several mechanisms for formulating strategies, ranging from production 'in-house' by one or a partnership of organizations, to the employment of a project officer or external consultants. These mechanisms each have different points for and against them which are not discussed here. Whichever method is chosen it is likely that a single lead agency or group of agencies will have an important role during the process in seeking the involvement of others, and in gaining their approval of its proposals.

The culmination of the formulation process is normally the production of a strategy document. This will often first be issued as a draft for consultation among the community of coastal users, and sometimes the wider public. The breadth of consultation will depend on the nature of the strategy being prepared.

Consultation is a part of the formulation process which warrants particular mention with regard to recreation. It is a fundamental need of any strategy which addresses recreation to make strenuous effort to embrace the views and needs of recreational participants. Contacts will always need to be established with local interests, which may be represented by clubs or associations and with the national governing body of sport. It is also important to make contact with regional sports organizations and federations where these exist. Lack of consultation has been a substantial criticism of some coastal strategy initiatives to date. There is no doubt that consultation poses a series of challenges, which include the following (based on Sports Council, 1994):

- Governing bodies of sport are voluntary organizations. They have few staff and with very few exceptions paid staff are based at the national office.
- At a local or regional level virtually all governing body committees and officers are voluntary. Committees may only meet every 3–4 months. While many regional and local committees run efficiently, this may not always be the case.
- The main purpose of governing bodies is to organize their sport, and thus involvement in coastal strategies is not part of their normal work. Governing bodies at a regional level will not always be well versed in environmental and planning issues, and expertise in this field will normally be at a national level.
- At a national level governing bodies are receiving increased and competing demands for time from a wide range of coastal initiatives. Some have found it particularly difficult to be able to respond to these demands within their staff resources. This is a fundamental constraint on the pace at which coastal management policy is able to develop, while adequately accounting for recreation. It is of particular concern that excessive pressure will mean that recreational involvement in plans will be reactive in nature, with initiatives seen more as a threat than as opportunities for sensible and balanced sport and recreation development.
- Many, probably the majority, of coastal recreation users are not members of an organized structure, be it a sports governing body or a club. Governing bodies of sport will normally be prepared to speak for their activity as a whole, including unattached users. However the need for direct contact with users will often exist.

The quality of any strategy for recreation is dependent on the efforts which are made to fully address consultation and account for the above constraints. The most important practical point with regard to consultation is that persistence and application will be required to achieve it properly. Contact should be sought on the users' own terms; this means:

- persistence in trying to contact recreational representatives;
- clear communication about the strategy initiative, the need for recreation to participate, and possible opportunities to benefit sport and recreation interests;
- a willingness to meet face-to-face on the users' own terms; for voluntary officers in particular simple measures like holding meetings in the evening can be crucial;
- preparedness to work to a timescale which user groups can respond to, and not to allow the drive to complete a written strategy shorten the consultation process.

12.4.3 IMPLEMENTATION

Implementation is where the work of agreeing a strategy is turned into action. This can include the development of practical projects, dealing with organizational issues, or agreeing planning and management policies. Regional strategies are likely to take a more broadly based approach than locally based plans. Because of the scale at which they operate and the quantity of information on which they may be based, it will normally be difficult for them to make effective recommendations at the local level. They are likely to set out a range of contextual information and set out broad policies for the development and management of recreation. In particular they can provide the framework for detailed policies to be worked out at a local level – either through management plans, or direct discussions between regulators and users. Some possible examples of the way in which regional and local initiatives relate are set out in Table 12.2 which may help to clarify this point.

The mechanism for implementing the strategy is important and needs to be considered at the pre-planning stage. Implementation implies change to a current situation, and change implies spending both time and money. Consideration and commitment must be given to providing these resources by all with an interest in seeing the strategy progress. It is important to establish continuity between the process of developing a strategy initiative, and the process of implementing it. There should be at least one agency prepared to act as an advocate and leader for the implementation of the strategy. A lack of a continued push for the strategy to move forward will increase the likelihood of the plan remaining on the shelf. The role of lead agency will normally be most easily taken on by a local authority, although other organizations may also perform this role. The appointment of a project officer is one potentially effective means of implementing a strategy. Where the strategy has been prepared by a project officer, that individual will have already established good working links with the range of organizations who will have a role in its implementation. It is therefore desirable, at least initially, that the same person continues to deal with the implementation phase.

12.3.4 REVIEW

We have already noted the uncertainty which surrounds current knowledge and predictions about sport and recreation on the coast, and the sometimes rapid changes in patterns of demand and activity which can occur. This means that any strategy must be sufficiently flexible to respond to changes which occur, and implies the need for regular review to be carried out. There is no fixed period after which a review will be necessary; if a strategy is being successfully followed, the need should become apparent to the key implementing parties who respond to it. Review requires a similar process to the creation of the original strategy, however because it builds on an existing agreement it should be less onerous to achieve.

12.4 EXAMPLES OF REGIONAL STRATEGIES FOR COASTAL RECREATION

This section describes examples of regional level strategies for coastal recreation, which illustrate the range of approaches which have been taken. Two types of initiative are examined: those which are strategies specifically for coastal recreation, and those which address recreational issues within wider coastal management strategies. Most, though not all examples are from England with an emphasis on the south-east. The strategies discussed are as follows:

12.4.1 RECREATION SPECIFIC STRATEGIES

• The Coastal Recreation Strategies of the Regional Councils for Sport and Recreation
• Development Strategies of Regional Sports Governing Bodies

Table 12.2 Examples of the relationship between policies and proposals in regional strategies and possible action at the local level. Action at the local level may be embodied in local management plans or in the policies of statutory plans, or taken forward through managing organizations and arrangements.

Example regional strategy policy	Possible regional strategy proposals	Possible local policies and proposals
A system of designated areas for fast powered water sports is required	• quantify demand • highlight activities • suggest possible locations for zones • identify key organizations	• confirm location of zones for different activities • propose bye laws • establishing education, monitoring and enforcement mechanisms
Facilities for sports clubs should be safeguarded and encouraged where possible	• set out needs • suggest action required • highlight main demands • identify key organizations	• new planning policies for club sites • identify possible options for new club facilities
Information on sport and recreation opportunities should be improved	• review existing provision • information requirements • mechanism for distribution • identify key organizations • project proposals	• contribute to regional or sub-regional initiatives • set up distribution system
Improved management of public launch points is required	• review existing facilities • review usage levels and demand trends • highlight management needs • propose management framework	• proposals for specific action on-site
Improved communication between recreational interests and other users is required	• highlight communication needs • propose communication mechanisms • propose projects: e.g. directories, fora	• establish consultative group as needed • contribute to regional/ sub-regional groups

12.4.2 RECREATION IN WIDER COASTAL STRATEGIES

- The Scottish Firths Initiative
- SERPLAN Coastal Planning Guidelines for the South East
- Strategic Guidelines for the Solent

12.4.3 RECREATION SPECIFIC STRATEGIES

- The Coastal Recreation Strategies of the Regional Councils for Sport and Recreation

The Regional Councils for Sport and Recreation (RCSR) were established in 1976. They were required to produce Regional Recreation Strategies which would take forward the national strategy for sport. The Department of the Environment (1973) set out guidelines on the form and content of the strategy. In the late 1970s the Sports Council requested the RCSRs to produce Regional Coastal Recreation Strategies. The general guidelines stated that they were 'to synthesize the recreational content of existing plans covering in more detail any aspect not adequately dealt with'. The strategies are based on the regional boundaries of the Sports Council and deal with all land, water and air sports which take place in the coastal zone.

A review of the Regional Coastal Recreation Strategies has recently been carried out into their relationship and influence on management plans on Heritage Coasts (Heritage Coast Forum and the Sports Council, 1993; Sports Council, 1992). This provides an excellent analysis of the issues and problems of integrating regional strategies with local management plans.

The report noted the strengths of the Strategies in dealing with a single aspect of the coast and in providing a digest of information about sport and recreation. However it also noted that they had been difficult to make use of by Heritage Coasts and it was suggested that the main reasons for this were:

- the adoption of zones based on local authority administrative areas or sports use of an area rather than resource characteristics, i.e. a demand rather than supply led approach;
- the non-critical stance of the strategies to existing policies of local authorities and others;
- the reliance placed on other bodies to take forward the proposals;
- lack of adequate policy on mechanisms to take forward the policies for increased provision.

The conclusions of the report included the following recommendations for how the Strategies might change in the future:

- The Strategies should give greater consideration of Heritage Coasts (and to conservation issues in general), and mechanisms should be proposed for communicating these changes to all relevant bodies.
- A clear policy on sport and active recreation in relation to Heritage Coasts should be articulated.
- The zones adopted should be more focused on the characteristics of the coastal resource. They should reflect changes in foreshore character, helping both the RCSRs and Sports Councils to develop policies based on both the conservation needs and recreation potential of the coast.
- Strategies should make recommendations on how policies proposed will be implemented.
- Because the policies proposed frequently relate to interests of other bodies, the endorsement of these policies should be actively sought, in order to commit partner organizations to the strategy.

The report also makes a series of recommendations for Heritage Coast management, including the following:

> [because] many prime sites and problem areas are near or adjacent to Heritage Coasts, a strategic approach to managing sporting activity on Heritage Coasts should take account of the management needs and potential of these areas. Heritage Coast Plans should therefore include reference to adjacent coastline in considering sport and active recreation.

Since the production of the report the recommendations have been adopted by the Sports Council, although no regional strategies have been reviewed to date. A Coastal Recreation Officer (the author of this chapter) has been appointed to implement the strategy of the Southern Council for Sport and Recreation, and details of how this project is being developed are given in the final section of this chapter.

12.4.4 DEVELOPMENT STRATEGIES OF REGIONAL SPORTS GOVERNING BODIES

Other than the Sports Council, the other bodies with the potential to develop regional strategies for recreation are the National Governing Bodies of Sport. The current constraints on the governing bodies have been summarized earlier in this chapter, and few strategies have been produced at a regional level. It is probable, however, that their role may increase in the future due to an increased emphasis on governing body-led action within government policy.

There are a number of potential advantages to governing body strategies. One is that they can be closely focused on the needs of a particular sport. This increases their potential to combine a regional perspective with practical proposals. A second is that the governing body is well placed to represent the needs of its activity, meaning that strategies should be able to be the most appropriate for the sport. However the resource limits and voluntary nature of regional governing bodies means that if they are to produce effective strategies they will normally require assistance from local authorities and others. The governing bodies also do not normally have a direct role in providing and managing facilities, thus there will be a key need for statutory bodies to participate in and recognize the strategies, and for the policies and action put forward to be realistic. Finally there may still need to be a wider framework which allows the demands of different activities to be integrated.

12.4.5 RECREATION IN WIDER COASTAL STRATEGIES

The alternative to producing standalone regional strategies for recreation is to deal with recreation within wider coastal strategy initiatives. The recent emphasis on integrated management of the coastal zone means that it is probably this sort of approach which is likely to be most widely adopted in the future. Three recent and on-going initiatives are discussed.

1. Recreation in Management Plans for Large Estuaries: English Nature's Estuaries Campaign

English Nature launched its Estuaries Campaign in 1993, under the banner of the 'Campaign for a Living Coast'. The relevant strategic policy statement is the *Strategy for the Sustainable Use of England's Estuaries* (English Nature, 1993).

The strategy covers the full range of estuary activities, including sport and recreation. The stated objective of policy for recreation is to: 'maintain and improve the sustainable enjoyment of estuaries by recreational users'. Estuary management plans are considered in detail in the following chapter. However, several strategies can be considered to be at least sub-regional, and cross a range of local authority and other organizational boundaries.

Two examples of the way in which recreation has been handled in some of the larger initiatives are as follows:

The Dee

A project officer is in post to develop an estuary strategy. A 60-member Dee Estuary Forum has been formed, and a sub-group of 16 members form the steering group for the project. The Sports Council, the British Association for Shooting and Conservation and the Tidal Dee Users Group are all represented. Three technical working groups have been formed to develop proposals for sport and recreation, one identifying issues, one evaluating management options, and one identifying recreation patterns and the difference between apparent and actual conflicts. Consultation has involved an extensive round of meetings between the project officer and interested parties, and invitations to local and national governing bodies to join technical working groups.

The Humber

Work on an estuary management strategy for the Humber began in January 1993. The work is being developed by an English Nature funded project officer. It is guided by a steering group and a smaller working group. The Sports Council is represented on the project steering group and it is considered that it would be appropriate to include further representation of sporting interests. So far the primary need for recreation is to bring together those involved to clarify issues and improve communication. Initially a topic group will be formed to produce a discussion paper on sport, recreation and access, the members will be drawn from local authority recreation officers, national agencies and user groups. The estuary strategy process is drawing on information and research from the Sports Council Regional Strategy and the National Rivers Authority.

The estuaries campaign is still a recent initiative and it will probably be several years before a full evaluation of its achievements and weaknesses will be achieved. From a recreational point of view the policy and approach advocated provides a possible framework for sustainable development of recreational opportunities. A number of the projects appear to be achieving progress. However concern has been expressed from recreational interests about the way in which some projects have been taken forward. Criticism has initially focused on inadequate consultation, and the workload imposed by a large number of initiatives. English Nature have sought to take on board the views of recreational bodies in reviewing the initiative, and it is hoped that measures including improved quality control and a more standardized consultation procedure may help realize a greater role for recreation as the initiative matures further.

2. Scottish Natural Heritage's Focus on Firths Project

Scottish Natural Heritage's Focus on Firths Project currently consists of four projects: Firth of Forth, Solway, Moray Firth and the Minch, each with a project officer. All the projects are pursuing integrated coastal or estuarine management, and the areas covered are very large. To achieve this integrated approach the work has focused on establishing partnerships to guide and coordinate the work on an equal-opinion basis. Effort is also being put into education and interpretation, working with local communities and increasing the profile of the various firths and their uses. Scottish Natural Heritage has taken a lead in appointing project officers for each initiative, in conjunction with local authorities and others.

In the Firth of Forth an Estuary Forum has been formed and consultation has led to the identification of the current issues and opportunities. Many recreational issues arose, and form the remit for a Tourism and Recreation Topic Group, which will research and produce a paper on the current situation with recommendations for the maximization of opportunities and resolution of issues.

Similarly in the Solway (a joint initiative with English Nature), the Solway Firth Partnership has been formed and a number of seminars have been held, including one on recreation. Again management objectives and principles will be developed through a topic paper and topic group.

In the Moray Firth the focus has been on education and interpretation. In 1993 a dolphin awareness initiative was launched, including a voluntary code of conduct for power boat and personal watercraft users, aimed at reducing disturbance. An accreditation scheme for the increasing number of dolphin-watching ventures is also being developed.

12.4.6 SERPLAN COASTAL PLANNING GUIDELINES FOR THE SOUTH EAST

SERPLAN is the London and South East Regional Planning Conference, and is a regional planning and transportation organization comprising local authorities in the South East and the London Boroughs. It has a role to produce regionally based planning guidance for its member organizations. It applies to the coast from Essex to the Isle of Wight. In response to PPG20 Coastal Planning (Department of the Environment, 1992), SERPLAN produced Coastal Planning Guidelines in July 1993 (SERPLAN, 1993). These provide an outline strategy for land use planning on the coast of the South East under a number of headings. Although recreation is not given a specific chapter it is referred to within the guidance within chapters on the undeveloped and developed coast. The policy guidance proposed related to recreation is as follows:

- Policy guidance 11: Coastal authorities within the region will be encouraged to draw up plans for the management of estuaries, Heritage Coasts and intervening stretches of coast which are subject to a concentration of pressures [including recreation].
- Policy guidance 12: Opportunities for access to and along the undeveloped coast for informal recreation should be encouraged subject to environmental considerations and in conjunction with sound visitor management.
- Policy guidance 19 [Developed Coast]: Opportunities for access to the sea for water-based sports should be supported subject to environmental capacity, residential amenity and in conjunction with sound visitor management.
- Policy guidance 20: Coastal authorities within the region should encourage the provision of a network of recreational harbours and marinas along the developed coast where this does not lead to unacceptable congestion and is compatible with other strategy objectives.
- Policy guidance 21: Local planning authorities should seek to conserve, manage and where appropriate, restore and reuse historic coastal buildings and landscape features. Where possible public access should be provided

SERPLAN guidelines note that the ability of statutory planning authorities to progress with many of the areas is limited and that cooperative action between organizations will be required. In an implementation checklist it sets out the roles which a range of partner organizations might undertake to achieve the planning guidelines.

12.4.7 STRATEGIC GUIDELINES FOR THE SOLENT

The project to develop strategic guidelines for the Solent provides an example of a project which is being developed through a non-statutory coastal group – the Solent Forum. The Solent Forum was established in 1992 and is a group of the principal interests in the Solent. Over 50 organizations are members. The Forum exists as a means of exchanging information and comment on all matters of strategic importance affecting the Solent.

The Forum is currently developing a project to produce strategic guidelines for the Solent. The intention is that these will establish the general direction for the whole of the Solent in terms of strategic planning and management, raise awareness of the main issues and set out the ground rules for liaison and consultation. It is hoped that, while the guidance would not resolve all the issues, it will enable unnecessary confrontations to be avoided. Recreation is one of a number of areas to be addressed. It is probable that a working group will be formed to identify the principal issues. It will then be for the Forum to agree on the issues to be researched and addressed by the strategic guidance, as a basis for developing future policy and action.

The involvement of Hampshire County Council in the project illustrates the way in which approaches to strategies are developing. The County Council prepared its own Strategy for Hampshire's Coast in 1991 (Hampshire County Council, 1991) which set out policies which would be pursued by the County Council on all aspects of the coast including land recreation and access, and water-based recreation. The strategy was limited to the responsibilities and policies of the County Council itself. Following the formation of the Solent Forum there is the opportunity to develop Solent-wide policies with the agreement of a wide range of organizations. Continuity is possible as the Council will be an active partner in the strategic guidance project and, although the policies within its existing coastal strategy will be the basis of its involvement, the process of development of strategic guidelines may mean that some of these will be changed during the process of dialogue and consultation.

12.5 IMPLEMENTATION CASE STUDY: THE SOUTHERN REGION COASTAL RECREATION STRATEGY

The Southern Region Coastal Recreation Strategy provides a case study of the implementation of a regional strategy for recreation, through the employment of a project officer. The appointment of a Coastal Recreation Officer within the Southern Region is a three-year joint project between Sports Council and Hampshire County Council. The post is based within the County Countryside and Community Department of the County Council and is jointly funded by the two organizations. The purpose is to implement and develop the Southern Council for Sport and Recreation's Coastal Recreation Strategy (Southern Council for Sport and Recreation, 1991) published as part of the Regional Strategy for Sport 1990–93.

The core responsibility is to 'provide a co-ordinated and integrated approach to the planning and management of coastal recreation and conservation in the Southern Region'. The project covers Hampshire,

Isle of Wight and Chichester Harbour and is guided by a small steering group. The priority work areas are as follows.

12.5.1 COMMUNICATION AND COORDINATION

The pattern of coastal recreation in the region is complicated and extensive, and the organizational responsibilities and consultative mechanisms which exist are diverse. A key priority of the project is therefore to be a common networking and information point for all those with interests in recreation on the Solent.

Other priorities of the work programme were devised to meet needs identified through consultation, to fit in with the existing work and responsibilities of others, and to develop opportunities for collaboration with different interests. This has resulted in a targeted practical programme of work, which aims to meet identified information, strategy and project needs. The main project areas are as follows.

Survey of Recreation at Coastal Sites

This project addresses an information need. A pilot survey was carried out in 1993 in order to assess the extent and levels of different coastal recreational activities within the Region. This drew on information gathered through a network of coastal site managers and repeat surveying has taken place in 1994.

Moorings and Marinas Information System

This project also addresses an information need. Consistent information is being collated on the provision of mooring and berthing facilities within all harbours in the region. The resulting information system will be held on geographical information system and will be available primarily as information to support the planning activities of local and harbour authorities.

Public Launch Points

This project too addresses an information need, develops strategy and seeks practical action. An audit of public launching facilities, including slipways, hards and beaches has been coordinated. This has identified the need to improve the condition of some sites to adopt a selective approach to promotion and to develop better and more consistent on-site information and interpretation. The importance of a strategic approach to public launch points is discussed further as a detailed case study below.

Assessment of Sensitivity of Coastal Sites

This project addresses a research need and contributes to future strategy. A study of the sensitivity of the coast is being coordinated which will seek to better understand the relationship of different recreational activities to the environment, and to clarify where key conservation concerns lie.

12.5.2 STRATEGY DEVELOPMENT

Work here aims to continue to develop the themes of the coastal recreation strategy through input into other statutory and non-statutory initiatives, and by working with governing bodies of sport. The main areas of emphasis are:

- contribution to the project to develop strategic guidelines for the Solent;
- encouraging the preparation of development strategies by the regional governing bodies of appropriate sports; advice has been given to the British Water Ski Federation who will be bringing forward their Regional Strategy shortly, and the Officer is also working with Royal Yachting Association Windsurfing on a strategy for windsurfing in the region;
- providing information and comment both directly and to Sports Council on statutory and non-statutory plans within the region, and on consultations and initiatives promoted by Government and national agencies, including English Nature's Sensitive Marine Area and Estuaries projects.

12.5.3 FUTURE STRATEGIC ISSUES FOR COASTAL RECREATION

Strategy needs to continue to develop and the following issues have been identified as some of the most significant with regard to the future of coastal recreation in the Southern Region. They provide examples of the sort of issues which coastal recreation strategies may need to respond to in the future:

- There is the need to increase the profile of coastal recreation, and countryside and water recreation in general. This needs to be seen as an equal priority in profile and resources with more formal sport and recreation.

- The abilities of regional governing bodies to take a lead in the development of their activities is a major controlling factor on the abilities to maintain a strategic approach to the development of activities. Moves to strengthen their role, and make better direct links between them, providers and conservation interests would be welcome.

- There are the wide range of, largely conservation-led, recent Government and government agency initiatives related to the implementation of EC Habitats and Species Directive, coastal zone and estuary management and sustainable development. The implications of future designation of Special Protection Areas and Special Areas of Conservation require particular attention and there is little information available at present on which to assess what the implications of new designations may be. Close attention is required so that the key needs to ensure their conservation objectives do not result in undue restrictions on sport and recreation.

- There is a broadening consensus that the Solent may be nearing capacity – at least during the busiest times of peak season. Further developments for recreation and increased participation will be possible, but within finite limits. Particular care is needed to ensure that they are well planned and managed and that they are acceptable in relation to environmental, safety and other users.

- Finding more space for watersports on inland waters within a time span of the next 10–15 years appears to be a pressing need which should figure highly within the strategic objectives for the Region. This may involve both maximizing use of existing waters within environmental constraints, and seeking access to new areas of water.

- Coastal erosion and the effects of sea level rise will continue to affect access at the coast in the foreseeable future, and the breaching of coastal footpaths will be a persistent feature of the next decades.

- There is a continuing need to improve the information base on coastal recreation. The experience of the last two years has shown that many coastal recreational activities are very sensitive to variations in the economy. The further complication is predicting the rise and extent of new activities e.g. personal watercraft. It would be helpful if there was some means of keeping a better watching brief on developments within the industry, but predictions of demand will continue to be very difficult.

12.6 CASE STUDY: MANAGEMENT OF PUBLIC LAUNCH POINTS – A PARTICULAR NEED FOR A STRATEGIC APPROACH

One of the principal areas of work in the Southern Region, as listed above, is the development of work related to public launch points. They provide a good example of an aspect of coastal recreation which requires a strategic approach, and experience of work in Hampshire is discussed below.

Public launch points are essentially sites on the coast which are available for anyone to use to get on to the water. A working definition is that they are:

> *sites where the general public may launch craft, through right, permission or custom, over the foreshore into tidal waters.*

Launch points include 'public slipways', which are built launching structures, 'public hards' which may be natural or maintained areas of hardstanding crossing the foreshore and 'beach launching' which is generally only used by portable craft. In addition to sites which are truly 'public', there may also be informal and unmanaged sites where it is possible to get boats on to the water.

In general, public launch points are provided by an organization which has built, or maintains the facility, and has designated it as being for public use. There is no general right of public access over the foreshore, so these organizations will normally have a leasing arrangement for the slipway with the Crown Estate (or other owner of the foreshore).

The law surrounding possible public rights at launch points is interesting, if arcane. It has been suggested public *rights* to launch may exist at certain types of launch points. This area of the law is discussed in detail by Phelan (1965). He suggests that to establish a general right over the foreshore, an established custom of use of a particular part of the shore would need to be demonstrated. He also suggests that the law would probably accept that public highways running down to the foreshore continue over the foreshore in a straight line to the sea. Phelan notes that the rights of the owner of land adjacent to the foreshore are superior to those of the public at large, and the former may include rights to launch. The precise rights of the public to launch are mostly untested in law, largely because the need to do so has not arisen.

Charges are made for launching at some of the public launch sites. It is not apparent that there are any general legal limitations on launch point owners regarding the imposition of charges. However in many cases it would be difficult in practice, as well as uneconomic and unpopular, to attempt to impose and collect launch fees. Harbour authorities have powers to charge harbour dues on craft using harbour waters. These may sometimes be collected at launch points, although they do not represent a launching charge *per se*.

Launch points have a fundamental importance within the coastal zone, for the following reasons:

● they represent the fundamental resource which allows much coastal recreation to take place. They are basic facilities which require recognition and supportive management.

It is important to stress that public launch points are not the only recreational launch points on the coast. Marinas and clubs may have their own facilities for example, and the launching activity from some clubs can be very significant. However:

● Some public launch points provide the launching facility for sailing, angling and other coastal recreation clubs.

Public launch points are also fundamental to planning and management of coastal recreation in relation to other uses.

● They are a fundamental influence on the pattern of recreation. Their management therefore is critical in influencing the pattern of recreation in the coastal zone as a whole.
● They provide key opportunities to contact launch point users with information on safety, conservation etc. In particular they are a focus for users who are unattached to club structures and for visitors who may be unfamiliar with a local area.

Despite their importance, however, there is often a gap between the potential and management needs of public launch points and the level, quality and consistency of attention which is paid to them. They are also owned by a range of different organizations so the levels and quality of management may vary and there is likely to be no organization with an overview of all the sites.

The following priorities for public launch points have been suggested:

Public launch points require a strategic overview

On any estuary or coherent stretch of coast the pattern of recreation normally transcends the administrative boundaries of most Districts and

Harbours. In order to move towards integrated management of coastal recreation an overview at sub-regional level is required.

Research and information on public launch points is essential

A first step must be to locate and document all the public launch points, so that there is a single database on the facilities, their quality, location and level of use and constraints. A survey in Hampshire found over 70 launch points in one county, but probably only half were particularly well used. The most important factors for a good launch point appear to be:

- a good condition and well maintained facility;
- proximity to attractive inshore waters;
- good car parking and shore based facilities;
- access at all states of the tide.

The management and promotion of different launch points should be linked

There are obvious benefits in managing launch points more as a single body of facilities than as a group of individual sites. Management and promotion should seek to distribute activities to sites where the facilities are best and most appropriate for their needs. This could also assist in separating activities which are incompatible, and is fundamental in the implementation of any zonation scheme for recreational activity.

Good quality and well maintained launch points are required

The promotion of adequate facilities for coastal recreation requires as a fundamental that much closer attention, and more resources are devoted to maintaining launch points which are a credit to the coast.

Public launch points should be a focus for good quality information and interpretation

The opportunities to focus good quality information and interpretation at public launch points should be grasped. These are sites which all non-club users will make use of and a natural focus at which to target information at groups who are otherwise difficult to contact. Attention to detail, and good quality design and writing which is aimed at the needs of recreational users is required. Public launch points have a particular role to play in educating recreational users about the environment in areas of nature conservation sensitivity.

A consistent and standardized approach to the provision of information to the public is required. Ideally this should be at a national level

Finally, consistency is all important. If users are to be reached effectively (many of whom may be tourists or very mobile) it is essential that we seek to follow some basic standards in terms of the content of information which is put over. National guidance on appropriate standards for coastal recreation signs have now been produced (Hampshire County Council *et al.*, 1995).

12.7 CONCLUSION

This chapter has provided a brief review of regional coastal recreation strategies and the range of forms which they take. It can only be an introduction to the subject, and has perhaps served to highlight how young many of the regional strategy initiatives are. More research on the effectiveness of regional strategies is certainly needed – but what is more important in the meantime is that those preparing strategies focus on ensuring they are effective. This means excellent consultation, the best possible links with partner organizations, integration with other planning and management initiatives, and an emphasis on achieving clear, appropriate and practical action. The measure of the success of regional strategies for coastal recreation will not be found within the pages of the strategy documents that are produced, but rather in the positive benefits they achieve for the quality, good management and where possible the quantity of recreational experiences within the coastal zone.

ACKNOWLEDGEMENTS

Many of the ideas and views within this chapter are the product of discussions with different organizations and individuals over several years. Particular thanks are due to Alan Inder from Hampshire County Council who made helpful comments on the manuscript, to Julie Amies, also of Hampshire County Council, to the Sports Council Southern Region, and to former colleagues at the Heritage Coast Forum in Manchester. I am grateful to Mark Jennison of Scottish Natural Heritage and to Meaghan Grabrovaz, Angela Moffat and Lynette Evans of English Nature for providing information which has been included above. The opinions expressed remain solely those of the author, and do not necessarily reflect the views of either Hampshire County Council or the Sports Council.

REFERENCES

Department of the Environment (1973) *Guidelines for Regional Recreation Strategies, Circular 73/77*, HMSO, London.
Department of the Environment/Welsh Office (1991) *PPG17, Planning Policy Guidance: Sport and Recreation*, HMSO, London.
Department of the Environment/Welsh Office (1992) *PPG20, Planning Policy Guidance: Coastal Planning*, HMSO, London.
English Nature (1993a) *Strategy for the Sustainable Use of England's Estuaries*, English Nature, Peterborough.
English Nature (1993b) *Estuary Management Plans: A Co-ordinators Guide*, English Nature, Peterborough.
Hampshire County Council (1991) *A Strategy for Hampshire's Coast*, Hampshire County Council, Winchester.
Hampshire County Council, English Nature, Sports Council, HM Coastguard (1995) *Coastal Recreation Signs*, Hampshire County Council, Winchester.
Heritage Coast Forum and Sports Council (1993) *Sport and Recreation on Heritage Coasts*, Heritage Coast Forum, Manchester.
Phelan, A. (1965) *The Law for Small Boats*, Charles Knight & Co. Ltd, London.
SERPLAN (1993) *Coastal Planning Guidelines for the South East*, The London and South East Planning Conference, London.
Southern Council for Sport and Recreation (1991) *Strategy for Sport 1990–93 Subject Report No. 8: Coastal Recreation Strategy*, Sports Council, Reading.
South Western Council for Sport and Recreation (1990) *Regional Strategy for Sport and Recreation in South West England Subject Report: A Strategy for Coastal Recreation*, South West Council for Sport and Recreation/Sports Council, Crewkerne.
Sports Council (1992) *Countryside and Water Recreation Factfile 3: Heritage Coasts: Good Practice in the Planning, Management and Sustainable Development of Sport and Active Recreation*, Sports Council, London.
Sports Council (1994) *Consultation with Governing Bodies of Sport on Estuary Management Plans: a guidance note for plan co-ordinators*, Sports Council, London.

Coastal Management Plans

13

13.1 INTRODUCTION

Implicit in the coastal recreational strategies, explained in the previous chapter, is the need for a comprehensive statement at a local level, usually relating to a specific site or area, to provide a framework for implementing practical management solutions for coastal recreation activities both above and below low water mark.

This guidance is often presented and coordinated in the form of a *management plan*. Such plans have been developed in a land management context for forestry enterprises, country estates and nature reserves as standard practice for many years. In 1974 the Countryside Commission extended the concept to the management of recreation with advice on producing management plans for Country Parks and, more recently, the Institute of Leisure and Amenity Management has produced a guide to management plans for Parks and Open Spaces (Barber, 1991). Management plans of this nature have been defined as:

> Site specific documents prepared by the controlling owner, occupier or manager of a piece of land, which guide the planning and management of that land. (Leay, Rowe and Young, 1986)

In this chapter the application of this approach to coastal recreation is examined. Coastal management plans for this purpose are deemed to include estuary and harbour management plans and heritage coast/AONB plans. Shoreline management plans, which are concerned primarily with coastal defence, and catchment management plans, designed to guide the development of water resources, are not included.

While these coastal management plans have all been compiled for particular stretches of the coast and, as a result, are not consistent in style or content, they do have a degree of commonality as follows.

Coastal Recreation Management Edited by Tim Goodhead and David Johnson. Published in 1996 by E & FN Spon, London. ISBN 0 419 20360 5

- They are non-statutory, relying on the voluntary principle and are designed to complement rather than provide any alternative to statutory development plans (Chapter 6).
- They are broadly similar in purpose and function and depend on the formation of local partnerships or existing arrangements for their implementation.
- They all attempt to influence complex multiple use and multi-responsibility situations where there is a perceived need for some control over the different activities but where other statutory controls are inadequate.
- They are based on agreed technical information often sourced and coordinated by independent consultants.
- They are self-contained, setting out both management decisions and the reasoning behind those decisions.
- They all require periodic re-appraisal and up-dating in the light of watersports developments and changes in the economic and institutional environments.

The distinction between coastal strategies and the range of different coastal management plans which incorporate coastal recreation is sometimes blurred. Indeed, several management plans for larger estuaries (such as the Mersey, Thames, and Wash) are more correctly defined as strategic documents. Management plans, which incorporate recreation issues, should not usually be concerned with whether or not recreational activity occurs at all in a particular area, but instead, they should set out how it is intended that recreational activities should be managed and developed.

English Nature point out that 'management plans need to be prepared within the context of adjacent stretches of coastline and the neighbouring hinterland, taking full account of regional and national needs' (English Nature, 1993).

A number of plans which have recently been drawn up are used to illustrate the management planning process. The chapter concludes by reviewing briefly two international case studies, by way of comparison, and then highlights a number of problems which coastal recreation managers, who are in the business of implementing management plans, still need to address.

13.2 WHY HAVE COASTAL MANAGEMENT PLANS AT ALL?

A fundamental problem within the coastal zone (as explained in Chapter 4) is the number of organizations with powers and responsibilities. Primarily as a result of this factor little positive management planning has taken place until recently. The House of Commons Select Committee Report (1992) identified the lack of a single body with overall responsibility and the authority to take an overview, as the chief reason behind overlap, confusion, omissions and piecemeal action.

While the idea of creating another body to oversee the coast has not found favour, it is clear that management is needed. This is particularly the case at certain pressure points, often in more sheltered waters, where spatial and temporal conflicts are experienced most frequently, both between informal and active recreation and between sports competing for water space (typically motorized v. non-motorized). With increasing participation and the emergence of new activities (Chapter 7) it is anticipated that these conflicts will worsen if no action is taken. However, a balance must be struck between maximum use/minimum control and limited use/maximum control. The accepted means for rationalization of decision making is the management plan.

The value of a management plan is to provide a 'memorandum' for an agreed framework of positive rather than reactive action.

Leay, Rowe and Young (1986) describe the role of the management plan as 'a vehicle for recording systematically the characteristics of the site, acknowledging explicitly its most valuable aspect and specifying objectives for the site's management which will be achieved through the proposals and work programmes which are outlined in the plan'.

The coastal management plan needs to combine different policies from a range of organizations and translate these into a 'set of instructions', acceptable to everyone, for the use of the manager(s) and in the 'best' interests of the water users.

As a result, since the mid 1980s much effort and enthusiasm has been put into developing management plans for the coastal zone in the UK.

Some key reasons why coastal management plans are now perceived as important are summarized below:

- To indicate priorities for management – the plan should help to focus advance planning, to determine what is achievable and where management effort needs to be concentrated. From any such evaluation manpower and resource priorities can be allocated. A further advantage of establishing these guidelines is evident in terms of establishing accountability.
- To reduce potential conflicts and improve safety – the plan should help the manager rationalize complex decisions and provide a spatial and/or temporal reference for different recreational activities.

- To improve the speed and effectiveness of existing decision making procedures.
- To inform users – while these management plans are non-statutory they should be publicized (in a simplified form) and thereby encourage a certain degree of self-regulation of unsafe, anti-social or conflicting activities.
- To provide continuity of management – the plan provides a documentary record of the site and its activities, including the effects and success of past management and how management keys into national and regional policy frameworks.

A sound plan will be a statement of policy for the future and a guide to the subsequent administration of the resource. It should describe clearly the objectives of management with the reasons for their adoption, the means for achieving those objectives and the specific management instructions which stem from them. (Countryside Commission, 1974)

13.3 PREPARATION AND CONTENT

The preparation of coastal management plans requires a systematic approach. To date, the most coherent advice has been produced by English Nature, who have published a 'Co-ordinators Guide to Estuary Management Plans' (English Nature, 1993). The DoE have recently commissioned a best practice on coastal management plains which should be available in 1996.

Kennedy (1994), using the development of the Thames Estuary Management Plan as an example, identifies the preparation stages shown in Table 13.1.

The projected timescale for this procedure is between two and four years. Management plans are then typically reviewed after an agreed time period and three to five yearly reviews are common. It would be inappropriate to set out a universal list of contents applicable to every coastal management plan. Each plan is specific to its site, managing agencies and subject focus. Furthermore, as pointed out by Bromley (1994) 'almost every organization that is responsible for managing land used for countryside recreation, or for advising those who manage such land, has its own method for preparing management plans'. This point is equally valid for coastal situations.

However, while detailed content will vary from location to location, many of the component parts are common to all such documents.

Table 13.1 Preparation stages in developing a coastal management plan

Stage 1
Scoping to identify the real issues for management. This involves information gathering to give a picture of the management situation prior to formulating the Management Plan. This stage may result in the production of a Preparatory Document, or Interim or Issues Report (e.g. New Forest District Council Coastal Issues Report, 1991) which serves as a consultation document, helping to shape and build support for the plan.

Stage 2
Planning what is desired as an outcome and how to achieve it; in effect the work programme for the management planning exercise.

Stage 3
Agreeing the Management Structure for the Plan is essential with any project where there are multiple responsibilities. An accepted format is the formation of a Steering Group or Working Party consisting of the primary decision-makers. The government advises that local authorities should take the lead in preparing coastal management plans (DoE/WO 1993), but funding and advisory agencies (e.g. Sports Councils, NRA, English Nature) are also typically members of any Steering Group. English Nature also envisages the formation of topic groups (e.g. Blackwater Estuary Management Plan), one of which should be for water-based recreation. In practice a range of different approaches have been taken and topic groups have not always been felt to be necessary. The Sports Council is generally supportive of the topic group approach, and has prepared a short guidance note suggesting a standard approach which might be adopted. The management structure for the Thames Estuary Management Plan Project is shown in Figure 13.1 by way of example (Kennedy, 1994)

Stage 4
Doing the work (i.e. analysis of information, formulation of objectives and production of a detailed action programme).

Stage 5
Presenting the Plan firstly as a draft for consultation, to allow for comment and public/user reaction, and then as a finalized document.

Leay, Rowe and Young (1986) set out the typical management plan format in the form of a flow diagram. A brief summary of their headings is given in Table 13.2.

It appears to be the case that non-statutory coastal planning initiatives are often unduly driven by the need to produce a document. This is something which must be resisted. The point is well made by Moffat and Paterson (1994), speaking about estuary management plans:

Often the primary aim is to have a completed management plan to be sent for public consultation by a specific date [. . .] In actual fact, the management plan document is not important for the management of the estuary. The process of drawing together statutory and non-statutory interests, setting up committees which together agree to and implement their future requirements, resolving conflicts on an ongoing basis, and directing and undertaking active management are the most important aims of estuary management.

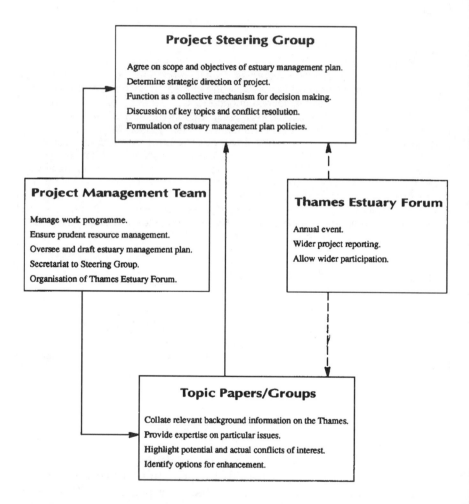

Figure 13.1 Thames Estuary Management Plan Project Structure. (Source: Kennedy, 1994.)

Table 13.2 Typical management plan format. (Source: after Leay, Rowe and Young, 1986.)

Aims:	Statement of intent reflecting strategic policies and the balance of interests
Survey:	Background information and baseline data which is both regional and site specific. This section usually includes both a description of the site and a detailed audit of the site's key features
Analysis:	Resolution of conflicting management proposals together with a consideration of opportunities and constraints, and an assessment of their importance
Objectives:	Specific, measurable and precise targets which can be priced and timetabled outlining courses of action
Prescription:	An overview of the work required to meet the management objectives together with resource requirements
Implementation:	A detailed action programme explaining how management objectives will be achieved and work executed
Monitoring and Review:	A record and assessment of action taken and proposals for reviewing the plan

While the preparation stages are important and largely determine the management plan's content the result should be a working document rather than merely a paper work exercise.

The importance of consultation and flexibility in order to achieve effective day-to-day management cannot be overstated.

13.4 CASE STUDIES OF MANAGEMENT PLANS FOR COASTAL RECREATION

This section describes some examples of coastal recreational management plans. Over 70 coastal management plans have currently been identified around the UK.

None of these is exclusively concerned with watersports, because, as this book explains, coastal recreational management is part of a complex mix of different issues.

As in the previous chapter two types of these initiatives are examined. Firstly, examples of those which are management plans whose main purpose is to manage coastal recreation are considered and then examples of integrated coastal management plans within which recreation features strongly.

The former are often driven by the safety concerns of controlling Port and Harbour Authorities and the latter are usually driven by the 'sustainability' concerns of local authorities and environmental organizations. English Nature, for example, have stated that their goal is to prepare plans for half of England's estuaries by number and 80% by area, by the year 2000 (English Nature, 1992).

The National Coasts and Estuaries Advisory Group (1994) have produced a Directory cataloguing coastal planning and management initiatives in England which lists a total of 90 entries.

13.4.1 RECREATION SPECIFIC PLANS

Milford Haven Waterway Recreation Plan

The Milford Haven Waterway Recreation Plan (1992) builds upon and updates an earlier initiative undertaken by the Milford Haven Port Authority in 1978. The 1992 Plan was conceived by the Port Authority together with a Working Group of local authorities and countryside agencies. Its aim is to provide a 'working document in managing recreational activities on the waterway' and to provide 'the basis for operation of the Water Ranger Service'.

A full range of water-based recreation activities take place on the Waterway both on an informal basis and as part of organized events. Organized activities include water-skiing and power boating championships, yacht racing and in 1991 Milford Haven hosted the Cutty Sark Tall Ships race. The Haven also provides some of the finest diving opportunities in Britain. The Port Authority estimate that recreation accounts for 90% of all craft movements. For management purposes the 28-mile Waterway is divided into the Upper Estuary, Middle Section and the Lower Waterway.

The survey phase of this Plan reappraised a number of issues. The first and most important of these was a survey of general recreational use and specialized sports giving detailed information on the spatial distribution of recreation and the frequency and timing of different activities. Other topics considered were conservation issues (landscape, wildlife, fisheries and water quality) and existing policies and controls, as they affected recreation.

An analysis of these issues lead to the formulation of objectives for both

- the recreational use of the water; and
- the development of new facilities.

Specifically, in terms of recreational use of the Waterway action is considered necessary to:

- zone high-speed motor sports;
- educate recreationists on the importance of wildlife and landscape conservation;
- improve safety information and ensure adherence to national codes of practice;
- continue to build a database of information on recreational use and its impact on wildlife, particularly bird populations;
- monitor water quality.

Potential for development of new facilities is defined as a need to:

- double new moorings and berths in the Middle Section;
- identify specific sites for new launch points and landing pontoons;
- raise awareness of recreational opportunities.

Management prescriptions put forward are applicable to the whole Waterway and locally appropriate management policies which, in the Plan, are presented as Area Studies.

Waterway wide prescriptions include:

- the introduction of a Water Ranger Service for a three-year term to develop liaison and advisory services for recreational users, assist with enforcement of bye-laws and help with monitoring and research;
- clearly defined permitted zones for aquaplaning sports (principally water-skiing and jet-skiing);
- the definition of 'Sanctuary Areas' for important nature conservation areas;
- promotion of safety by improving publicity of local conditions and safety considerations and the consideration of local zoning policies;
- biannual surveys of recreational use, together with annual ornithological surveys;
- compliance with NRA water quality standards;
- new development of moorings and berths in appropriate locations;
- consideration of individual launching and landing developments on their own merits;
- information dissemination through liaison with other bodies, contact with users and the development of information boards.

Implementation details and monitoring procedures are not stipulated.

The Recreation Plan has now been in place for three years. During that time a jointly funded Water Ranger has been employed by the

National Park Authority. The Ranger's role has been primarily educational and advisory. The Plan is thought to be accepted by 90% of recreational users. Visitors to the Waterway respect both the principles and the bye-laws (although as always a small minority of visitors and locals elect to disregard them!). However, the Water Ranger post is not to be renewed in 1995.

Experience of implementation suggests that the Plan correctly concluded that 'the vast majority of activity on the water requires little or no additional supervision or control, since users generally exercise their right of navigation in a responsible way'. In reality only an occasional enforcement presence (say two staff in a rib) for perhaps ten hours a week during the summer is needed, rather than a full-time Water Ranger. Furthermore, the Port Authority are perceived by their partner organizations as unwilling to be seen to be encouraging 'unnecessary' over-regulation.

The plan is therefore a useful decision-making framework. On the whole the prescriptions put forward are working well. It would appear that, at present, recreational activity is not enough of a problem to warrant rigorous enforcement action. Indeed, aggressive enforcement is deemed as inappropriate and, given the size of the waterway, education of recreational users is perhaps more cost-effective. Specialized safety and conservation information has been produced for specific sectors (e.g. canoeing and kayaking), by the National Park.

Poole Harbour Aquatic Management Plan

Poole Harbour is a large natural, sheltered and relatively shallow harbour within which a range of recreational activities often conflict and have the potential to increase in intensity. Recreation is competing for water space with equally valid commercial and environmental uses. The Poole Harbour Aquatic Management Plan: Consultation Draft (Dorset County Council. 1994) is a first attempt to provide a management framework, based upon the strategic advice of a series of management policies formulated in the 1980s and revised in 1991 (Poole Harbour Management Policies, 1991).

The Plan is a peculiar hybrid of part Issues Report and part Management Plan. Its formulation was coincidental with a bid by Poole Harbour Commissioners to introduce a 10 knot speed limit throughout the Harbour. Poole Harbour RNLI station still had the unenviable position as the UK's busiest in 1994. The Secretary of State would only confirm this new bye-law if areas were formally demarked for high-speed activities (namely water and jet skiing).

Background or survey information within the Plan comprises an analysis of the status of three key elements (environment, recreation and commerce) with the aim of evaluating:

- the characteristics of the harbour and distribution (in time and space) of the various uses and interests and how these are likely to change over time;
- the inter-relationships between the various uses, the mutual benefits and conflicts;
- the current mechanisms for safeguarding interests and resolving conflicts; and
- the effectiveness of existing management regime of the Harbour and any additional management powers or measures which are needed.

Part of this process involved compiling access and activity maps for different recreational activities and providing quantitative data on levels of use in order to evaluate the relative importance of activities. Seasonality of recreational uses was also considered. An impact analysis was then used to identify conflict between various elements and their specific activities.

While not exclusively dedicated to coastal recreational management, the emphasis of this Consultation Draft Management Plan is the segregation of recreational water activities from those of the commercial port and from each other. It also aims to confine recreation to areas where the impact on wildlife will be least damaging.

The Plan sets three clear objectives:

---

1. protection and maintenance of the special natural features of the Harbour;
2. promotion of the sustainable and wise use of the Harbour for commerce, recreation and amenity; and
3. the provision of a framework for the coordinated management of the Harbour.

The prescription for the Aquatic Management Plan is expressed as a Zoning Plan, the intention of which is to incorporate, as far as possible, existing controls for those activities where a means of management already exists (e.g. wildfowling), and which is enforced by Harbour Bye-laws. The result has been a simple Recreational Zoning Plan within which certain areas are dedicated exclusively for specific watersports (the Plan identifies zones for jet skiers, waterskiers, windsurfers and sub aqua). Main channels are nominated to separate commercial and recreational craft and an emphasis is placed on clearly informing users of the relevant regulations which govern their activities, in particular, speed limits.

The Zoning Plan is shown in Figure 13.2.

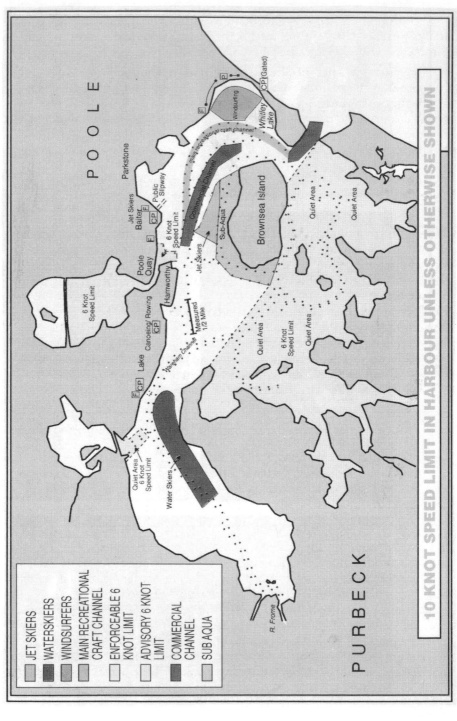

Figure 13.2 Poole Harbour Recreational Zoning Plan. (Source: Dorset County Council, 1994.)

The Management Plan also recommends consideration of:

- the formation of a Liaison Committee supported by a wardening system;
- registration and identification of vessels;
- interpretation and information provision;
- additional on-shore facility provision;
- a charging system for water access;
- on-going monitoring of effectiveness of the Zoning Plan and its attendant measures.

At this stage implementation and monitoring details, for the above, were not worked up.

Public reaction to the Consultation Draft Plan (Poole Harbour Commissioners, 1994) criticized the lack of consultation, lack of justification and the data used to formulate proposals. The practicality of the zoning was also seriously questioned, particularly

- the juxtapositioning of the jet ski and subaqua zones (in reality part of the sub aqua zone is a popular mooring area and it is sailors who object to the noise of nearby jet skiers); and
- the positioning of the jet ski area, half a mile offshore and astride three designated channels – recreation, small craft and commercial shipping. With jet skis also confined to one common slipway they are effectively banned in theory from inshore areas. In practice this element of the zoning is not working.

With the support of EU funding, a Project Officer was appointed to undertake a series of consultations; collect baseline information over a typical summer, and then redraft the Management Plan to produce a finalized document. Work during 1994/95 concentrated on building up a local database to counter the Consultation Draft Plan's perceived shortcomings. It included a major aerial and questionnaire survey to chart the variety and position of craft over several busy weekends (Fairgrieve, 1995) and a report by the RSPB to evaluate recreational disturbance to breeding birds. This work which confirms several of the initial criticisms (i.e. existing activity zoning is not strictly observed; proportionally approximately 90% of the craft using the harbour are yachts and motorboats; and Poole Harbour is not reaching its 'capacity' for absorbing waterborne recreation) will help justify the final Management Plan. A clear conclusion is that it is the 'issue of access to and into the water which is itself the major determinant of Poole Harbour's capacity for recreational activities'.

Likely proposals are the construction of a second public slipway and shoreside facilities (showers, toilets, etc.) and changes to the zoning plan including extending the quiet zone, repositioning the personal water craft zone within inshore waters, simplifying the permit system for waterskiing and abandonment of the sub-aqua zone.

Perhaps the most difficult management challenge is yet to be faced – the promotion of the redrafted Plan. Poole attracts recreational water users from a local, regional and national catchment area. Work to raise awareness and promote the Management Plan initiative has already been undertaken, with some success, but simply 'getting the message across' and liaising with all parties will have significant future resource implications.

13.4.2 RECREATION WITHIN INTEGRATED MANAGEMENT PLANS

Brief summaries are given below of three well established initiatives. They all feature in the National Coast and Estuary Advisory Group Good Practice Guide (1993) and each, in their own way, can claim to be ground-breaking in terms of coastal management planning within the UK. All three are also important (and heavily designated) conservation areas within which the intensity of recreational activity is thought to be increasing.

Chichester Harbour Management Plan

Chichester Harbour Conservancy, formed in 1971, has in the past and continues to be a leading UK player in the development of solutions for the management of coastal water-based recreation. The Conservancy has a well-established staffing structure and significant volunteer support (1540 volunteer man days during 1993/94 were estimated to equate to an input of £46 000). A strength of the Conservancy's work is the emphasis placed on surveys establishing quantitative information upon which to validate management decisions. The most relevant of these to the subject of this book are surveys of recreation (the most recent by Fecher, 1993), but similar resource audits have been published for landscape, ecology and economic and cultural resources.

The Chichester Harbour Management Plan (Chichester Harbour Conservancy, 1994) replaces the 1983 Amenity Area Plan, which sought to balance different recreational interests. The Management Plan has a much broader aim, seeking to foster wise use of resources, sustainability and consensus, as well as balancing all interests. It also provides the context for a number of smaller site specific management plans.

Objectives are defined in terms of policy, function and area. The Plan lists 27 Policy Objectives. These include, for example, statements which summarize the Conservancy's future policy with regard to personalized water craft, sailing and boating, and water skiing as three separate objectives. Objectives by function are then listed and prioritized (High=1, Medium=2, Low=3) with the highest priority objectives divided into essential and opportunistic (i.e. to be undertaken if the right circumstances and opportunities arise). The Function Objectives for water-based recreation (WBR) are illustrated in Table 13.3.

Table 13.3 Chichester Harbour Management Plan: function objectives for water-based recreation

(a)	Provide additional jetty facilities for water, essential fuel and pump out at Emsworth and Itchenor	1
(b)	Improve facilities for visiting yachtsmen through an opportunistic increase in visitors' mooring sites	2
(c)	Adapt the existing pontoon moorings at Itchenor to accommodate a further 15 vessels and incorporate on the pontoons the existing A1 moorings	2
(d)	Provide pontoon visitors' berths at Emsworth	2
(e)	Provide improved shored based WC and shower opportunistic facilities at public landing sites	1
(f)	In order to reduce congestion caused by swinging moorings, and to reduce the extent of the mooring areas, replace them, where appropriate, with pontoon berths unconnected to the shore	2
(g)	Provide support for seamanship training under sail and power vessels	3
(h)	Introduce good-seamanship award for sail and power vessels	2
(i)	Review water-based patrol systems essential	1
(j)	Review policy on moorings every three years through the Mooring Working Party	2
(k)	Continue to discuss with the Chichester Harbour Federation and sailing clubs essential way of reducing congestion at peak times	1
(l)	Produce an information leaflet for distribution to windsurfing centres setting out a code of practice	2
(m)	Produce a leaflet direction at owners of personal essential water craft and speedboats, launching from public hards, indicating restrictions on their use	1
(n)	Promote a harbour Code of good water user opportunistic practice	1

The Plan then divides the Harbour into 26 'Area Objectives Sites' and statements which are essentially management plan prescriptions are put forward, together with a 'consultation list' of interested parties, for each area.

Implementation and costs are covered in a separate chapter of the Plan. This section attempts to relate income projections to management plan implementation costs but does not provide a detailed action programme. Monitoring however, is clearly specified. Data on seven indicators, one of which is recreational water users, are to be monitored to provide essential feedback and a reporting/updating procedure is stipulated.

Taw Torridge Estuary Management Plan

The management plan for this major river estuary in North Devon was developed from a study carried out by environmental consultants in 1992. This study was in effect an information gathering exercise and an analysis of the main coastal issues – recreation conflicts; conservation, water quality, development pressures erosion and the water table. A Consultation Draft Summary report was published in 1993 and the final Management Plan in 1994 (W. S. Atkins, 1994). The management plan is seen as the basis for detailed management and control of the estuary. A jointly funded Estuary Manager was appointed in 1995, for whom recreational issues are a first priority.

The Taw Torridge Estuary Management Plan is part of English Nature's Estuary Initiative. It clearly identifies recreation and environmental objectives; defines geographical management areas; and identifies local priorities for these areas. From this, a rationale for specific proposals is developed. For example, an area for jet skiing, outside designated swimming areas, is defined – where access and car parking is good and a launching lane can be demarked. Jet skiing is then restricted in all other sites. The Plan also includes a table with a summary of implementation proposals.

In practice, however, the recreational zoning of jet skiers is proving difficult. Both jet skiers and the Parish Council, who have control of the foreshore access, are unhappy with the Management Plan proposals for jet ski zoning. As a result the Estuary Manager has decided to initiate further consultation, using a more pro-active approach, to establish a grass roots ownership of the Plan and a refinement of the zoning. This example illustrates the importance of marketing the Plan and further modifying it in the light of experience. The implementation proposals in this case provide a useful starting point, or set of ideas, but they must be acceptable to all recreational groups.

Norfolk Coast Project

Management plans for Heritage Coasts, being largely land-based, are the most established of the UK coastal management plans. The North

Norfolk Heritage Coast Management Plan was first prepared in 1981 and the latest version in 1989. Countryside management policies, to conserve habitats and landscape as well as managing tourism, were extended to include the Norfolk Coast Area of Outstanding Natural Beauty (AONB) in 1991, and the initiative has now become the Norfolk Coast Project.

The management planning process, is directed by a Joint Advisory Panel (Countryside Commission, local authorities and parish councils) and is being implemented by a Project Officer, responsible to an Officer Working Group.

The Heritage Coast Management Plan presents a policy and action framework for integrated countryside management (i.e. habitat management of saltmarshes, sand dunes and shingle together with informal recreation) of defined areas. The emphasis, in terms of water-based recreation, is not on the water area but concentrates on maintaining access and initiating projects to, for example, reduce recreational conflict. The 'second phase' of Heritage Coast Management Plans is currently underway and the Countryside Commission's aim is to involve more people and relate the management of heritage coasts to the coastline as a whole (Countryside Commission, 1991).

For the Norfolk Coast recreation issues have also been specifically addressed by a separate Visitor Management Strategy which incorporates a simple zoning policy. The Consultation Draft version of the Visitor Management Strategy was presented in 1994 as 'a new approach to managing tourism and recreation'. Following public comment the revised and simplified document has now been published (Norfolk Coast Project, 1995).

Recreation is considered alongside policies on, for example, traffic and transportation, pollution, and information and interpretation. Watersports are set in context with other recreational activities, taking place within the AONB, including beach use, bird-watching, cycling and horseriding. Measures put forward to improve recreational management of watersports include codes of practice; an emphasis on self-regulation and cooperation; and the provision of information and education at launch sites and other key points.

13.5 INTERNATIONAL COMPARISONS

Management of water-based recreational activity in Chesapeake Bay in the USA has been studied by Selwyn (UK CEED, 1994). This research highlights different administrative arrangements, management planning and financial provisions. Chesapeake Bay is the largest estuary in North America and its recreational boating activity is intense.

The Maryland State Boating Administration, formed in 1988, is responsible for the planning and management of all boating and recreation. State boating regulations are enforced by the Natural Resource Police and all motorized watercraft (including PWCs) have to be registered. The Administration's funding is derived from 'directed' taxes, paid by the boaters themselves, including a 5% excise tax on the sales of all new and second-hand boats. This funds both the planning and management function and a Waterways Improvement Fund.

As part of their role the Administration has drawn up 'Comprehensive Vessel Management Plans' for three of the main rivers feeding the Bay. Selwyn suggests that this has been a learning process. Simple, clear, more enforceable management restrictions are considered more popular and locally effective than the complex arrangements which were drawn up initially.

The implementation of management objectives is achieved through:

- speed limits;
- 'minimum wake zones' in protected areas;
- noise level limits for noisy sports such as water skiing;
- zoning of specific activities;
- information (using buoyage) on the water and explained in a general leaflet.

Simplification of speed limits is a good example of what has proved achievable in practice. The first plan incorporated five different speed limits, changing according to the time, day and season, based on safety records. In subsequent plans this has been simplified to a general 6 knot limit.

Management planning for coastal areas is however perhaps most advanced in Australia. Inscribed on the World Heritage List in 1981, Australia's Great Barrier Reef is the largest single collection of coral reefs in the world. Biologically it supports the most diverse ecosystem known to man and this diversity reflects the maturity of an ecosystem which has evolved over millions of years. The reef is managed as a multiple-use protected area by the Great Barrier Reef Marine Park Authority (GBRMPA), established in 1975, with day-to-day management being undertaken by the Queensland National Parks and Wildlife Service.

The Great Barrier Reef Marine Park Act of 1975 established the legal basis for the management of the reef and the GBRMPA is working to both a 25-year strategic plan and a current five-year corporate plan (1993–98). Management planning is based on a three-tier system consisting of zoning, site management plans for heavily used areas (e.g. Whitsunday region) and permits for any tourist operation or facility. The Park is divided into four sections, each of which has its own zoning plan of eight zones ranging from general use (most activities allowed) to preservation (almost no-one can go). The zoning plans, first completed in 1988, provide for conservation and reasonable use by limiting some activities, separating conflicting activities and excluding unacceptable activities. Public participation has provided an essential input.

Within the Park, tourism is the largest commercial activity in economic terms with 24 island resorts catering for approximately 1 million visitor nights annually (Ottesen, 1992). Large high-speed catamarans provide trips to island and outer reefs which are used extensively for watersports, snorkelling and reef walking. A 'user pays' charge, levied on commercial tour operators, was introduced in 1993, after four years of consultation, to help fund management.

Park rangers check permits and patrol islands but Alcock (1992) sees a 'well designed education and extension program' as essential for management plan implementation. For the GBRMPA this includes:

- regular direct contact with reef user groups;
- public participation programmes (media events, public meetings, liaison groups, displays and advertising);
- effective 'social marketing' of management plan decisions (i.e. educating users as to what is allowed and why).

The principle adopted in Australia is that if people help develop management plans this generates commitment, improves effectiveness and, in the long-term, saves money (for a full discussion see Cubbay, 1989).

13.6 CONCLUSION

Water-based recreation features strongly in a range of coastal management plans. They are all relatively recent and the examples detailed here can only give a flavour or the range of initiatives underway. Management plans are a useful tool where many activities are taking place and no one controlling body is responsible for their management. Within the UK however, a number of problems in implementing these management plans remain largely unresolved.

Firstly no 'best solution' administrative framework has emerged. Where a separate statutory body has been formed, as with the Great Barrier Reef Marine Park Authority in Australia and Chichester Harbour Authority in the UK, this is seen to be effective and efficient in management terms. But formation of a new statutory body for each management plan area would be costly and unrealistic.

Joint ownership of a management plan requires some form of steering, liaison or management group. Any such body must then have a means of implementing the management plan. MacDonald (1994) stresses the importance of bye-laws. He suggests that while 'bye-laws can be – and to a large extent have been – operated in isolation from an overall set of agreed policies for an area within which such bye-laws operate [. . .] the main way (and, in some cases, the only way) in which the policies and proposals of management plans can be achieved is through bye-laws'. But bye-laws are limited in terms of their control. Currently, for example, speed limits can be imposed but activities such as jet skiing cannot be banned from a particular area. Bye-laws also need to be enforced which raises cost implications.

Harbour masters, with the authority vested in their position, are well placed to manage most water-based recreational interests. Other managers, unable to implement management plan objectives using regulations, have to look to other methods. Many interested parties, not least the recreation groups themselves, feel that most conflicts between different recreational uses can best be sorted by cooperation and voluntary agreements (see DOE/WO 1993 for a full discussion). Codes of conduct and provision of information in various forms (leaflets, notices, press releases) are an accepted, if not always effective, and cost-effective means of implementation. In many cases around the UK the first Project Officers, Estuary Managers and Water Rangers are in post. Past experience of countryside management plans indicates that initiatives which hinge on an individual to implement them are often only as good as that individual's enthusiasm, and it will be interesting to monitor the effectiveness of these appointments.

In any event everyone is agreed that successful management solutions are unlikely to be achieved using heavy-handed 'top-down' management planning with its emphasis on regulation and policing. Estimating recreational carrying capacity is an imprecise science. It may be that, as yet, in many places management objectives (and thus management plans) for controlling recreational use are not required. Environmental interest groups maintain that they are, before environmental damage becomes irreparable. The Royal Society for the Protection of Birds (RSPB) particularly would like to see legislation to control the recreational use of estuaries and coastal waters. In response the RYA is preparing submissions to all the estuary management projects underway to 'ensure that the voice of the recreational user is heard' (*The Times*, 21.6.94). A key role of the management plan is to avoid this sort of polarization between different interest groups. Recreationalists, who to date have enjoyed largely unrestricted access to water space, are perhaps the most likely group to resent any activities being imposed on their activities. As with coastal strategies, consultation, and the endorsement of the management plan by as many interested parties as possible, is therefore vital to enable effective management. In many cases the lead body has needed to act as an 'honest broker', approaching individual interests, rather than convening group meetings which can result in entrenched positions. Chichester Harbour Authority's 'scientific' approach – periodic monitoring of indicators and comparisons with national trends in an attempt to define carrying capacity – must also be recognized as good practice.

To date, perhaps due to a combination of the factors discussed above, most coastal management plans have failed to address the detailed implementation of objectives (how and when work should be done). They have also largely failed to specifically identify who should pay! Management planning is not simply an information-gathering exercise but must incorporate or be combined with some form of business plan based on an agreed budget. Resistance from recreational users to management planning is also very probably linked to fears that they will be made to pay for the privilege of partaking in their sport, as happens via the boating tax in Chesapeake Bay and the permit system employed by the Great Barrier Reef Marine Park Authority. Andrew (1992) made this point when considering management proposals for the Exe Estuary. He questions 'Who bears the costs of management? Will it be the recreational user, who, at the present time is paying very little for use of the water space; and, if there is to be self-financing estuary management, is it equitable that we just charge the water users?'

The number of plans being produced indicates that, despite these implementation problems, management plans will continue to be put forward as means of coordinating decision-making in the coastal zone. At the very least plans provide a focus for action and a means for raising awareness. It should be remembered, however, that any plan is only a stage in an on-going management process. Its success largely depends on the degree to which it can be integrated with existing controls and interests. The active support of as many organizations as possible with a vested interest in the management plan area, together with effective collaboration and communication is clearly essential.

ACKNOWLEDGEMENTS

Thanks are due for many helpful comments received from professionals currently involved in formulating and implementing coastal management plans. Particular thanks to Charles Mathieson, Ranger Service Officer, Pembrokeshire Coast National Park; Michael Hyslop, General Manager, Milford Haven Port Authority; and Rhona Fairgrieve, Harbour Survey Project Officer, Poole Harbour Commissioners.

REFERENCES

Alcock, D. (1992) Management of the Great Barrier Reef Marine Park. *Current*, 1(2).

Andrew, D. (1992) The Exe Estuary. In *Coastal Planning and Management*, Conference Proceedings, Winchester, 27 November 1992, Hampshire County Council, 13–16.

Barber, A. (1991) *A Guide to Management Plans for Parks and Open Spaces*, Institute of Leisure and Amenity Management, Reading.

Bromley, P. (1994) *Countryside Recreation*, E & FN Spon, London

Countryside Commission (1974) *Advisory Notes on Country Park Plans*, CCP 80, Countryside Commission, Cheltenham.

Chichester Harbour Conservancy (1994) *Chichester Harbour Management Plan*.

Countryside Commission (1991) *Heritage Coasts: Policies and Priorities 1991*, Countryside Commission, CCP 305, Cheltenham.

Department of the Environment and Welsh Office (1993) *Managing the Coast: A Review of Coastal Management Plans in England and Wales and the Powers Supporting them*, DoE.

Dorset County Council (1994) *Poole Harbour Aquatic Management Plan: Consultation Draft*, Dorset CC, Dorchester.

English Nature (1992) *Caring for England's Estuaries: An Agenda for Action*, English Nature, Peterborough.

English Nature (1993) *Estuary Management Plans: A Coordinator's Guide*, English Nature, Peterborough.

Fairgrieve, R. E. (1995) *The Poole Harbour Survey, 1994:* Report of the Harbour Survey Project Officer, Poole Harbour Commissioners.

Fecher, S. (1993) *A Survey of Recreation in Chichester Harbour.* Chichester Harbour Conservancy.

Gubbay, S. (1989) *Coastal & Sea Use Management: A Review of Approaches and Techniques.* Marine Conservation Society.

House of Commons Environmental Select Committee (1992) *Coastal Zone Protection and Planning*, HMSO, London.

Kennedy, K. (1994) *Producing Management Plans for Major Estuaries, the Need for a Systematic Approach. Case Study – The Thames Estuary*, Conference on Management Techniques in the Coastal Zone, University of Portsmouth: 24–5 October.

Leay, M., Rowe, J. and Young, J. D. (1986) *Management Plans: A Guide to their Preparation and Use*, Countryside Commission, CCP 206, Cheltenham.

Moffat, A. and Paterson, C. (1994) *Using the Co-ordinators Guide*. Unpublished conference paper.

MacDonald, K. (1994) *Controls over Marine Recreation in the Coastal Zone. Is the Existing System Adequate*, Conference on Management Techniques in the Coastal Zone, University of Portsmouth: 24–5 October.

Milford Haven Port Authority (1992), *Milford Haven Waterway Recreation Plan*, Port Authority, Milford Haven.

National Coasts and Estuaries Advisory Group (1993) *Coastal Planning and Management: A Good Practice Guide*, NCEAG.

National Coasts and Estuaries Advisory Group (1994) *The Directory of Coastal Planning and Management Initiatives in England*, NCEAG.

New Forest District Council (1991) *Coastal Issues Report*, NFDC.

Norfolk Coast Project (1995) *Visitor Management Strategy for the Norfolk Coast*, Norfolk County Council, Norwich.

Ottesen, P. (1992) Tourism in the Great Barrier Reef Marine Park: How is it managed and who pays? Proceedings of a National Conference, *Heritage Management: Parks, Heritage and Tourism*. Royal Australian Institute of Parks and Recreation, 4–9 October, 131–41.

Poole Harbour Commissioners (1994) *The Aquatic Management Plan for Poole Harbour: Summary of Responses to Consultation Process*, October 1994, Unpublished.

Poole Harbour Management Policies (1991).

The Times (1994) Sailors vie for clear water', 21.6.94, p. 9.

UK CEED (1994) *Steering a Balanced Course*, BMIF.

W. S. Atkins Planning Consultants (1993) *Taw Torridge Estuary Management Plan*, Torridge District Council.

Legislation or Self-Regulation

14

14.1 INTRODUCTION

In recent years there has been much debate as to whether legislation should be introduced into coastal management over a wide number of issues from proficiency standards to development control. Central to this debate has been the philosophy of self-regulation. In brief the key issues have been:

- whether to extend planning jurisdiction offshore or promote voluntary coastal management plans;
- whether to introduce compulsory proficiency standards for skippers of recreational craft or rather to leave it to organizations such as the Royal Yachting Association (RYA) to promote education and training;
- whether boats should be registered centrally, rather like cars, for security reasons or alternatively should security marking of equipment be left to the industry and users;
- whether the environment should be protected through legislation or by the adoption of voluntary codes;
- whether safety standards in watersports should be left to the national governing bodies to administer or be centralized through a state organization; and
- whether navigational regulation, instituted for commercial reasons, should be extended to some areas currently freely enjoyed by all (this is currently being debated for the Western Solent where Associated British Ports (ABP) has applied to the DOT to extend its regulatory authority).

This chapter considers three of these specific subject areas within which the legislation or self-regulation debate is ongoing. The intention here is to present the issues rather than suggest any solutions or judgements.

Coastal Recreation Management Edited by Tim Goodhead and David Johnson. Published in 1996 by E & FN Spon, London. ISBN 0 419 20360 5

The first area of consideration is that of health and safety. An acknowledged role of the coastal recreation manager is to minimize the risks which are an inherent part of coastal recreational activity. As with any leisure activity, there is a balance between the way in which risk is minimized and freedom to pursue the challenge of the sport. A precautionary principle should obviously be adopted by individual participants. Managers can help by providing information to make participants more aware of risks. However, in a training environment, such as a sailing school or outdoor activity centre, where the manager is personally liable, a more proactive approach is under consideration. The current debate centres around whether or not water-based activity centres should be registered and regularly inspected.

Secondly, training requirements for water-based recreation activities in the UK are currently a matter of individual choice. Voluntary training competences promoted by the RYA are acknowledged to be of a high standard but there is no legal requirement for water users to gain set levels of proficiency unless using small craft commercially. In the interests of safety and good management should all coastal managers and water users reach agreed proficiencies and, if so, at what level?

Thirdly, if coastal recreation, like all other sectors, is to work towards sustainable development, environmental management considerations should be agreed. At present the only obvious area where an environmental management system could be applied is in the marina facility context. In theory good environmental practice should enhance the quality of the facility but at a cost. Environmental auditing and environmental management systems are currently voluntary options for managers to implement. In the future they could well become mandatory.

Finally, the use of information technology is reviewed in the context of resolving some of these conflicts.

14.2 HEALTH AND SAFETY TRENDS FOLLOWING THE LYME BAY CANOE TRAGEDY

The world of outdoor education and watersports teaching has evolved rapidly over recent years. A number of Local Education Authority centres have closed as education budgets are delegated to schools and the gaps being left have, in some cases, been filled by commercial operators. At the same time there has also been a formal recognition of the value of outdoor education, demonstrated by the inclusion of outdoor and adventurous activities in the national curriculum for physical education. A prominent issue facing the industry is that of the safety of children undertaking activity courses and the regulation of the centres providing these opportunities.

The events of 22 March 1993, when four young people from Southway School in Plymouth died in the canoeing tragedy, while on a school activity course at a centre run by Active Learning and Leisure Limited in Lyme Bay, have brought the industry and all aspects of safety into the public and media spotlight. The deaths of the four young people was not an accident, but the result of criminal neglect.

Following the subsequent trial into the case, details were reported in *The Times* (9 December 1994) and the *Guardian* (9 December 1994) and then by the British Canoe Union (BCU, 1995). The tragedy occurred when a group of eight pupils and their teacher were led on a proposed canoe trip along the coast by two unqualified 'instructors' from the centre. The canoes that the pupils were using were not fitted with spray decks, and no flares or radios were carried to enable communication with the shore to take place. It also appears to have been the case that the 'instructors' had not obtained any weather or tidal information, nor had they informed the Coastguard of the proposed trip. During the outing the group found themselves drifting further out to sea with several members of the group capsizing and their canoes becoming swamped. Eventually all the children ended up in the water.

The centre manager made a search of the coastline when the group did not arrive at their destination, but it was two hours later before the Coastguard service were informed that the group was missing. The Coastguards were initially given misleading information regarding the experience of the instructors and the equipment being carried. Tragically, following a long search and rescue operation, four members of the group did not survive.

Following the deaths, the manager of the centre and the managing director of ALL Limited were charged with manslaughter and the company was charged with corporate manslaughter. On the 8 December 1994, Peter Kite, the managing director was found guilty of manslaughter and sentenced to three years in prison. ALL Limited was found guilty of corporate manslaughter and fined £60 000 (the first successful prosecution for corporate manslaughter in British legal history). Joseph Stoddart the centre manager, was found not guilty of the charges against him as the jury were unable to reach a majority verdict.

The tragic events at Lyme Bay led to a public outcry over safety at activity centres. In March 1993 the Activity Centres Advisory Committee (ACAC) was set up by the English Tourist Board as an independent body of experts, with the task of setting up a code of practice. The Outdoor Activity Providers code of practice was published in April 1994. It was hoped by many, including members of the government, that this code of practice would provide the framework for self-regulation of the industry.

The formal government response to the Lyme Bay tragedy was announced on 11 November 1993 by John Patten MP, the then Secretary of State for Education, in the form of a four-point action plan: This advocated:

(a) an immediate survey of outdoor activity centres followed by a programme of inspections by the Health and Safety Executive (HSE) over the next two years;
(b) making publicly available factual information about the inspections and any enforcement action arising from them;
(c) new comprehensive and detailed guidance by the Department for Education (DFE) with assistance of HSE, to provide information to schools and local authorities on the lessons which they should draw from Lyme Bay; and
(d) changes in documents concerning schools' Articles of Government to make explicit the legal duty of care concerning health and safety. (DFE 1994)

This four-point plan placed an onus for health and safety on the schools by making governors of schools corporately and legally liable for the safety of children from their school while on activity courses. The guidance described in the four-point plan was published by the DFE in 1994 in the form of Circular 22/94. But with no registration system in place for centres, schools are currently forced to try to evaluate the safety standards at centres for themselves, despite in many cases not having the expertise to make value judgements. In practice schools can often only establish a centre's safety credentials by sending a suitable questionnaire to the centre before the visit or by arranging an inspection by the school or local authority.

The inspection programme described in the four-point plan was carried out by the HSE and Local Authority inspectors. During the first year a total of 211 outdoor activity centres were visited. The interim report on the first year of inspections was published in January 1995. The HSE (1995, p. 7) reported that:

The overall picture which has emerged from the findings is that safety standards in the majority of centres are good... Nevertheless, some areas for improvement were noted and appropriate action was taken to deal with both serious and less serious concerns.

During their inspections the HSE (1995, p. 9) found that '76% of the 158 centres with 5 employees or more had a written safety policy'. Therefore 38 centres did not have such a written policy. The report also states that '92% of centres had procedures and equipment in place to deal with emergencies.' Therefore 13 centres did not. Furthermore the report notes that '84% of all centres ensured that formal or informal training was provided for their instructors'. Therefore 25 centres did not ensure such training occurred.

In the words of David Jamieson, Member of Parliament for Plymouth Devonport, in the House of Commons, 27 January 1995.

> I wonder how many of us would fly in an aeroplane knowing that 16% of pilots had not received training and 24% of airlines did not have a written safety policy.

Following campaigning by many members of the public and from within the industry, David Jamieson, MP, in whose constituency Southway school is situated, introduced a Private Member's Bill titled 'Activity Centres (Young Persons' safety) Bill'. The contents of the Bill relate to activity centres which offer activities for young people under the age of 18. The Bill, if it successful in reaching the statute books, will require all centres providing courses for people under 18 to register with a central body every year, stating the activities to be offered and the level of qualification of the instructors. The central body will then decide on accreditation. It will have the power to inspect any centre during the accreditation process and will carry out periodic inspections over a longer period of time.

The Bill had its second reading on 27 January 1995, a week after the publication of the HSE interim report. At this time the Government decided to support the Bill and move away from its previous stance of supporting self-regulation.

Thus regulation of centres is currently a major issue facing the industry. The initial response from many following the Lyme Bay tragedy was to call for greater legislation. However some still believed that it was not necessary to hold a register of centres, and that the cost of such a scheme was prohibitive. In this instance it appears legislation is the winner. In the words of Justice Ognall, the judge who presided over the Lyme Bay canoe trial:

> The potential for injuries and deaths are too obvious to be left to the inadequate vagaries of self-regulation.

It is probable that the Activity Centres (Young Persons' Safety) Bill will reach the statute books during 1995, supported by the Government and a majority from within the industry including ACAC. It is hoped by Mr Jamieson, MP that the requirements of the Bill will take effect from early 1996.

14.3 TRAINING

While water-based leisure is part of the Leisure Industry, to date it has not been acknowledged as an entity, probably because of its fragmented and diverse nature. Nevertheless, it can claim links with at least seven of the nine leisure industry lead bodies. Incidents such as the Lyme Bay tragedy involving the loss of life often provoke questions as to the level of qualification of those in authority.

The recent expansion of employment opportunities within the leisure industry has been significant. Employment in sport and recreation rose by 106% between 1960 and 1983. By the late 1980s sport and recreation, including sports-related employment was estimated to be at 376 000, making it the sixth largest employment sector in the UK. The CNAA Review of sports related to leisure (1991) stated that 'in response to this growth there has been a rapid, and largely unplanned, increase in vocational education, oriented towards employment in the leisure industries'.

But Flemming (1992), suggests that 'the leisure and tourism industry is fragmented and diverse and has always suffered from a lack of co-ordinated training and no cohesive qualifications framework'.

The development of management and subject specific training is reviewed below.

14.3.1 MANAGEMENT TRAINING

The last 15 years has seen a turmoil of development in management training. Some of this has impacted on maritime leisure.

In 1981 the then Manpower Services Commission produced its New Training Initiative, part of the strategy of which was the identification of standards for training by industry and the need to establish a more relevant qualification structure. As a result of this, the National Council for Vocational Qualifications was established in 1986. In the same year, the Pegasus project was launched by the British Institute of Management and the Department of Education and Science to help undergraduates identify and develop their potential management skills through vocational training and counselling.

The Management Charter Initiative, the operating and marketing arm of the National Forum for Management Education and Development, was introduced in 1988. The Management Charter Initiative defines a clear structure for the education and training of all levels of management.

General developments in education and training are also attempting to address this need to establish a more relevant qualification structure. Issues such as experiential learning; vocational emphasis; student ownership of their own education and training; life-long education and training; and development of unconventional education pathways are manifest in the introduction of:

- TVEI (Technical and Vocational Education Initiative);
- CPVE (Certificate of Pre-Vocational Education);
- RSA (Royal Society of Arts 'Education for capability');
- BTEC (Business and Technical Education Council skills/competence/ outcomes),
- NVQs and GNVQs.

There is an increasing acknowledgement that individuals cannot be assessed simply by the number of GCSE/A level (or equivalent) certificates acquired. There is more to an effective labour force than cognitive competence.

Assessment criteria now include such requirements as experience, attitude and behaviour. In many cases, inclusion of Accreditation of Prior Experiential Learning (APEL) contributes to a more accurate applicant profile. Traditional full-time higher education for the 18+ student must now be considered as only one of many routes to a management career.

The management education debate is ongoing. During the 1980s, however, much was written about graduate shortcomings. Management development in particular was highlighted because it is generally held that a significant proportion of the supply of managers comes from graduate recruitment. Traditionally, the British have seen the skills of management as predominantly intuitive and looked to, for example, classical scholars, to further their development. But in 1984, the Institute of Manpower Studies called for the UK government and industry to attempt to match the vocational and educational training in West Germany, the USA and Japan.

The Manpower Services Commission and NEDO commissioned Coopers & Lybrand Associates to produce a report entitled *A Challenge to Complacency*, which found that British managers were largely unaware of their companies' training programmes compared with their European rivals. Training was seen as an 'overhead to be cut when profits were under pressure'. Further evidence was provided by a series of reports (such as Handy, 1990) which can be seen as the triggers to the action of the late 1980s and early 1990s.

BTEC has, since its inception, stressed the need for skills development to run concurrently with the cognitive process. It encouraged a move away from the traditional compartmentalization of subjects to a cross-modular approach which encompassed increasing experiential learning that was vocationally relevant. Seven skills areas have been identified:

1. managing and developing self;
2. working with and relating to others;
3. communicating;
4. managing tasks and solving problems;
5. applying numeracy;
6. applying technology;
7. applying design and creativity.

A key document concerning training and the leisure industry is the Yates Report from the Recreation and Management Training Committee, 1984, established to address the problem of appropriate education and training in the industry. Its terms of reference were to consider training of staff in both public and private sectors, with reference to all forms of sport and recreation.

This report emphasized the problem of transmitting a coherent message from such a multi-disciplinary industry. It looked at management development and could not identify a systematic approach to training. Yates found a poor geographical spread of courses, many lacking vocational relevance. Many managers were totally unaware of course provision, which was mostly intuitive and not based on empirical evidence. Little or no obvious career progression was apparent, and limited attention had been paid to the needs of graduates regarding their future careers.

Evidence of more pre-career training was found in the public sector; with the private sector preferring 'in-career' training, often taken to mean learning 'on the job'. Yates identified the need for specialist skills which she believed to be generally the same throughout the industry. The 'generalist/specialist' debate has been echoed throughout the 1980s. No conclusion has yet been drawn and the argument has continued into the 1990s. The case is well put by Coalter (CNAA, 1991) who draws on evidence from a study of graduates five years on (Coalter and Potter, 1990). This work maintains that most relevant higher education courses have a degree of vocationalism allowing students to specialize in certain areas within the industry. There is still nevertheless a tussle between those who value and would fight to maintain high academic rigour in degree courses, and the push by most students for greater vocational relevance.

Given the high degree of 'vocational fit' between courses and subsequent employment it is essential that academics respond to these demands and take into account the (changing) vocational needs. (CNAA, 1991)

Torkildsen (1986) stressed 'education for jobs yes, but education also for self discovery'.

Within the sport recreation and leisure degree courses, evidence from Coalter and Potter (1990) and the CNAA courses review (1991) suggested that there was at that time no recognized entry level for graduates.

This is in part a reflection of the lack of standardization of job titles and responsibilities in Local Government Leisure services, the relative immaturity of the commercial sector, the general underdeveloped understanding and appreciation of the value of many of these degrees. (CNNA, 1991)

Coalter argues that many employers have experienced unrealistic expectations about entry levels from graduate recruits.

The following skills/characteristics can be identified as being what many managers in the water-based leisure industry would look for in recruits:

- practical water skills,
- communication skills,
- organizational ability,
- decision-making ability,
- self-motivation,
- an understanding of management accounting,
- reliability,
- problem-solving expertise,
- teaching skills.

In a recent research study enquiring as to employer needs, practical water skills received the largest vote from the smaller firms within the industry (Hill, 1993). The larger firms, however, still stress the need for the more general management type skills.

According to Flemming (1992), much of water-based leisure is at about the same state of development as sport and recreation was 10 to 15 years ago with regard to understanding and use of management skills. He sees the future as a gradual evolution helped among other factors, by constructive and sympathetic dialogue between the industry and higher education.

14.3.2 TRAINING AND EDUCATIONAL COURSES

Water-based training is unusual in that it is dominated by initiatives promoted by National Governing Bodies (associations sponsored by their members). Mainly in the last five years a range of vocationally specific courses have also been developed. An overview of the different courses available in the UK is given below.

National Governing Bodies

Associations such as the Royal Yachting Association have developed comprehensive training packages for watersport instructors. The RYA are considered world leaders in this field. The RYA Dinghy, Windsurfing, Powerboat and Yachtmaster Instructor awards have become very much industry standard qualifications, in particular the Yachtmaster certificate. Any young person at the start of a water-based career is advised to build a portfolio of these certificates or their international equivalent.

GCSE/A Levels

Some schools and colleges offer GCSE certificates in Nautical Studies or similar. These offer a base of theory and case study. On their own they will not lead to much but as a stepping stone to a more advanced qualification they are invaluable.

BTEC

There are a wide variety of BTEC courses in Leisure Studies from first/national diploma to higher national diploma together with specialized water-based courses. Where these are linked with work experience the take-up of these students by industry has been very impressive. The BTEC courses are in a period of transition with the introduction of GNVQ and NVQ. It is not totally clear how they will develop in the future.

City and Guilds

These courses tend to be very vocationally specific, with some boatbuilding courses for example holding very successful nationally recognized reputations.

National Vocational Qualifications/General National Vocational Qualifications

GNVQs and NVQs are very much in vogue at the moment. Heavily promoted by the government they have been adopted by some sporting associations and many colleges. The emphasis is on the student developing skills and proving competence. Proving the latter by providing evidence has made these initiatives very difficult to implement. The dinghy and windsurfing RYA training schemes have incorporated NVQs into their schemes. It is very early days yet but it does seem that NVQs in particular do have a future within water-based leisure training.

Degree courses

It is now possible to take degree courses in maritime leisure management. These courses perhaps offer the young person the greatest investment for the future. Courses vary considerably and it is critical that young or mature students pick the right course for their needs and the needs of the employer.

Leisure management training at sailing schools

These training courses could be criticized for being only a package of National Governing Awards, however they do have a place, particularly where the student is unable to go to college or university through a lack of academic qualifications.

Institute of Leisure and Amenity Management (ILAM)

ILAM has developed a well-respected package of Continuing Professional Development programmes. Anyone involved in water-based leisure management is advised to consider joining this organization.

14.4 MANAGING ENVIRONMENTAL IMPACT: THE CHALLENGE FOR MARINAS

Previous chapters have explained the rapid growth of leisure-related activity around our coasts. In many cases this has also had a profound impact on the environment. Again it is argued by some that this impact can be managed through the concerted efforts of the various water users; but others maintain that the state should legislate. This section examines potential environmental management measures for marinas.

Boat users and marina operators should, in theory, be in favour of sensible environmental controls since water and environmental quality are important to maintaining the quality of their recreational enjoyment. Marina operators need to preserve business, therefore water quality is of primary environmental concern (ICOMIA, 1993). A number of European marina developments also coincide with coastal areas of outstanding natural beauty and ecological importance. Thus it is also appropriate for marina sites to operate in an environmentally aware manner, whereby these ecosystems can be protected.

Sound environmental management requires a proactive approach to environmental issues by the marina management. There is, however, a reticence towards introducing formal environmental management techniques among some coastal recreational managers for the following reasons. Firstly, it is felt that there is no economic advantage. Secondly, managers do not consider that their operations are causing environmental damage. Thirdly, an environmental approach is difficult to put into practice since most coastal recreation currently operates in an environmental management policy vacuum where few statutory guidelines exist.

On balance, in future, the introduction of an appropriate environmental programme to protect the coastal ecosystem is likely to preserve business since, 'a cleaner more healthy environment should enhance recreational boating activities and a desire for more people to participate in recreational boating' (ICOMIA, 1993, p. 7). There is also a realization that environmental considerations will play an increasing role, particularly in marina development, as sites for formal recreation become more difficult to locate and develop.

14.4.1 A MECHANISM FOR ENVIRONMENTAL MANAGEMENT

Environmental auditing is a check on any aspect of environmental management which is made during the operational period of a facility. It should not be confused with environmental impact assessment (EIA) which is an evaluation of possible environmental effects during the planning stage prior to operations. Thus environmental auditing provides an indication to management of how well the administrative organization, systems and equipment of a company are performing in reducing and/or controlling environmental impacts. If this is to be achieved, it requires above all the full commitment and cooperation of those involved.

Auditing is an integral part of any Environmental Management System (EMS). 'The underlying objective of environmental management is to provide a structured and comprehensive mechanism for ensuring that the activities and products of an enterprise do not cause unacceptable effects in the environment' (ICC, 1988, p. 14). The framework for this has already been defined by BS 7750 and the EC Eco Management and Audit Scheme.

In theory a company which operates in an environmentally conscious manner will be more energy-efficient and cost-effective. There will be an awareness of the need to avoid activities which could cause environmental degradation. Such incidents, if allowed to occur, could be costly in terms of damage to the ecosystem, fines, remedial treatment and public opinion (Rennis, 1993).

For these reasons alone, marina operators should consider the protection of the surrounding environment as a key business issue. The CBI considers that environment protection requires a management approach which:

- understands the issues and associated impacts on operations;
- develops policy to deal with the issues;
- sets targets/objectives to achieve this policy;
- measures performance against targets to identify variation;
- implements improvement plans.

A business approach should be adopted to identify problems and solutions and 'more importantly implement those solutions without waiting for legislators... to force action to be taken' (Chambers, 1993, pp 6).

Companies are becoming increasingly sensitive about environmental performance information being forced into the public domain. In particular they are anxious to avoid attracting the scrutiny of regulators and loss of business due to public concern. The introduction of an EMS to a company should reduce this sensitivity, since it will ensure compliance with regulations and the meeting of public environmental expectations (Elkington, 1988). Environmental management goes beyond pollution control to consider all operational impacts on the environment and health and safety considerations. This includes emissions to air, discharges to water, minimum energy waste, environmental credibility of suppliers and the establishment of a management structure (Rennis, 1993). Importantly it will ensure the protection of employees and customers.

Table 14.1 Environmental issues for marinas

Area of concern	Issue or pollutant	Effect
Construction materials	Glass reinforced plastic (GRP)	Atmospheric emissions of styrene causing photochemical pollution with health and safety implications
	Timber	Use of non-renewable tropical hardwoods
	Marine paints	Atmospheric emissions of volatile organic compounds which have health and safety problems for workers
Bacterial/viral contamination	Derived from sewage	Health implications for other water users (e.g. bathers and windsurfers)
Discharges to marinas and surrounding waters	Oxygen demanding wastes and organic enrichment (derived from sewage, organic debris and oil	Aestetically unacceptable to customers. Causes damage to marine ecosystem due to deoxygenation of water column and eutrophication
	Hydrocarbons	Aesthetically unacceptable to customers. Bioavailable and toxic to marine life
	Antifouling paints	Heavy metals and biocides are bioavailable and toxic to entire marine ecosystem and not just target organisms
	Storm drainage	Contaminates marina basins and surrounding areas with above wastes
Litter	Plastics, paper, glass, cans etc.	Waste of readily recyclable materials. Aesthetically unacceptable to customers. Damaging to marine ecosystem due to smothering or ingestion
Physical disturbance	Dredging, anchoring, construction of facilities	Damages or removes benthic communities. Releases contaminants from sediments

In 1991, the British Marine Industry Federation (BMIF) sponsored an industry environmental initiative. The initiative has published advisory guidelines for boat users (Cook, 1992), and an environmental review of the industry culminating in the publication of an environmental policy statement in 1994, 'Steering a balanced course'. Problems as perceived by the industry are identified together with a series of recommendations. A summary of these impacts is given in Table 14.1. They can be subdivided into maintaining the aesthetic appeal of the environment for boat users and addressing specific issues when they occur, such as the TBT problem. The main recommendations of this exercise were to encourage:

- use of renewable boat building materials;
- avoidance of oil spillages and discharge of marine lavatories;
- reduction in noise and nuisance to other boat users;
- enhanced materials management in maintenance and construction areas (i.e. operators should be familiar with and comply with Duty of Care regulations);
- boatyard and marina staff to undergo training so as to be conversant with environmental responsibilities related to their work (BMIF, 1994).

14.4.2 ENVIRONMENTAL POLICY FORMULATION

In order for a company to implement a programme of environmental management a list of goals and instructions are needed for the manager to follow. These guidelines or Environmental Policy (EP) reflect compliance with regulations and the need to minimize issues identified by an initial review of the operation. The policy can be either general, stressing commitment to safeguard the environment, or specific, stipulating quantitative objectives (Rennis, 1993). The EP should define the marina operator's response to environmental issues and underline the commitment to meet any future legal requirements. It is more than a statement of a company's good environmental intentions, 'it is a set of measures intended to work together to achieve a specific goal, in this case the improvement of the environment' (Woolston, 1993, p. 53). It is also important that the EP be communicated to all levels of the company hierarchy (Woolston, 1993). It is no good for example for just the company directors or marina manager to know about the EP, if staff are still hosing antifouling paint chippings into the dock.

The problem at present is that there are no specific standards which could be incorporated into an EP for marinas or boatyards. Some existing Water Quality Standards have been applied sporadically to marinas. These are contained in the EC Bathing Waters Directive. However, such standards were not designed for marinas and do not include all the pollutants found there and thus do not fulfil all the requirements of a marina/boatyard EP. The present situation of applying the directive without modification to facilities is likely to bring marina operators into conflict with other interest groups such as fishermen or environmentalists, since these guidelines do not meet those necessary to preserve livelihoods or the environment. The standards should, however, be incorporated as part of a broader policy since they address the specific issue of sewage contamination.

It seems likely that the EP for a boatyard or marina should be a combination of general and specific objectives. General guidelines to preserve the aesthetic appeal for customers juxtaposed with specific standards to deal with issues such as antifouling, oil pollution or sewage from marine lavatories which cause degradation of the coastal ecosystem.

While there are no specific guidelines covering UK marinas/boatyards, there is, however, the Environmental Quality Objectives (EQO) system employed by the NRA and Scottish River Purification Boards (RPB) for coasts and estuaries. An EQO is a statement concerning the conservation of water quality for a particular activity. The NRA operates eight types of EQO, each related to the use of 'controlled' waters.

The priority objective of all EQO's is that current water quality should not decline so as to disrupt the present ecosystem. Secondly, EQO 1 (Basic Amenity) and EQO 2 (General ecosystem conservation) should apply to all waters. For a marina Environmental Policy, EQO 1 and EQO 2 could provide the basic guidelines, with the others being applied as the situation dictates. For example if the marina was adjacent to a shellfish bed EQO 5 would be applied. It should be noted that, as the present law stands, legal action could be taken against a marina/boatyard if it broke the guidelines of EQOs 1 and 2.

The aim of these is to protect the aquatic environment. In addition they do prescribe guidelines to preserve the aesthetic quality of waters but these are poorly specified. At present, the aesthetic objectives of the EC Bathing Waters Directive are complied with. These include:

● no abnormal change to water colour;
● no lasting foam;
● no visible film of oil;
● no specific odour.

In addition there should be no sewage derived debris .

Guidelines from other countries are more specific with regard to aesthetic controls for recreational waters and could be applied to marinas (e.g. Health and Welfare Canada, 1990 and US EPA, 1987) (MacDonald *et al.*, 1992)).

The probable policy objectives of a marina should consist of three sections. The first will address the aesthetic aspirations outlined by the BMIF, with modifications from international and national EQOs. The second will be a general statement on the protection of the coastal ecosystem meeting the EQOs 1 and 2 of the NRA (Table 14.2). Thirdly, it will set quantifiable criteria for specific pollutants or issues as raised by the BMIF.

14.4.3 TOWARDS AN ENVIRONMENTAL MANAGEMENT SYSTEM (EMS) FOR MARINAS

The identification of environmental issues together with the formulation of policies to tackle them forms only the first part of the EMS. The setting up of a management structure will designate responsibility and authority among company employees. Their brief will be to ensure compliance with the Environmental Policy and to take action to remedy non-compliant situations. A management plan will be a programme to achieve the targets and objectives outlined in the EP. A member of staff will be designated responsibility for achieving each objective (Rennis, 1993)

Methods and procedures for reaching the targets and objectives should be designed by an EMS management team, probably with the help of outside consultants. The EMS process is a cyclical management strategy which incorporates the following features.

Manual and documentation

All information should be collated into a manual. This will be provided as a reference for all levels of management. It will contain the marina environmental policy, objectives/targets, procedures to meet them and a review programme. Also contained within the manual will be the roles and responsibilities of staff. Reference should also be made to other management systems, such as Health and Safety. A description of the monitoring procedures should be documented, together with the level of compliance to be attained.

Table 14.2 National Rivers Authority Environmental Quality Objectives

1. Basic amenity	Maintain water quality so as to prevent public nuisance arising from visual and smell problems
2. General ecosystem conservation	(a) For waters receiving no substantial effluent discharges directly or indirectly: Maintain water quality so as to protect all aquatic life and dependent non-aquatic organisms such that the ecosystem is typical of waters with those physical characteristics and latitude. It is implicit that objective (a) includes all the sub-objectives outlined in (b) where applicable.
	(b) For waters receiving substantial discharges: Maintain or improve receiving water quality to such a condition that:
	(1) It supports a variety of aquatic life and dependent non-aquatic organisms
	(2) where appropriate, fish and shellfish are protected
	(3) where appropriate, it supports a benthic fauna essential to sustain sea fisheries
	NB Specific species and habitats may need more stringent protection on a local basis because of their particular value as an environmental resource. This will include SSSIs, RAMSAR sites, Marine Nature Reserves, fisheries and shell fisheries including beds designated under the EC Shellfish Directive
3. Migratory fish	Maintain water quality so as to protect passage to and from fresh water of all relevant species of migratory fish where this is not prevented by natural physical barriers. To include eels but not marine species which use parts of estuaries or coastal waters for breeding grounds
4. Commercial harvesting of fish	Maintain water quality such that commercial marine fish quality shall be acceptable for human consumption as determined by the appropriate competent authorities. This objective relates only to suitability for human consumption; the general health of shellfish themselves is protected under Objective 2 above
5. Commercial harvesting of shellfish	Maintain water quality such that commercial shellfish quality shall be acceptable for human consumption as determined by the appropriate competent authorities. This objective relates only to suitability for human consumption; the general health of shellfish themselves is protected under Objective 2 above
6. Bathing	Maintain water quality so as to protect those engaged in bathing. This should include those activities related to bathing
7. Other water contact related recreation	Maintain water quality so as to protect those engaged in water contact-related recreation
8. Other uses	Maintain water quality so as to protect all other recognized uses which are affected directly by water quality and which are not incorporated in other objectives. This objective should only be applied where positive water quality management is practised. For example this would not include abstractions unrelated to water

Control and verification

Control and verification methods will be employed to ensure the system is working. This will safeguard that a marina's operations are routinely checked against the guidelines of the EP and regulatory requirements.

Records

Environmental records should be kept to extend targets/objectives, record the results of audits, review the EMS and structure staff training.

Audits

The effectiveness of the EMS should be evaluated at periodic intervals using environmental audits. These can be general reviews of the system as a whole or specific investigations of individual areas (for example it could review specific processes, such as refuelling or boat maintenance areas). This will insure that a marinas environmental risks are minimized and liabilities reduced (Royston and McCarthy, 1988; Johnson and Hill, 1995).

The audit can also take different forms. A compliance audit will evaluate if the site is meeting the appropriate legal requirements. Acquisition audits are another example. These are used to ensure that a new site for purchase by a marina operator does not have an environmental liability which could increase operating costs, for instance contamination due to past industrial use.

Reviews

The EMS should be reviewed periodically to ensure that the system is effective. The results can be published for customer or public relations (Rennis, 1993).

The incorporation of EMS into the management procedure of a marina or boatyard business has a wide range of advantages. It will ensure compliance with regulations and laws. The environmental considerations and aesthetic aspiration of customers will be met, a key consideration in the age of the 'Green Consumer'. Most importantly the application of an Environmental Management System will protect the environment, the enjoyment of which is the principal business asset of the boating industry.

14.5 INFORMATION TECHNOLOGY

Finally the modern manager has a developing armoury of information technology facilities at his or her fingertips to aid in the resolution of conflicts. In the last ten years the use of word-processors, databases and spreadsheets have become common in most offices. In the future information retrevial is likely to become more graphic with the introduction of information systems that can reprint spatial dimensions.

The Internet has meant that private-sector databases are easily accessible between organizations. Thus the RYA, BMIF and conservation groups could access each other's information to further the common good.

Geographic Information Systems (GIS) are being developed that can run on a modern PC and have applications in coastal recreation safety, training and environmental management. Information can be layered on for example an electronic chart which will display:

- safety zones;
- moving craft;
- records of craft ownership;
- records of boat-owners' licences;
- display security alerts;
- display records of environmental quality.

The modern harbour master will soon be able to view the integrated issues of commerce, leisure and the environment all on a VDU screen.

To most of us a map or chart is such an everyday tool that we rarely think about what it actually is and the information it includes. More importantly, perhaps, we are extremely unlikely to ever give a thought to what information it excludes. Professionals at the Ordnance Survey or Hydrographic Office will have made those decisions for us. The key reason they will have decided to include or exclude information is because the map or chart simply cannot display it all. The system of symbols, despite its attempts to encode information in a precise and concise way, will eventually fail if too much information for any given location is displayed at once. The result is merely clutter and confusion.

This exclusion of information is not a problem when the needs of the user can be ascertained clearly and only the pertinent information displayed. Thus car drivers need road maps which highlight and include road- and vehicle-related information, pilots need maps with air corridor and overhead cable height information, walkers need footpath maps and geologists need details of the underlying geology and ignore all of the above information. This situation is not confined to the land as, for example, conventional charts will show active seabed cables but will exclude old, inactive cables. For the majority of users this is fine but for the trawler man who could lose his nets (or even his boat!) through snagging such a cable, knowing the position of all cables, active or inactive, is critical and so the Kingfisher series of charts shows them all.

This selectivity of information can also be a problem when the user specifically wishes to interrelate information, as is normally the case when considering any management decision. For example a new leisure facility will raise questions about the existing road network, geology, land usage, planning constraints, environmental importance, land ownership, catchment area and population statistics. All this information will probably be available on individual specialist maps but not on a single, combined sheet. In the past integration of such information required manual preparation of overlays from the specialist maps for use on a master, base map. Using these overlays the decision-maker was then able to assess the answers to questions such as:

- What other facilities are there within a defined radius of the proposed location?
- What is the population size, type, need in the vicinity of the site?
- Is the area geologically suited to the development?
- Are there any planning constraints?

Clearly then paper maps or charts are sub optimum sources of data in this respect as they are not able to display all the available information for a location on a single sheet. The search for a more ideal solution has led to the development of Geographic Information Systems (GIS) and Electronic Chart Display Information Systems (ECDIS).

Geographic Information Systems may appear to be a recent phenomena but have in fact been under development since the mid 1960s. Despite almost three decades of work in the area there is still no clearly agreed definition of when a computer system is or is not a GIS (Martin, 1991).

In general terms GIS Systems are exactly what they say they are – systems which manage and manipulate information on the basis of its geographic location. More specifically Martin (1991) states that they may be said to have the following characteristics:

(a) Geographic: They are concerned with data relating to geographic scales of measurement, referenced by a coordinate system to locations on the surface of the earth.
(b) Information: They enable questions to be asked of the geographic database to obtain information about the geographic world.

(c) System: They are structured in a systematic way allowing data to be managed and questions to be posed.

This, while useful, does not fully define the computer-based systems to which the term GIS is now generically ascribed. A specifically computer-based systems definition given by Marble in his 1984 paper reproduced in Peuquet and Marble (1990) states that a GIS has and must perform efficiently in four main areas:

1. a data input subsystem;
2. a data storage and retrieval subsystem;
3. a data manipulation and analysis subsystem;
4. a data reporting subsystem.

Marble further adds that a fifth area must shortly be added to this list of essentials, namely an explicit interface to spatial modelling activities.

Thus we might conclude that a GIS is a computer-based system capable of accepting and storing geographically referenced data in a way which allows easy data retrieval, manipulation, analysis and display, and also facilitates the use of this information in spatial modelling exercises.

While the concept of what is GIS is relatively easy to define the implementation of that definition is a much harder task. Data model type, structure, format and analytical algorithms all need to be considered as the interaction of these elements will determine the GIS's functionality. It is beyond the scope of this book to explore these questions of implementation in detail but in order to illustrate the complexity of the problem some of the common errors associated with GISs and their causes are considered.

Like any information system a GIS is only as good as the data that is put into it. However, with GIS the problem is compounded by the fact that the information not only has to be right, it has to be in the right place. This is especially important when entering data from surveys undertaken at different times for the same area. For example if one wished to input information on an area's specific storm water drainage system into a GIS, following work to extend the sea outfall, it would be logical to use the maps made for the system when it was installed. For the majority of the land-based sewage systems these were made in Victorian times. But for new outfall they will be more recent. Input as separate entities these would appear to show the system accurately. However, linking them together to get the overall picture might show that the seaward end of the system does not connect to the landward side. We know this is not true and the only explanation is that the absolute positional accuracy of the Victorian survey is different to the modern one. The cartographer is then faced with the dilemma of either assuming the whole survey was subject to the same, constant, positional error and correcting all the data for it or of assuming that the error is variable across the area. In the latter case the only recourse is to resurvey the whole system using modern techniques, a costly exercise.

This type of positional error is extremely important as it allows a single entity to exist in two different locations at the same time, which is clearly impossible. To overcome this requires rigorous analysis rules to cope with the positional uncertainty, a resurvey of all the information to be inputed into the system or a guarantee that all data for any point are input using exactly the same positional reference. For clearly identifiable objects this is comparatively simple but for less tangible features such as land boundaries and contour lines it is an extremely complex task. A whole range of factors need to be considered such as:

- The age of the data – when and how were they surveyed?
- The map/chart scale used to represent the object, especially important when data are digitized in from paper charts.
- Observation density – how much information are the contour lines based on?
- Positional accuracy – how accurately does the surveying technique define position?
- Descriptive accuracy – Qualitative or quantitative description?
- Natural variation – might the shift in position between surveys be real?

These errors are source data errors which are not inherent in the GIS itself but fundamentally affect its usefulness.

To run the most basic information system on a computer a minimum of 8 megabytes of RAM is required on at least a 486 DX2 machine in order to operate a Windows organized database, spreadsheet and word-processing package. To run more sophisticated geographical information systems the operator has to decide whether to use a DOS or a UNIX operating system. With the DOS system the minimum hardware requirement would be a 21 in high-resolution monitor, 16 megabytes of RAM and a hard disk of at least 500 megabytes. The cost of this technology is currently between £1500 and £3000. The UNIX system, sometimes known as a workstation, provides much more power and speed as it represents what is basically shrunken mainframe technology. However, this comes at a current cost of between £8000 and £100 000.

GIS software tends to be written on its own graphic platform. Most is written in C language. In coastal areas the technology is already available to adapt electronic charts into GIS systems by layering them as a series of two-dimensional images. These can be further developed for the display of three-dimensional information.

GIS also shows great potential for use as a pictorial database presenting information in geographic form for use by the coastal manager. Underpinning the basic map or chart a series of layers can represent for example environmental quality, recreational zones, ownership rights, rent due and rent paid. Such a GIS application could also be used to predict areas of conflict between water space users by using appropriate data.

14.6 CONCLUSION

The 1993 Lyme Bay incident has resulted in a period of introspection for watersport training. National governing bodies have reviewed their inspection procedures to see if they needed tightening up and there have been further calls for legislation. Against this the voluntary providers of watersport training have been outspoken in advocating self-regulation as a more practical solution than legislation in providing safety standards. The UK Government finds itself in a dilemma in that to introduce mandatory safety standards may be extremely costly and could devastate parts of the British Marine Industry. On the other hand incidents such as the Lyme Bay tragedy should never be allowed to happen again. The Activity Centres (Young Person's Safety) Bill is only the tip of the iceberg in terms of potential legislation and the debate is likely to go on well into the next century.

Qualifications alone will not guarantee employment in the maritime leisure industry. Practical skills and national governing awards are vital. A vast number of courses have sprung up in the last three years. Leisure managers now have to view training as a long-term commitment in a rapidly changing world. It is wrong to assume that one qualification or skill will be a passport to any particular job. Anyone considering joining the maritime leisure industry will have to accept that continuing professional development will be required. Within this commitment will be a 'cocktail' of self-development including, a sound basic education, national governing body awards, management and supervisory training, sea and work experience and perhaps most of all an overriding level of common-sense. Some of these skills, attained by those already working on the water, may have been gained over many years. Present developments in NVQ assessment will enable these people to receive formal credit for their experience.

The debate as to whether proficiency training and assessment should be centralized is likely to rage on. The main obstacle to this is the problem of resolving how the 'vast army' of volunteer trainers associated with watersports could be replaced and at what cost. It is likely that there will be some change with further harmonization with the European Union.

From the case study in this chapter it is clear that the environmental impact created by marinas can be measured and those measurements in some way acted upon. All leisure activity is likely to have some environmental impacts, some of which might be regarded as acceptable and others unacceptable. Monitoring is the key to taking informed decisions as to whether or not to take action. Again there is one train of thought that feels that government standards should be introduced while others feel that self-regulation is the way forward. The legislation versus self-regulation debate is at its most contentious perhaps in the environmental arena where values are so difficult to rationalize and 'cultural perceptions' abound.

Ultimately information technology could help resolve many of the conflicts in the self-regulation/legislation argument. GIS represents a powerful tool for use by the coastal manager. The acquisition of compatible data is currently a problem. The technology exists but acquiring data is time-consuming and costly.

In any event the success or failure of coastal recreation managers in influencing and resolving the many conflicts apparent in the coastal zone will eventually have a significant influence on determining the balance between legislation and self-regulation for water-based leisure on the coast.

REFERENCES

Health and Safety Trends

Activity Centre Advisory Committee (1994) *Outdoor Adventure Activity Providers Code of Practice*, ACAC.
British Canoe Union (1995) *Canoe Focus*, BCU.
DFE (1994) *Safety in Outdoor Activity Centres*: Guidance Circular 22/94, Department for Education.
Guardian (1994) Basic errors led to tragedy at sea, 9 December, p. 3.
House of Commons Minutes, 27 January 1995, Hansard
HSE (1995) *An Interim Report into Safety at Outdoor Activity Centres*, Health and Safety Executive.
Jamieson, David (1995) *Brief Notes on David Jamieson's Activity Centres* (Young Persons' Safety) Bill, House of Commons.
Knight, Kathryn (1994), Catalogue of mistakes that led to drownings, *The Times*, 9 December.

Training

CNAA (1991) *Review of Sport, Recreational and Leisure Degree Courses*, CNAA Pub.
Coalter, F. and Potter, J. (1990) *Recreational, Management, Training Needs*, Sports Council.

Coopers & Lybrand (1980) *A Challenge to Complacency.*
Flemming, I. (1992) Industry led bodies – what are they?, *The Leisure Manager*, 34.
Handy, C. (1990) *The Age of Unreason,* Arrow Publications.
Hill, Z. (1993) *An Analysis of Appropriate Management Skills for the Water Based Leisure Industry,* unpublished.
Torkildsen, G. (1986) *Leisure and Recreation Management,* E & FN Spon, London.
Yates Committee (1984) *Recreational, Management, Training Committee Final Report.*

Managing environmental impact

BMIF (1994) *Steering a Balanced Course: The Boating Industry and the Environment.*
Chambers, N. (1993) *The Environment as a Business Issue – Threat or Opportunity,* Environmental Management Unit, CBI.
Cook, P. (1992) *A Guide to Boating and the Environment,* The British Marine Industries Federation.
Elkington, J. (1988) The Environmental Audit: Holy Grail or essential management tool, *Industry and the Environment,* **11**(4).
GESAMP (1990) *The State of the Marine Environment,* Blackwell Scientific Publications.
ICC (1988) ICC position paper on environmental auditing, International Chamber of Commerce, *Industry and the Environment,* **11**(4).
ICOMIA (1993) *Marina Design and Development with an Environmental Conscience,* International Marina Conference, 1993.
Johnson, D. and Hill, R. (1995) Environmental auditing of marinas and boatyards. In W. Blain (ed.), *Marina III, Planning, Design and Operation,* Computational Mechanics Publications, Southampton, 143–9.
MacDonald, D. D. and Smith, S. L. (1992) *The Development of Canadian Marine Environmental Quality Guidelines,* Marine Environmental Quality.
Rennis, D. S. (1993) Environmental Management Systems in ports and harbours, *The Dock and Harbour Authority,* **73**(841).
Royston, M. G. and McCarthy, T. M. (1988) The environment management audit, *Industry and the Environment,* **11**(4).
Woolston, H. (ed.) (1993) *Environmental Auditing: An Introduction and Practical Guide,* The British Library.

Information technology

Cadoux-Hudson, J. and Heywood, D. I. (eds) (1992) *Geographic Information 1992/3,* Taylor & Francis, London
Martin, D. (1991) *Geographic Information Systems and Their Socioeconomic Applications,* Routledge, London.
Peuquet, D. J. and Marble, D. F. (eds) (1990) *Introductory Readings in Geographic Information Systems,* Taylor & Francis, London.

Summary

Many of the subject areas considered in this book are part of a dynamic picture. The framework for the management of coastal activities is not yet fully agreed or developed. The situation is made even more complex because the issues concerned affect and can be affected by so many different organizations and individuals. The following paragraphs present a brief summary of the main issues covered in this book.

Recent history shows a tremendous expansion in coastal water-based recreation. There is no reason to doubt that this will continue. Demand for watersports participation is likely to come from an expanding middle-aged group who have a greater commitment to an active lifestyle, and from the continuing concern of all age groups with physical activity. Activity holidays, both in the UK and abroad, are set to become increasingly popular with more people looking for interesting, varied and challenging leisure pursuits.

The role of the coastal recreation manager is yet to be fully recognized. The title can be conferred on a range of existing professionals, such as the activity centre manager in charge of a range of watersports; the waterside business person incorporating coastal recreation in a mix of leisure and service enterprises; the recreational planner tasked by a local authority to resolve potential conflicts; and the Port Authority manager balancing the needs of recreation with commercial shipping requirements. A broad spectrum of people also regard themselves as having an input to coastal recreation management as part of a wider remit. These include officers of sports governing bodies; officers of regulatory bodies such as the NRA and environmentalists with a special concern for the coast. The pressure for water-based recreation is also driving the need for coastal zone management to increasingly remote locations around the UK.

Improved protection and safety equipment has enabled participation in coastal watersports all year round. But this is no substitute for a working knowledge of wind, waves and tides. The danger involved with working with natural elements must always be an important consideration.

There is evidence of increasing pressure on resources in prime locations. This is especially true of estuary mouths at peak times (e.g. busy summer weekends). More work is needed to establish recreational carrying capacity guidelines for coastal waters. The public is also increasingly aware of the health effects of water pollution and leisure pursuits themselves can adversely affect the environment. An understanding of the planning system is important in order to integrate coastal zone management properly with existing regulations.

So called 'new sports' included windsurfing, jet skiing, parascending and even 'banana riding' present a range of management problems primarily concerned with the difficulty of controlling individuals who may need little in the way of associated support facilities. This can also be said of more recent developments in small sailing craft.

A new range of exciting hi-tech boat designs came on to the market in the 1990s with boats between 3.5 and 5 metres sporting accessories such as twin trapezes and assymmetric kites. Boats such as the RS 400, Laser 4000, Laser 5000 and Buzz, range in price from £4000 to £8000. Their image is quite different from the more traditional mirror, enterprise and wayfarer dinghies. While requiring a fair level of expertise all these sports have an exciting new appeal. However, the cost of much of the hi-tech equipment is pushing some sports out of the reach of many would-be interested participants.

Sea schools are a traditional seedbed for watersports activities. They also provide employment for many coastal recreation managers. The long-term viability of sea schools has to be questionable, however, due to a number of influences:

- business being taken away by 'new sports' and the increase in small craft participation;
- the effect of political changes and local management for schools resulting in decreasing budgets for outdoor recreation;
- public-sector cutbacks affecting local authority and national centre outdoor activity provision.

On the other hand potential legislation requiring mandatory certification levels of competence for watersports participation could boost income and revitalize their role.

The demand for mooring provision for yachts is difficult to ascertain. Most recreationalists consider the existing provision in the UK inadequate and cite state-supported schemes in Europe by way of comparison. Existing marina operators also need to concentrate on quality of service. Further redevelopment of waterfront areas is likely with locations such as Hartlepool, Portsmouth and Liverpool being possible locations. There is significant potential for high-profile events (e.g. Enza around the world in 80 days and the Ultra 30 Grand Prix) to attract more media coverage of yachts and yachting. In addition, significant target groups (e.g. ethnic groups, women) are yet to participate in any great numbers.

Recreational users must often share coastal and harbour waters with commercial shipping, creating the possibility of potential conflicts of interest. It is the role of the competent harbour authority for an area to implement management measures, such as bye-laws and Vessel Traffic Services, to ensure safety for both groups of users by minimizing this potential conflict. With education, cooperation and careful planning, commercial and recreational activity can safely take place side by side.

Increasingly the recreational resources of coastal waters need to be related to those inland. In particular the convenience of power boating is likely to continue to develop.

Further research is needed to establish the value of coastal strategies. There is a need to acknowledge management systems developed over centuries which already work in practice. Guidance at regional level is however welcome and continues to be developed in several areas. This is accepted as a way of tackling a range of issues which might otherwise not be rationalized.

Over use and conflict at a local level has prompted the production of coastal management plans. There is a danger that these initiatives may become too bureaucratic and overly complex. Management plans, which essentially apply land management practice to water areas, have been adopted with enthusiasm by environmentalists but are often received with scepticism by recreation groups.

The current coastal recreation management debate concerns the issue of whether coastal recreation should be subject to more legislation or continue to rely mainly on self-regulation. Public concern over safety in outdoor pursuits following the Lyme Bay tragedy in 1993 has prompted calls for the former. Alternatively the application of technology may increase safety without the need for additional legislation. Application of environmental management systems to marine facilities and security systems are also both areas where legislation is likely to affect the coastal recreation manager's obligations.

Index